The Miegunyah Press
This is number eighty-nine in the
second numbered series of the
Miegunyah Volumes
made possible by the
Miegunyah Fund
established by bequests
under the wills of
Sir Russell and Lady Grimwade.
'Miegunyah' was the home of
Mab and Russell Grimwade
from 1911 to 1955.

HOMES
IN THE SKY
APARTMENT LIVING IN AUSTRALIA

HOMES
IN THE SKY

APARTMENT LIVING IN AUSTRALIA

CAROLINE BUTLER-BOWDON AND CHARLES PICKETT

Photography by Max Dupain and Eric Sierins

THE
MIEGUNYAH
PRESS

HISTORIC HOUSES TRUST

short street

THE MIEGUNYAH PRESS
An imprint of Melbourne University Publishing Limited
187 Grattan Street, Carlton, Victoria 3053, Australia
mup-info@unimelb.edu.au
www.mup.com.au

Published in association with the Historic Houses Trust, The Mint,
10 Macquarie Street, Sydney, New South Wales 2000, Australia
www.hht.net.au

Produced to coincide with the exhibition *Homes in the Sky* held at the
Museum of Sydney from 12 May to 26 August 2007

First published 2007
Text © Caroline Butler-Bowdon and Charles Pickett 2007
Design and typography © Melbourne University Publishing Ltd 2007

Edited by Cathryn Game
Designed by Phil Campbell
Typeset in Avenir by Phil Campbell
Printed in Singapore by Imago

National Library of Australia Cataloguing-in-Publication entry

Butler-Bowdon, Caroline.
    Homes in the sky: apartment living in Australia.

    Includes index.
    ISBN 9780522853162.
    ISBN 0 522 85316 1.

    1. Apartments—Australia. 2. Apartments—Australia—
    History. 3. Apartment houses—Australia. 4. City and
    town life—Australia. I. Pickett, Charles, 1950– . II.
    Title.

643.270994

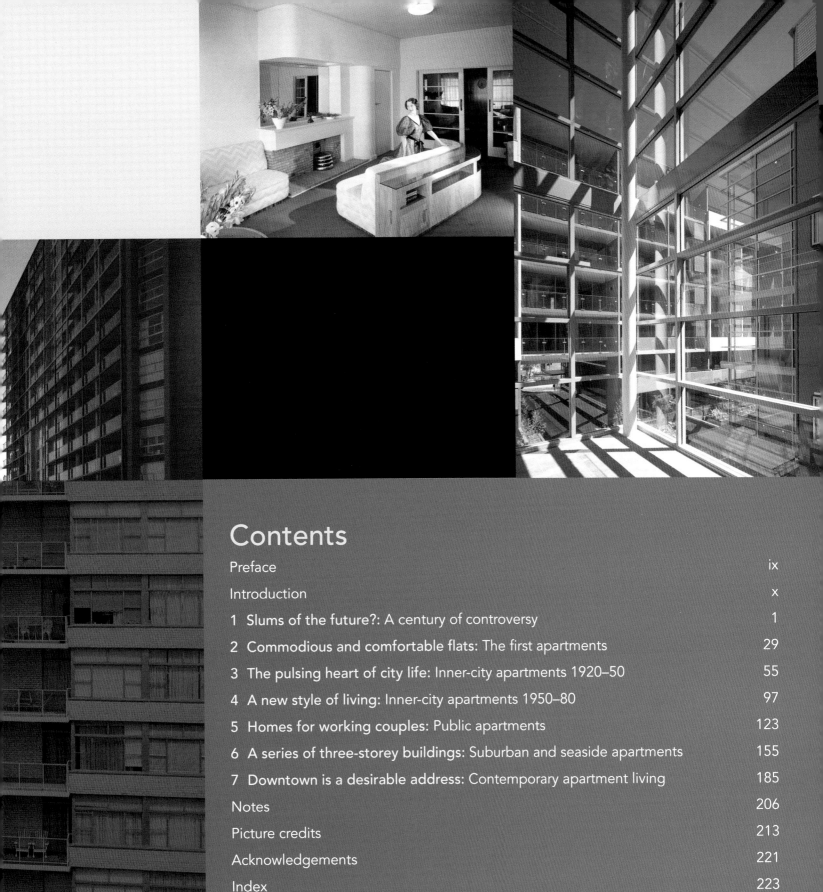

Contents

For Dr Phillip Kent (1958–2003)

Preface

When I was invited to write this preface my first reaction was 'what a great idea—I wish I'd written this book', but this changed almost instantly to 'no, it's a book I am dying to read rather than to write'. And Caroline and Charles have written this remarkable and overdue book—the first on this hitherto neglected part of Australian cultural history.

I was asked to do the preface because I once noted in an essay that I'd lived in about forty apartments in my life (I have done a more careful count and, excluding houses, hotels, friends' sofas, boarding houses, army barracks and clubs, and including only residencies of a week or more, it's closer to fifty).

I suppose the big distinction aesthetically between an apartment and a house is that a house is its own singular building and the exterior design and location is an expression of your aesthetic self and, more often, a statement also of wealth and status. True, some apartment buildings are grand and make a statement about the status of those who live there but some of the most delightful apartments I've known were in nondescript or even shabby buildings (these flats are often passed on from friend to friend).

With an apartment it's usually only the interior that can be an expression of yourself. With a furnished (or serviced) apartment you gain a type of anonymity or shedding of self (if you think that shedding of self is a good thing—I find that it sometimes is).

When furnishing my present apartment in Kings Cross (which as the book notes, is one of Australia's first grand apartment precincts), I followed the romantic design principles of early twentieth century Vienna: '... a person who is fortunate enough to possess an object of exquisite design, say a vase or cigarette case, will in time experience a revolution in his environment, set in motion by this object, which will transform his surroundings and ultimately himself ...' (author unknown, from *Deutsche Kunst und Dekoration*, 1906).

I created the interior of my apartment around some prints by the 1920s artist Marie Laurencin (Gertrude Stein's favourite painter), whose work I'd discovered when living in France and which I brought back with me. It was around these prints and their mood and spirit that I furnished and organised the apartment.

Usually, in a block of apartments you can hear faintly (or not faintly enough) people moving upstairs or next door, or you hear water or steam running in pipes, or doors slamming—or the sounds of personal drama. After a while these sounds are accommodated into the ambience of your living, some might even become comforting—giving a sense of being near to people without being required to interact with them (except when you are evacuated from an apartment building, say in case of fire, where a camaraderie sometimes shows itself among the residents thrown out into the street as well as curiosity about who we are and what we look like, sometimes standing there dressed in sleeping clothes and clutching jewellery boxes or wallets of personal papers or, in my case, my laptop).

There is a short story from the 1940s by John Cheever called 'The Enormous Radio' about apartment living in Manhattan. The young couple '... lived on the twelfth floor of an apartment house in the East Seventies between Fifth and Madison Avenues ...' They purchase a new radio and find to their fascination that by some technical quirk the radio broadcasts the lives of people in the other apartments in their building. They overhear '... demonstrations of indigestion, carnal love, abysmal vanity, faith, and despair ... and one woman in this building is having an affair with the superintendent ...'

Apartment living can be like that. But it can also be a decision to live without knowing anything about the others in the building. Interestingly, Charles and Caroline quote from a novel written by Australian writer Dymphna Cusack, who describes the way the city sounds outside an apartment also become part of its ambience.

More than any other way of living, apart perhaps from becoming a recluse, an apartment offers flight from the prying village, and as the beautiful title of this beautiful book says, a flight to a 'home in the sky'.

Frank Moorhouse
Sydney, November 2006

Introduction

Today more flats than houses are being built in Melbourne, Sydney and Brisbane. A third of Sydney households live in medium and high-density housing, and apartments form significant minorities of Melbourne's and Brisbane's dwellings. Urban demographers predict that by 2030, 45 per cent of Sydney households will be living in flats.[1]

Flats have always been a minority dwelling form in Australia, but for most of the twentieth century living in flats formed a popular alternative to the suburban cottage. At mid-century flats accounted for almost a fifth of occupied dwellings in Sydney, Australia's largest city.

Yet a recent history of 'European' housing in Australia ignores flats 'because this form has only become significant in relatively recent times'.[2] Perhaps significance in this context is less about facts than about culture. In his seminal history of Australian domestic architecture, Robin Boyd stated: 'Australia is the small house ... The suburban way of life and the aspiration to own and occupy a detached house have long been Australian characteristics.'[3]

Since Boyd wrote these words in 1952, the association between the suburban cottage and Australian history has become even more of a nationalist touchstone. Despite its popularity, apartment living remains excluded from the patriotic embrace. The historian and urban activist Miles Lewis, for example, argues that 'the flat, or today the unit, is an alien concept in Australia ... it is a dwelling form which was introduced to this country belatedly and not always satisfactorily. Even now there remains a degree of suspicion towards a form of accommodation historically occupied by fast livers, welfare recipients and European refugees.'[4] In reality, apartments have a longer Australian history than majority home ownership, the 'Anzac legend' and many other touchstones of national identity.

The architect Peter Brew writes: 'Flats and their architects remain outside official histories ... Flats pose a problem for our invariably nationalistic historians because they do not affirm the egalitarian myth of the nuclear family with Hills Hoist and mortgage.'[5] As symbols of urban cosmopolitanism, apartments continue to attract critics. A recent study of inner-city Brisbane criticises apartment names and marketing 'which references other cultures and other inner city lifestyles', rather than those of Brisbane or Australia.[6]

Against this background, it is not surprising that *Homes in the Sky* is the first history of apartment buildings in Australia. Compared to the considerable literature on the Australian house and the heritage significance of particular architectural styles of houses, the history of Australian apartment architecture has been primarily confined to survey volumes.[7] Studies of individual architects also contain useful material yet, despite the close association between apartments and architects, architectural historians have consistently favoured the small house as the most important interface between professional design and public culture.[8]

The publication of *Homes in the Sky* is well timed. In Australia today apartments and urban consolidation policies are at the centre of controversy over the future size, social composition and urban character of our cities. The increasing number, variety and dispersion of apartment buildings exemplifies contemporary urban change.

This phenomenon is not unprecedented. Throughout their history, apartment buildings have formed the architectural cutting edge of social and cultural change. Apartments have provided an architectural context for the emergence of social groups distinct from the suburban mainstream, including the mid-century 'bohemia' of Kings Cross and St Kilda, the beach culture of the seaside suburbs and the gay movement of more recent times.

Given the size of its largely undocumented subject, *Homes in the Sky* cannot offer comprehensiveness; we have focused on purpose-built apartment buildings rather than converted houses and other structures. In addition, *Homes in the Sky* focuses on the major apartment cities of Sydney and Melbourne. Sydney occupies more pages because it has been the home of the majority of Australia's apartments. Apartments were also popular in the smaller capitals of Brisbane and Perth, and these histories are also acknowledged. The vignettes about contemporary apartment life are located in Sydney in an attempt to provide a snapshot of apartment dwellers in the Australian capital with the highest concentration of apartments. Throughout we have attempted to balance recognition of individual structures with the several dimensions of an overall history.

Finally, we should point out that the terms *flat* and *apartment* are used interchangeably throughout the volume, despite their different histories and inferences. Historically, a range of terms has been used to describe multi-unit housing, including *tenement*, *apartment*, *flat*, *home unit* and *apartment house*.

The word *apartment* dates from the European origins of apartment living in the cities of the Roman Empire. In the first centuries after Christ, 'city planners in Rome erected thousands of multiple dwellings called *insulae*, or islands'.[9] The typical *insula* was three to four storeys high, but some were built as high as seven or eight storeys. Shortage of space meant that the multistorey apartment blocks became the preferred form of housing. They generally employed identical facades that followed identical floor plans and heights.[10] *Apartment* comes from *appartimenta*, from the Latin verb *partire* meaning to divide or to share. The term appears in English in the seventeenth century, a derivation of the French *appartement*.[11]

Flat originates in the old Scottish *flaet*, which was used as early as the twelfth century to denote an 'independent set of rooms'.[12] The word was also used in England and Australia to refer to floors in buildings. Its origins have also been found in the Old High German *flaz*, meaning 'level'.[13] Although the term *flat* was seen to have a vulgar sound in the USA by the beginning of the twentieth century, it continued to be employed in Australia.[14] The term *home unit* became popular during the 1960s, when strata title laws made individual ownership of apartments possible; the association of flats with renting had lent the term a pejorative tone.

Apartment was also used in Australia throughout the twentieth century, although it was usually reserved for the upmarket end of the property spectrum. In 1938, describing a flat in Wentworth Towers, *Decoration and Glass* gushed: 'The word "flat" seems strangely inadequate … almost incongruous … in this generous inspiring *apartment* crowning Point Piper … Truly, the term "FLAT" is inadequate.'[15]

Slums of the future? A century of controversy

In 1925 Charles E. W. Bean, author of the official Australian history of the 1914–18 war and main creator of the 'Anzac legend', wrote of his fears if apartment living were to become popular. According to Bean: 'a very great danger has again crept in … the danger lying in the areas of flats which are fast springing up in some suburbs. In these regions the children are again turned out into the streets … for their normal playground, and areas are being created which will almost certainly become slums within present lifetimes.'[1]

Bean believed that apartments posed the same 'national danger' as 'those streets of endless terraces which during more than half a century were allowed to grow up unchecked in many other countries, fatally affecting the physique and cramping the growth of their peoples'. In contrast, the Anzac soldiers were the product of suburban cottages, 'fairly well spaced, with gardens—about the healthiest next to country life itself for the growth of our people'. If flats replaced cottages, Bean warned, 'the "Anzac" stamp will pass from among us'.[2]

Bean did not lack for supporters. For decades, a wide variety of opinion-makers queued up to denounce apartment living—politicians and churchmen, trade unionists and journalists, academics and film-makers. More than forty years later, a minister of the New South Wales Government repeated Bean's taunt: 'These home unit blocks … will become the slums of the future.'[3] In 2006 Sydney Lord Mayor Clover Moore opposed new apartment towers on a former industrial site with the words: 'You are just looking at the slums of the future.'[4]

The 'Australian dream'

Australia's first apartments were built at the start of the twentieth century. Since then the popularity of apartments has grown to the extent that they comprise a third of Sydney's dwellings, a quarter of Melbourne's and almost a fifth of Brisbane's.[5] This transformation of Australian cities has not happened without opposition. Opponents of apartment development characterised them as a challenge to the 'Australian dream' of house ownership and suburban living. In the apartment debate much more was at stake than aesthetics and convenience. To many Australians, the future of the nation was in the balance. Specifically, apartments were widely considered to be hostile to family life.

Until the 1950s, there were two strands to this debate. With few exceptions Australia's first purpose-built flats were aimed at the wealthy. Moreover, with rentals of flats being higher on average than those of houses during the 1920s and 1930s, the association between apartments and wealth was long-lasting. In contrast, flats for workers were the subject of passionate debate: 'It was … a crying shame that tenements were ever put in the Rocks area. The residence of the workman should be in the suburbs, where he might have his own garden for his children to scamper around in the sunlight.'[6] These are the words of John Burcham Clamp, architect of some of Sydney's first apartment blocks, including Wyoming in Macquarie Street and Montana at Cremorne Point, which were designed when he was briefly in partnership with Walter Burley Griffin. Clamp took advantage of the 'very decided demand on the part of the better class of people in Sydney for flat accommodation'.[7]

As far as respectable society and published opinion was concerned, apartments were alternatively a symbol of respectability and progress or a potential blight, depending primarily on their social setting. The debate about workers' flats flared first.

Tenements and workers

In 1900 Sydney had only just overtaken Melbourne as Australia's largest city, but it was the first to be confronted with a distinctively metropolitan conjunction of urban problems. Plague, congestion, class conflict, public and private squalor inspired decades of urban soul-searching.

The sense of foreboding evident in new-century Sydney was expressed by the town planner J. D. Fitzgerald's warning that 'a City, which has the most beautiful site in the whole world, is running the risk of becoming one of the ugliest, the most backward, and the most disease-stricken; while its commercial future is imperilled'.[8] The Federation decade saw the first debate between the competing ideals of low-density suburbs and compact apartment blocks, which have formed the familiar elements of urban controversy for the past hundred years.

The victory of suburbia looked far from assured in 1902 when the New South Wales Government confronted the problem of rehousing

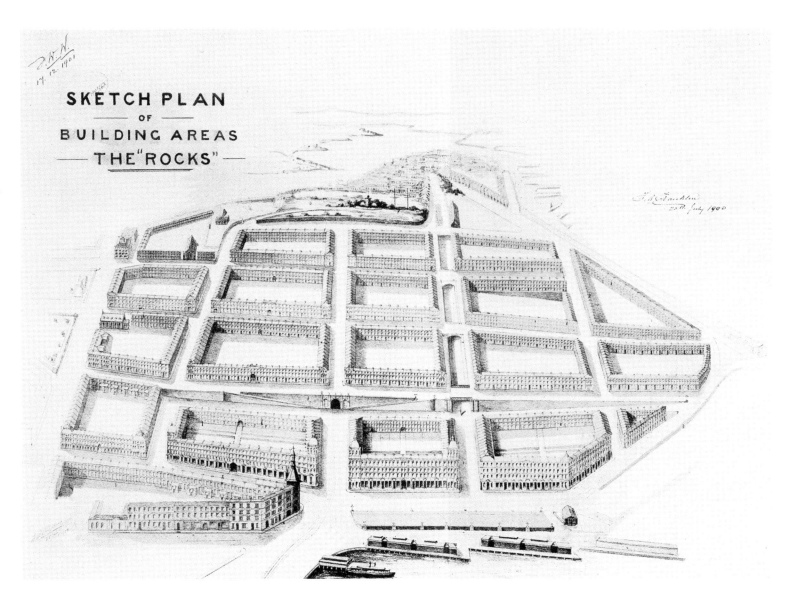

SKETCH PLAN
OF
BUILDING AREAS
—THE "ROCKS"—

the population of Sydney's plague-stricken Rocks district. Having resumed the entire precinct, the government debated the most appropriate form of new housing for dock workers and their families. The
initial plan was for two 'great tenement dwellings', each occupying an
entire block and together housing 4000 people: 'Imagine a building
five storeys high, the facades of stone and as architecturally imposing
as the Victoria Markets or the Post Office … and some idea may be
gained of the magnitude of the undertaking.'[9]

In Australia around 1900 apartments usually conjured up images of
the tenement block. In industrialised cities from Berlin to Glasgow to
New York the urban context was defined by a dense hub of tenement
blocks of six or seven storeys.[10] Typical of the type of domestic space
provided by the tenement was a three-room domestic space, no more
than 30 square metres in total. The front was a multifunctional room,
which often served as a place of earning during the day, then dining
room and then parlour. The middle room was the kitchen, and the

⬆ 'Imagine a building five storeys high.' Plans for complete demolition and
rebuilding were the initial, anxious response to bubonic plague outbreaks
in Sydney's Rocks district. This proposal envisaged massive blocks of
workers' flats.

third room was the main bedroom, which was stuffy and dark and had
no external access. There was no enclosed toilet or bathroom. Facilities were shared among families, with often as many as twenty people
using the same toilet.[11]

Tenements were demonised by Charles Dickens and others as
'rookeries: urban catacombs in which an entire family might share a
single room with nothing more than an oblique view of daylight, surrounded on every side by neighbours in similar circumstances'.[12] Yet
many tenements were built by charitable organisations such as London's Peabody Trust, and they were a decided improvement on
squalid slum housing. They had supporters in Australia, such as the

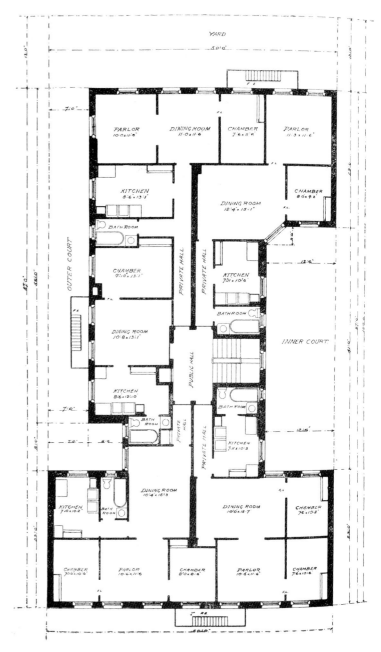

The tenement blocks of the USA and Europe formed the background to Australian debates about flats. These two New York examples were illustrated in a 1913 New South Wales Government inquiry into appropriate housing for Australian workers.

Reverends Boyce and Campbell, who both argued for 'the erection of tenement blocks on the lines of those in English cities, but with larger balconies' in Chippendale, Surry Hills and other 'congested and ill-planned areas'.[13] J. D. Fitzgerald advocated for 'the workman … the modern tenement flat, not the hideous barracks of some English towns, but a modern flat, as much isolated and convenient as the most modern hotel'.[14] Fitzgerald argued that the 'Hotel Australia is, after all, a tenement house on a grand scale'.[15]

However, among submissions to the Royal Commission for the Improvement of the City of Sydney and Its Suburbs in 1908–09, the majority view was expressed by Mrs Dwyer of the Trades Hall Council, who said that 'the flat system tended to destroy family life, and was not conducive to morality'. The royal commission agreed that 'on social or hygienic grounds, workmen should be encouraged to live in separate houses in the suburbs'.[16] It concluded that tenement blocks with shared facilities 'will never do other than burden the rates and produce a race of feeble physique that can never be the backbone of the nation. The real remedy, and the only one, is dispersion from the centre and development of suburban areas.'[17]

The controversy about workers' flats contrasted with the small number built by governments. After terrace-style workers' flats were built in The Rocks, the Sydney City Council constructed Australia's first multi-unit public housing in Chippendale in 1914. The flats were named after the New South Wales Governor Lord Strickland, who

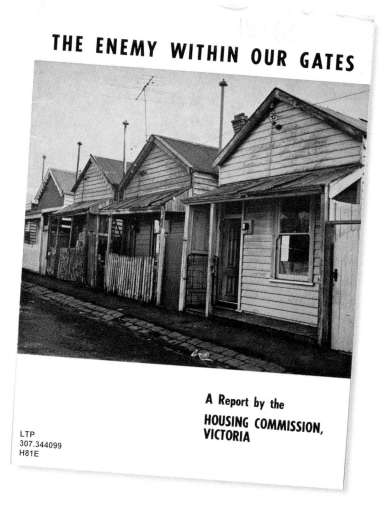

THE ENEMY WITHIN OUR GATES

A Report by the
HOUSING COMMISSION,
VICTORIA

LTP
307.344099
H81E

↑ 'Most complete and comfortable …' Completed in 1914, Strickland Flats was the first large public housing apartment building in Australia.
↗ Until the 1970s the Housing Commission of Victoria used images of poor quality housing to justify its 'slum clearance' and flat-building program.

observed at the opening ceremony that 'the flats seemed most complete and comfortable … The health of the people would be improved, and in that way the council was engaged upon a good work.' The Lord Mayor emphasised that the council 'was merely keeping pace with the policies and practice of the cities of England and Europe … They could never produce an imperial race from slums.'[18]

Needless to say, the Strickland Flats attracted critics, notably J. J. C. Bradfield, Chief Engineer for the Sydney Harbour Bridge and City Railway. Bradfield argued that the new railways could solve 'overcrowding in the city … The only available ground where a breath of air is obtainable is the street, and the children's playground is usually the gutter.'[19] In contrast, a rapid transit system would make available suburban living 'where the children can enjoy fresh air and sunlight in healthy surroundings'.[20] Bradfield singled out the 'Workmen's Residential Flats' at Chippendale as a faulty response to the slum issue: 'These flats are certainly well built, and proper attention has been paid to the supply of baths and adequate sanitary conveniences. But there are no gardens, no yards, and, as will be seen, the family washing is often dried by hanging on the balconies, or from the windows.'[21]

Slum reclamation

Sydney City Council built three more blocks of workers' flats during the 1920s, but this program was unique. No other municipal or state government followed suit until the late 1930s. Instead, Australian workers were constantly told of their good fortune in housing. Describing a new London flat development, *Building*, the journal of the Master Builders' Association, commented, 'workers in Australia, who enjoy the privileges of living in dainty little cottages remote from neighbours and 15 feet from street alignment, with a plot of grass, tree or garden between them for "breathing space", have no idea what their brother workers in England put up with in the way of housing …'[22]

However, the issue of workers' housing was kept alive during the 1920s and 1930s by crusading churchmen, journalists and politicians. Most influential was Oswald Barnett, a Melbourne accountant and lay Methodist who published and lobbied extensively for 'slum reclamation'. Governments' main response to housing shortages was to encourage home-ownership, a successful strategy in new suburbs. However, renting predominated in inner-city areas, and was one of the factors in their continued branding as slums.

'Slums of the future.' The subject of bitter controversy before their construction in 1938, the Erskineville public housing flats attracted support from tenants and neighbours in 2002, defeating a Housing Department plan to sell the estate to make way for higher-density housing.

In 1936 Barnett persuaded the Victorian Government to create a Housing Investigation and Slum Abolition Board, with himself as a member. Its first report stated: 'These unwholesome conditions sap the physical fitness of the children and develop their mental processes along lines of abnormal quick-wittedness in the lowest ideals. In these areas there are thousands of children who are condemned by the circumstances of their environment to worse than physical death—to slow-warping influences of poverty, to filthy conditions, and to other evils and dangers which it is easier to imagine than enumerate.'[23]

As well as poverty, slum reformers feared the social consequences of slum living. A difficulty was that condemnations of decaying inner-city terrace houses were more or less identical to those of flats. As

Barnett's investigations began, the Member for Footscray told the Victorian Parliament that 'we should investigate the great apartment buildings being erected in Melbourne', claiming that they were un-likely to 'cater for the comfort and welfare of the young'.[24] Fear that an apartment solution might recreate the 'slum' problem dogged Barnett and other campaigners.

This argument confronted the New South Wales Government in 1936, when it created a Housing Improvement Board with the aim of encouraging local councils to follow their English counterparts and take partial responsibility for housing the poor. The Housing Board's first major project was a public housing development in the inner sub-urb of Erskineville.

Although the language of 'slums' was simplistic, there is no deny-ing the poor quality of the housing suffered by many city residents. An officer of the Housing Improvement Board pointed out that the board had inspected Erskineville houses 'where the damp reached six feet up the walls which, in some cases, showed a patchwork of moss. In one

house the carpenter, who removed the flooring boards for the health officer, dropped his hammer through the aperture … It disappeared into two feet of water.'[25]

Despite this, Erskineville Council refused to approve or contribute to the scheme because it involved the construction of flats. Although the aldermen agreed that the new flats would be more 'habitable' than the residents' present homes, 'it was decided to oppose any scheme which involved the construction of flats in the municipality' as those 'forced into the flats would be robbed of their privacy', and 'the encouragement of the flat system would tend further to reduce the birthrate'.[26]

There is no doubt that the council expressed the opinions of many of its ratepayers. A petition of Erskineville residents opposing the flats included the argument that 'FLATS on moral and religious grounds have a definite tendency to make people limit their families by birth control methods, which has a definite injurious tendency on the health and morals of married peoples … If we desire to populate Australia with Australians we must encourage them to propagate.' The expressed preference was for 'semi-detached cottages or some other such design that will give each family a definite form of home life embodying a backyard to each home'.[27]

Dr Norton, Catholic Bishop of Bathurst, joined the Erskineville debate, arguing that flats were a means by which 'the modern social system had made property the privilege of a small class. The mass of mankind was shut out from its pleasures … Small wonder if masses had turned Socialist or Communist, and demanded the abolition of property altogether.'[28] He was supported by the Reverend S. A. McDonald, general secretary of the Sydney City Mission, who criticised 'the wiping away of little homes' for barrack-like flats. Novelist Kylie Tennant replied that 'the little homes in question are smut-grimed hovels, some of them built over an old typhoid swamp'.[29] Most of the extensive public comment was critical of the council, which reversed its decision after the Housing Board offered to bear the entire construction cost of a third of the planned proposal.

The Erskineville controversy emphasised that although middle-class flat life could be tolerated or even celebrated, flats for workers inflamed political and social anxieties. A *Sydney Morning Herald* editorial noted the 'curious paradox' that the planned flats inspired 'such a distrust of flats when flats are being built at record rates in the more fashionable parts of the city and suburbs'.[30]

A 'real home'

Similar criticisms were made of the effects of flats on the family life of the better-off. The Melbourne architect John Henderson wrote that 'a furnished flat can never become a real home … The apartment dwellers spend a great deal of money in order to escape from the monotony of their more or less unsympathetic surroundings …'[31]

Another architect critic was Florence Taylor, editor of *Building*. Despite her apparent feminist credentials as Australia's first qualified female architect and editor of an influential industry journal, several of Taylor's early opinion pieces condemn flats for their diminution of women's domestic role: 'The flat dweller, because of her environment, becomes flaccid and unwomanly, losing physical, mental and moral tone … for the whole of the circumstances of her existence, as well as her condition, make her a coward, afraid to face the discomfort of pain and motherhood.'[32]

The feminist Women's Reform League took a similar line, arguing that 'life in city flats became a factor in a diminishing birthrate. Flats and no families seemed to be the growing evil of society.'[33] A 1919 editorial in the *Evening News* decried 'the huge development of the "flat" system in the last decade in metropolitan Sydney', arguing: '[T]he creation of these great "insulae," as the ancient Romans called them, will harmonise, indeed, with another feature of modern life, the limited family, but that does not coincide with the broad interests

'Flats in those days were looked upon as evil.' Cavendish Hall was one of several Kings Cross flats to be home to the poet and journalist Kenneth Slessor. The 1920s block suggests quiet respectability rather than the lurid bohemia imagined by Slessor's mother.

of the State. A country that urgently needs population should not countenance any system which favors a low birthrate.'[34]

But these arguments threatened the new independence of middle-class women. It was widely recognised that apartments offered women at least a partial release from domestic drudgery. Instead of the 'management of a household which our benighted, unemancipated grandmothers were wont, stupidly, to look upon as a labour of love', *Art and Architecture* believed that the 'women of to-day have other outlets for such energy as they possess—and hence the demand for flats'.[35] While media moralists worried about the relationship between flats and childlessness, more and more middle-class women eagerly embraced flat life. A *Sydney Morning Herald* Women's Section writer observed: 'It is curious how many of us agree that living in a flat is the so-called wrong way of life. But we do continue to live in them, and they spring up on every side like mushrooms after rain. So their advantages in modern life must outweigh their supposed evils after all!'[36]

To women between the extremes of wealth, apartments offered an opportunity for independence and a more diverse life than was offered by the suburbs. In her novel *Time Enough Later* Kylie Tennant celebrated the independence of flat living: ' "We'll get a flat", she said

warmly, "at Kings Cross. It's so continental, so full of interesting people and unusual little shops. I like the colour and gaiety of the street stalls and the cafés." '[37] Such a 'bohemian' lifestyle continued to incite disapproval. In his novelistic memoir of between-wars Melbourne, *My Brother Jack*, George Johnston captured the mood of the times: 'There was something excitingly sordid about this particular visit … Uncle Stan at that time lived in one apartment of the first block of flats ever seen in Melbourne. It was in St Kilda Road, and of red brick, with leadlight windows. The novelty of this kind of communal living was regarded in the somewhat staid city of Melbourne as having distinctly immoral qualities, and I remember how we entered the lobby with Mother holding my hand very tightly …'[38]

The young Kenneth Slessor encountered similar parental attitudes in 1920 when beginning his career as a journalist, poet and flat-dweller. His brother Robin recalled:

Well to our dear mother the idea of taking a flat was only one step away from announcing he was going to shack up with a prostitute, because flats in those days were looked upon as evil, something really evil. For a boy of nineteen to take one was beyond mother's comprehension and she complained bitterly that he was paid far too much money and threatened to go and ask them [the *Sun*] to reduce his salary which of course she didn't do. But Ken left home and took his little unit somewhere or other around Darlinghurst or Kings Cross.[39]

For many single people flats offered a chance to escape boarding houses, suburban lodgings and hotels, which were home to perhaps a tenth of the population during the 1920s. Melbourne's Prahran municipality alone had 536 boarding houses in 1920.[40] The novelist Hal Porter experienced the petty tedium of life as a lodger: 'I find out that, behind the starched curtains and the half-drawn blinds and chipped prisms of privet and brassoed doorbell, lies a slum world run largely by Methodist widows, English, unintelligent, shrewd as pickpockets, a world where milk is poured into cups before tea is, where electric-light bulbs are thirty-watt, bananas black, apples shrivelled and flecked with acrid beauty spots, lavatory paper a scandal sheet …'[41]

The popularity of flats during the 1920s and 1930s produced alarm in many quarters. A disjuncture emerged between published opinion and urban reality. More than 70,000 apartment dwellings were built in Sydney between the first and second world wars. In 1911 flats represented just 1.5 per cent of private dwellings in Sydney; by the 1940s they accounted for 19 per cent—almost a fifth—of all private dwellings. In Melbourne the increase was less spectacular—by 1947 flats formed a tenth of the southern capital's dwellings—but more than enough to excite political and journalistic condemnation. In both cities apartment buildings spread rapidly into suburban areas.

⬆ One of the first 'talkies' to be made in Australia, the 1933 feature *The Hayseeds* used many of Sydney's most photogenic locations, including the roof of Bellevue Gardens flats at Potts Point.

⬅⬅ Apartment living has never lost its popular association with unconventional lifestyles and 'permissive' sexuality. The 1970s television soap opera *Number 96* explored all the angles.

⬅ 'Mrs Chisholm … is wearing a Lanvin model, made of heavy morocain.' Set in Darnley Hall apartments, Elizabeth Bay, Russell Roberts' 1935 portrait was one of many to use apartments as a setting for society and fashion photography.

Suburban rebellion

Ku-ring-gai was one of several Sydney suburban municipalities that attempted to ban apartment buildings entirely. According to Ku-ring-gai Alderman McFadyen, 'The flat dweller belongs to the floating population of the big cities and is of no value to the community, as a flat is not a home.'[42] Most of the protesting councillors represented wealthy harbourside suburbs, such as Vaucluse, Woollahra, Waverley, Mosman and Balmoral, where rising land values and views made apartments an attractive investment. Aldermanic agitation produced the Local Government (Amendment) Bill of 1928, which allowed local councils to 'prohibit the erection or use in a district for the purpose of a "residential flat"'. Councils could, however, prohibit flat buildings only in specified areas, not an entire municipality. Even these rules did not apply to the City Council, with the result that Kings Cross apartment blocks frequently occupied entire sites. A City Council alderman complained in 1939 that 'Kings Cross is fast becoming a slum area' owing to the lack of ventilation and space between apartments.[43]

The bill received support, particularly from the conservative side of politics, with Woollahra Alderman and Member of Parliament W. F. Latimer arguing that flat construction should be restricted to the city: 'Woollahra flats are a menace to the moral welfare of the community.'[44] Woollahra Council succeeded in forcing the redesign of some apartment proposals, yet by 1937 'about 50 per cent of the property on Point Piper is either flats, boarding houses or private homes that have been converted into rooms for letting'.[45] After continuing municipal protests, the New South Wales Government during the 1930s gave councils some discretionary powers over the design of flats before producing the *Local Government (Regulation of Flats) Act 1940*.[46] Although the new laws introduced site coverage limits for large apartment blocks, the focus remained on setting building setbacks from site borders.

In contrast, Melbourne's building laws were already more thorough in stipulating the retention of open space around buildings. They were stringently enforced by Melbourne City Council, with the result that few large apartment blocks were constructed in and around the city.[47] Apartments became an element in the competing reputations of the two cities. In a 1934 description of Sydney's 'modern flats', Melbourne's *Australian Home Beautiful* declared: 'Sydney has always, to some extent, been the home of the flat-dweller. For this a variety of reasons may be suggested, the most popular one being that the Sydney-sider is more easy-going and less home-loving than his Melbourne brother.'[48]

The eastern states debate was closely watched in Perth, where flats were becoming plentiful. In 1938 the Western Australian Government instructed a royal commission to consider whether Perth's building laws were sufficient to control these 'slums of the future'.[49] Harold Krantz, a young architect already synonymous with apartment architecture in Perth, argued that 'public antagonism' to flats 'has been stirred up by

⬆ Apartment buildings feature in the work of many artists, perhaps because they often provided their homes. In *The Heights of Darlinghurst* the artist and broadcaster Gladys Owen depicted Kingsclere and Byron Hall above her usual subjects, the threatened buildings of old Sydney.

↗ 'Here may be seen the great residential region of the flats of Darlinghurst.' Elizabeth Bay photographed from the air for *The Home* magazine, 1936.

↘ *Building*'s editor Florence Taylor was a prominent opponent of apartment living until her attitude changed, in part because of her own experience as a flat-dweller after being widowed in 1928. Taylor proposed many grand urban visions, including this plan to transform 'the slum area of Woolloomooloo' with multistorey flats.

so-called housing reformers … not willing to concede our democratic rights to live as we please'. He went on to argue that 'the architectural possibilities of flat buildings … are far greater than those of unending rows of small villas on small allotments. A city of flats is infinitely more exciting aesthetically …'[50]

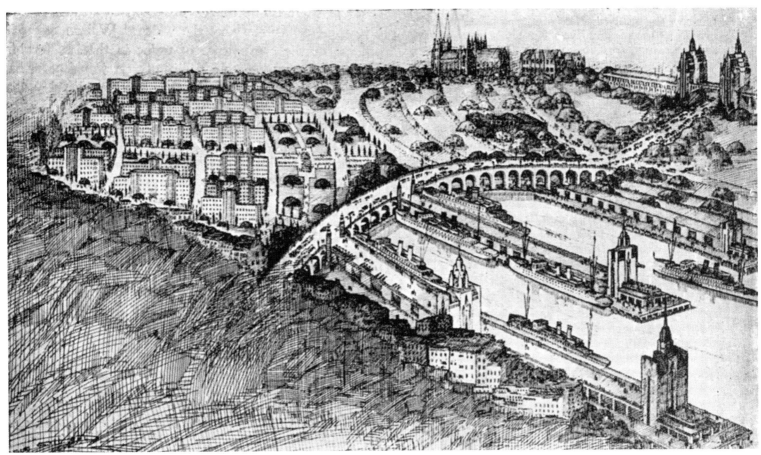

Partly owing to its prominent location near Sydney Harbour Bridge, Blues Point Tower has provoked debate since its completion in 1962. Embodying many of the debates surrounding apartments in Australia, the building has been a reliable space-filler for the Sydney media. Every Sydneysider has an opinion about Blues Point Tower. For example, Frank Sartor, former Sydney Lord Mayor: 'It's not a thing of beauty, indeed it's the converse, it bears no relationship to its environment … If it was in my power and I could do it with no cost to the taxpayer, I'd get rid of it.'[1]

Blues Point Tower is probably the best-known building designed by Harry Seidler, who is one of relatively few architects to build a public reputation largely on the basis of apartment design. Seidler regarded Blues Point Tower as one of his best buildings, and was always prepared to defend his creation.

The controversy and personalisation of the building has obscured the tower's rationale. The uncompromising modernity of Blues Point Tower resulted from Seidler's study of the views and aspect of Blues Point, which is 'surrounded on three sides by water'. He rejected 'a long slab-like building orientated North–South … its long glass facades would be undesirable since the Northern view … is poor and complete

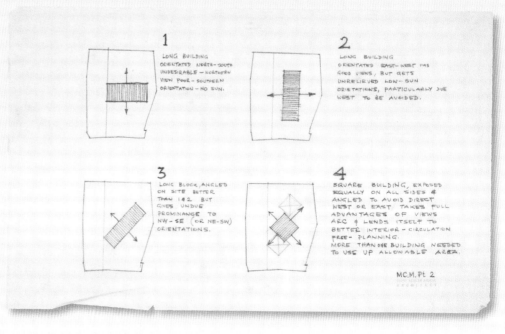

southern orientation is undesirable [i.e. lack of sunlight].' Other orientations had similar problems, whereas a square tower 'exposed equally on all sides, set diagonally, angled to avoid direct West or East orientations, takes full advantage of the view-arc and makes it possible for a high percentage of flats to have double exposure, i.e. views in both directions'.[2] In addition, the tower's small footprint allows generous public space and foreshore access at its base.

Comprising twenty-three residential floors totalling 168 dwellings, Blues Point Tower was Australia's first strata-titled apartment building, and it ushered in an era in which apartment living was allied to the 'Australian dream' of home owner-ship. Although some of its flats have been amalgamated to create larger spaces, the modesty of its materials and the small size of its dwellings have always been somewhat at odds with the building's reputation and its unmissable profile. Yet they are crucial to the logic of Blues Point Tower—to strike a blow against urban sprawl and for demo-cratic enjoyment of harbourside living. Harry Seidler: 'They are humble small apartments … it didn't have marble floors or a con-cierge or any of that stuff. It was meant to be accessible to people of average means. It just has the best views in Australia.'[3]

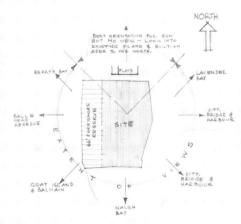

Modernist visions

The 1950s are regarded as the most passionate decade of the Australian love affair with suburban living. For the first time a majority of Australian families held the title deeds to their home. The decade was also another episode in the cottage/flat debate, fuelled in part by the new self-confidence of Modernism and its enthusiasts.

Architect Samuel Lipson, experienced interpreter of international trends, was among those to report that 'Australia will never catch up on its housing lag while it neglects to build flats … Australia is lagging far behind because all the emphasis is on individual homes.'[51] In Europe a wave of apartment building was compelled in part by the need to house those left homeless by the war as well as a fresh political idealism. In Australia the housing shortage created by the 1930s depression and the war incited similar idealism, with governments finally accepting responsibility for housing the poor and poorly housed. Although the new housing commissions built suburbs as well as flat complexes, suburban expansion began to attract criticism as an enemy of the modern, rationally designed city. The most influential exponents of this case were émigré architects, including Frederick Romberg and Harry Seidler, who fled Europe during the 1930s and 1940s.

Seidler arrived in Australia in 1948 having completed a student project on apartment design at the University of Manitoba and Harvard studies under Walter Gropius. He was shocked to find cities composed of brick cottages 'utterly alien to a country with a climate of such small temperature variations as those prevailing in the South Eastern part of Australia'. Seidler had no doubt that exposure to contemporary European architecture would challenge local prejudices: 'People here don't like flats, mainly because of the monstrosities that were built in the past … Australians would lose their prejudice against flats if they saw these developments.'[52]

By the 1950s some former critics, notably *Building*'s editor Florence Taylor, became converts to apartment living. Taylor complained:

> our people are compelled to live in drab outer suburbs, when thousands and thousands could be afforded Harbour views and at the same time live close to the city, which would result in an immense saving in transportation … Our antediluvian building laws proclaim 'a residential area' of the most beautiful districts, but permit only one favoured tenant to occupy one cottage on most valuable land, which could and should be shared with others in well-built and architecturally beautiful flats …[53]

Denis Winston, professor of town planning at the University of Sydney, was another to call for the reversal of the 'fashionable flight from the centre to the suburbs, the escapism which has always marked the decline of civilization'.[54] Winston spent the 1950s complaining that 'the home has become a kind of talisman making it difficult socially,

politically and even financially … to build any other than a three bedroom textured brick bungalow, one and half hours from the office with a picture window to frame the view of the "septic," and a lifetime to pay off the mortgage!'[55] Sydney's Lord Mayor, Harry Jensen, conceded that 'huge blocks of flats' could be 'a major answer to the housing problem'.[56] At the same time a variety of Australian writers, notably Barry Humphries, Patrick White and George Johnston, mocked the suburbs as cultural wastelands.[57]

This tide of argument provided the intellectual ammunition for Australia's post-war apartment boom. Although delayed until the late 1950s by shortages of building materials, labour and capital, the apartment building frenzy that then engulfed the construction industry dwarfed its predecessors of the 1920s and late 1930s. 'All over the metropolitan area ultra-modern blocks of home units are springing up, sparking off a new way of life,' a *Sunday Telegraph* feature on apartment living observed. 'Low-density living has been presented as giving better living conditions—even as an Australian trait—but increasingly people are finding the suburban sprawl no longer to their liking.'[58] In 1970, for the first time in any Australian city, more flats were built in Sydney than houses.

The backlash

Sydney's post-war apartment boom threatened a 'wall-like effect of continuous high slab buildings parallel to the foreshore'.[59] Architects were among the critics: 'Mr Seidler said the present redevelopment by individual real estate operators and builders would ruin the Harbourside suburbs unless it was properly planned. At present, new apartment blocks were going up on any site, blocking out each other's views of the water …'[60] Harry Seidler was also scathing about the 'rows and rows of flats and home units' being built in the suburbs, 'their regularity separated only by "shooting gallery" spaces between them'.[61]

Yet Seidler remained identified with the apartment boom and its failings. The architect and cartoonist George Molnar was an early critic of urban consequences of Seidler's many apartment projects: 'Most of these blocks are not only unrelated to the ground they stand on but are definitely hostile to it … As the blocks of flats grow larger the scale set by the units of habitation disappears and the façade becomes a play of patterns of glass and solid, geometrical and inhuman.'[62]

Local campaigns opposed apartment developments in several suburbs, reflecting the renewed desirability of the inner suburbs: 'Over the past five or six years terrace houses have been "taken over" by authors,

➲ Commissioned by architects, builders, journalists and advertisers, Max Dupain depicted flats from many viewpoints. This photo illustrated a 1956 *Australian House and Garden* story about flats as a 'background for bachelors … the old-fashioned idea that men can't look after themselves goes by the board these days …'

In 1962 Dupain used models and a North Sydney block of bachelor flats in a photo advertising windows and doors.

The photographer David Mist arrived in Australia from England during the 1960s, quickly making himself at home both in Sydney's fashion world and on the roof of his Kirribilli bachelor flat. The association of flats and pleasure was ultimately more convincing than Modernist logic.

artists, architects and actors, who have bought houses, often in conditions which at first sight look beyond repair, and "done them up".[63] This cultural shift embraced some 'slum' areas, notably Paddington and Balmain, Carlton and Fitzroy, which were reborn as sought-after addresses. Gentrification of old suburbs saw urbanity become associated with heritage houses rather than with new apartments.

These circumstances created several confrontations; the most notable being sparked by Victoria Point, a large apartment development proposed for Victoria Street, Potts Point. The project brought together Frank Theeman, a first-time property developer who had recently sold his successful clothing business, with a newly desirable street

composed of large Victorian terraces. It provoked an unusual alliance between squatters, urban conservationists and unionists led by Jack Mundey of the New South Wales Builders' Labourers Federation.

A former footballer and building worker, Mundey had joined the Communist Party and become a union activist during the 1960s primarily out of concern for the exploitative and dangerous conditions prevalent in the booming construction industry. By the time he became secretary of the BLF in 1970, Mundey and his supporters had developed a form of socially conscious unionism, in which urban and social issues were legitimate reasons for industrial campaigns. As well as its architectural heritage, Victoria Street was still largely tenanted by workers and retirees,

and the BLF's 'Green Ban' on construction work was aimed at protecting low-cost housing as well as the street's architectural character.

Although the original proposal for three forty-five-storey apartment towers was greatly ameliorated to a smaller development that retained most of the existing terrace houses, conflict continued over Theeman's use of hired thugs to evict squatters and tenants.[64] The consequences were explosive and violent, including the still unsolved disappearance of the department store heiress Juanita Nielsen, a prominent supporter of the Green Ban. Theeman eventually withdrew from the stalemated controversy. The events also provided the background to two successful feature films, novels and other fiction.

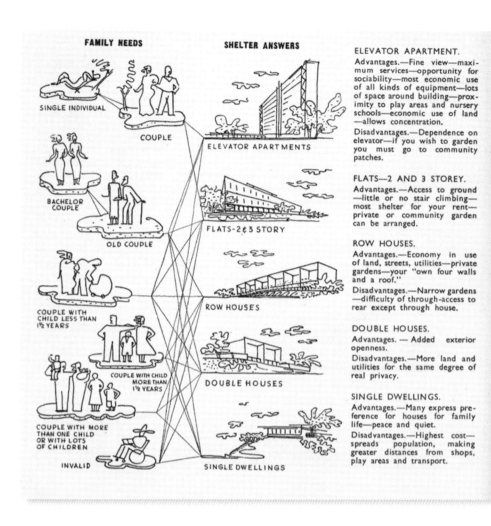

FAMILY NEEDS

SINGLE INDIVIDUAL

COUPLE

BACHELOR COUPLE

OLD COUPLE

COUPLE WITH CHILD LESS THAN 1½ YEARS

COUPLE WITH CHILD MORE THAN 1½ YEARS

COUPLE WITH MORE THAN ONE CHILD OR WITH LOTS OF CHILDREN

INVALID

SHELTER ANSWERS

ELEVATOR APARTMENTS

FLATS—2 & 3 STORY

ROW HOUSES

DOUBLE HOUSES

SINGLE DWELLINGS

ELEVATOR APARTMENT.
Advantages.—Fine view—maximum services—opportunity for sociability—most economic use of all kinds of equipment—lots of space around building—proximity to play areas and nursery schools—economic use of land —allows concentration.
Disadvantages.—Dependence on elevator—if you wish to garden you must go to community patches.

FLATS—2 AND 3 STOREY.
Advantages.—Access to ground —little or no stair climbing— most shelter for your rent— private or community garden can be arranged.

ROW HOUSES.
Advantages.—Economy in use of land, streets, utilities—private gardens—your "own four walls and a roof."
Disadvantages.—Narrow gardens —difficulty of through-access to rear except through house.

DOUBLE HOUSES.
Advantages. — Added exterior openness.
Disadvantages.—More land and utilities for the same degree of real privacy.

SINGLE DWELLINGS.
Advantages.—Many express preference for houses for family life—peace and quiet.
Disadvantages.—Highest cost— spreads population, making greater distances from shops, play areas and transport.

MOLNAR 19 2 81

SORRY. I THOUGHT IT WAS A DOLE QUEUE.

◄ Architect and senior executive of the newly created Commonwealth Housing Commission, Walter Bunning typified the idealism and rationality of mid-century Modernism. His 1946 diagram matched dwelling types with social groups.
⬆ The year 1981 saw both an economic and employment downturn and the completion of the luxurious and expensive Kincoppal apartment block at Elizabeth Bay. The coincidence produced a typically sardonic comment from architect and cartoonist George Molnar.

Jack Mundey later reflected: 'I think that a compromise on medium density housing would have been a good thing, with a guaranteed percentage of low income earners having permanent occupation. It didn't happen … In the late 1970s, Theeman's financiers, CAGA, started to put up expensive home units in his name …'[65]

Although leadership conflicts saw the BLF drop its Green Bans on contentious projects in 1975, its activities during the early 1970s fundamentally altered urban planning and attitudes in Sydney. Urban and heritage considerations gained decidedly greater influence with governments, architects and the public. Australia's first heritage protection laws were one of the results.[66] During the 1970s most Sydney councils introduced new building regulations that restricted the height, site coverage and other elements of new apartments. In municipalities where apartments were concentrated, such as Woollahra and North Sydney, control of apartment development became a major local issue.

A telling indicator of the new climate occurred in 1982, when the cartoonist Patrick Cook published a cartoon titled 'Harry Seidler Retirement Park', caricaturing apartment buildings designed by Seidler, who was by then Australia's best-known architect. The cartoon showed box-like structures with small apertures through which people were being fed. Cook explained that the structures were inspired by Seidler's buildings, notably Blues Point Tower, Seidler's signature harbourside apartment tower. At the back of the structure a man was removing excrement with a shovel and putting it into a cart, surrounded by flies and filth.

Weary of attacks on his work, Seidler brought an action for defamation against the *National Times*, publisher of the cartoon. Testifying during the case, Cook claimed the cartoon made three points against Seidler's buildings: 'that in his opinion they were ugly, induced claustrophobia and were severely functional'. Cook described Blues Point Tower as a 'hideous … offence against the Harbour'.[67] Seidler lost the case and the appeal.

The case, which brought two of Australia's leading cultural personalities into a courtroom, entertained the public intermittently for months. Its result was confirmation of a more aesthetically driven ambivalence about apartment buildings, a contrast to the more moralistic criticism of former years.

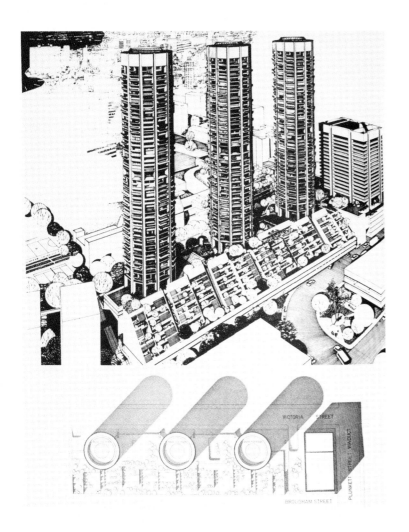

PROPERTY & DEVELOPMENT
CARRY THE OBLIGATION
TO EXPLOIT

In Memory of Victoria St Kings Cross

NO TO THEEMANS
MILLION DOLLAR DREAMS

↖ The first proposal for the major flat development in Victoria Street, Potts Point. The development was thwarted by one of the first union 'Green Bans' rather than by Sydney's liberal development laws.

↑ 'In memory of Victoria St, Kings Cross.' Jan Mackay's poster commemorates the bitterest controversy of Australian development history. Although the Green Ban era was short-lived, it encouraged more critical assessment of apartment design.

← Donald Crombie's 1981 *The Killing of Angel Street* used the Victoria Street conflict as source material for a contemporary urban thriller. *Heatwave*, directed by Phillip Noyce and starring Judy Davis, was a more commercially successful interpretation.

When completed in 1994, Melbourne Terrace was a confirmation of Melbourne's urban rebirth. Forced by the 1980s financial roller-coaster to confront its tired public and economic infrastructure, Melbourne made the decision to restore urban fabric and lifestyle and to re-establish the city as a desirable urban address. The new urban self-consciousness was expressed in several ways, including new public buildings and spaces. It also inspired a new generation of city apartments.

Nonda Katsalidis came to Australia from Athens as a boy: 'I always felt I was wrenched away … Melbourne in the 50s and 60s wasn't a very interesting place … I grew up living above shops in Carlton and Fitzroy, some very tough streets but it was alive. I hate the suburbs, it's a disease …'[1]

Despite his European longings, Katsalidis conceded that 'the culture has changed. It's come alive.' His own part in this change was the design of a series of landmark apartment buildings, beginning with Melbourne Terrace. Several Melbourne architects were already recycling local materials and symbols, creating structures that embraced the city's history and design vernacular. Katsalidis took this process a step further and avoided homely localism in favour of cosmopolitan borrowings, most obviously the quasi-Classical sculptures guarding Melbourne Terrace's four main entrances.

More programmically urban is Melbourne Terrace's exterior of street-level retail spaces mixed with a palette of materials, collaging a monolithic building—the Terrace occupies an entire city block—into a series

of patterns and colours. Despite its urbanity and generous balconies, the Terrace's sixty-five apartments are notable for their spaciousness and privacy, a quality heightened by the block's division into four distinct buildings titled Equus, Roma, Mondo and Fortuna. For Melbourne Terrace residents, city living does not require the sacrifice of suburban space or amenity.

Melbourne Terrace played a part in revitalising the Queen Victoria Market precinct, partly owing to its high-profile residents, who included the architect. Representing a more expressive and playful urbanism than Seidler's austere rationality, Melbourne Terrace restated the appeal of city living.

⬆ Harry Seidler, photographed here by Eric Sierins in 2005 with a model of his Perth Emu Brewery apartment complex, was one of a small number of architects who personified apartment design.

↗ Patrick Cook's 1982 cartoon dramatised divisions in middle-class opinion about the aesthetics and morality of apartment living.

Tower blocks

The new climate had its greatest influence in the field of public housing, where it created a reconsideration of 'slum reclamation' and its consequences. Many 'slum' dwellers had never been in favour of rehousing. *Poor Man's Orange*, Ruth Park's popular 1940s novel of inner-city life, drew on this sentiment: ' "Nobody asked if we want to be chucked out of our houses ... This is where we belong," said Delie definitely. Thus, while the rest of Sydney was reading the papers and thinking how nice it would be for the poor Surry Hills people to live in decent places at last, the poor Surry Hills people were fuming ...'[68]

Melbourne's inner suburbs were remade with a ruthlessness not matched in other Australian cities. During the 1960s the Victorian Housing Commission built twenty-one high-rise estates, featuring forty-five tower blocks housing about 14,000 people.[69] The commission's chairman was not moved by local opposition: 'People always resented being forced from their slum houses. But, after it had happened and they were re-housed, they realized it was for their good.'[70] As the Melbourne activist Kay Hargreaves observed, 'the Housing Commission may have set some sort of record in continuing to rely on a set of social and economic assumptions made in the nineteen thirties'.[71]

By the end of the 1960s residents' action groups were active in all of the areas affected by Housing Commission plans. As well as a concern to maintain communities and social networks, these groups were motivated by a new appreciation of the architecture and character of inner-city housing and its increasing value. At the same time, tower blocks were accused of creating youthful deprivation similar to the slums they replaced. A 1971 *Age* exposé of 'high-rise kids' reported:

There are kids in Melbourne who have never used a knife or fork or a tablecloth, who have never seen beans or a piece of cabbage, who don't know the names of animals, apart from dogs and cats ... Every apartment visited during this survey has its TV going at the time, regardless of whether it is morning, afternoon or night. Everybody seems to be watching the screen, from preschool kids to those rare beings who hope to go on to university.[72]

The Victorian and New South Wales governments ended their high-rise public housing program during the 1970s. Both housing commissions began the decade with ambitious plans for tower block construction in the inner suburbs. By 1975 most of these plans were in abeyance, thanks in part to an international backlash against high-rise public housing.

Consolidation

A century ago suburban living was promoted as a panacea to the social and public health malaise afflicting cities, which was dramatised in Sydney by the bubonic plague outbreaks of 1900. Decades of debate focused on the culture and aesthetics of suburban living, united by agreement on its centrality to the 'Australian dream'. In contrast, apartments struggled for credibility and approval as a legitimate way of living.

The period since the 1980s has seen a dramatic reassessment of these attitudes. The cost of providing transport and other infrastructure forced governments to reconsider their commitment to suburban expansion. In addition, suburban expansion is today frequently viewed as a culprit in a potentially severe crisis of urban environment, transport, affordability and liveability. As a result, city fringe land for cottage building is released slowly, in favour of higher-density development within existing boundaries. Apartment development is favoured by urban consolidation policies.

By 1990, for the first time in decades, the population of central city areas had begun to increase. The continued flight to the suburbs, still the major dynamic of Australian urban development, now competes with the lifestyle of public consumption and urbanity. A Melbourne developer summarised the city apartment market as follows: 'And that has been a major push both in young people starting out wanting to buy into the excitement, and also a large market, the empty-nester market, people late-forties, fifties, kids moved out of home, downsized, coming back to where things are—cafés, restaurants and such-like—they're wanting to buy into that lifestyle as well.'[73] Similarly, the popularity of apartment living among European and Asian immigrants has broadened the apartment demographic.[74]

↑ 'Aerial view of slum reclamation'. Public housing towers are the most prominent structures in this 1970 view of Melbourne's suburbs.

Urban consolidation is the setting for the contemporary apartment versus cottage—or McMansion—argument. Several academics and journalists have argued that government promotion of apartment living is founded in cultural prejudices rather than economic or ecological pressures. According to the opinion columnist Michael Duffy, the result of urban consolidation is 'the destruction of the traditional suburban way of life that has suited the vast majority of Sydneysiders. Governments have been assisted in this by certain planners and

Apartment living Marinco Kodjanovski

A thirty-something bachelor, Marinco Kodjanovski has lived in apartments since he moved out of home at the age of twenty-eight. The most recent apartment is a studio of 45 square metres in inner-city Sydney, which is basically one room.

The son of Macedonian migrants, Marinco was born four days after their arrival in Sydney to make a new life for the family with only a few bags and some blankets. Growing up in the archetypal suburban house and garden in Sydney's inner and outer west, Marinco views his years living in apartments as definitely temporary: 'I hate apartments. I'm only living in this studio because it's close to work, and I'm saving money to buy a large house. My aim is a house with three garages so that I can keep my Ducati motorbike, my everyday car and my dream car, a 1965 Mustang. And I want water

views and a balcony from which I can throw a rock into the water. I will keep working hard until I can afford it.'

Marinco bought his ninth-floor apartment not long after the building was completed in the 1990s. Part of an adaptive reuse complex common in this part of town, it has 144 apartments and a communal gym and lap pool for residents. The reasons he likes the inner city are that it's close to his work in a photographic studio and that it's a great place to eat and drink. 'The studio suits my current lifestyle. I'm out a lot pursuing a range of interests—fishing,

mountain-bike riding, socialising—so it's very convenient. I like the privacy of it. I don't want to know anyone in the block because I have plenty of friends and a busy life. I just come and go. But one day when I'm married with kids I will leave apartment living far behind. I want some space with room for the kids to play backyard sports, such as cricket, like I did as a child. This is what Australia is all about. This is what my parents dreamed of, and I share their dream; having some space, a nice house, a view and a good quality of life.'

Housing Project No. 84, by the Italy-based Australian artist Jeffrey Smart, captures the generic nature of public housing developments throughout the world. According to Jeffrey Smart: 'Travelling on long haul flight Syd-Bangkok and the woman alongside me had a small tapestry frame and was forming … a lot of coloured knots, something like squares, and it led me to *Housing Project*.'

environmentalists antipathetic to that tradition, indeed contemptuous of the suburbs. They desire to change our cities into a green fantasy of Paris … They speak of bringing the vibrancy of Manhattan to Sydney, and contrast this dream with the tedium of ordinary life in a freestanding house with a garden …'[75]

The campaign against urban consolidation is more strident in Melbourne than Sydney. Generic and widely dispersed public housing towers created a strong reaction against high-rise apartments, which was accompanied by something of a return to pre-1939 anti-apartment opinion. But whereas public housing was confined to working-class areas, urban policy now encourages apartment development in affluent established suburbs, creating alarm among Melbourne's well-off.

Formed in 1997, the 'Save Our Suburbs' movement has gained a high public profile, largely through a series of campaigns against apartment developments, including a sprawling 128-apartment complex in the inner suburb of Fitzroy. Opposition to this development was primarily based on its inconsistency with existing building scale: 'Fundamentally Fitzroy is low rise and I think people like it like that.' The architect of the project, Ivan Rijavec, pointed to its environment-friendly credentials while offering a different response to suburban scale: 'Melburnians are height-phobic when really they should be pancake phobic. Flat, pancake development leads to consistency and mediocrity.'[76]

Other disputes have taken place in wealthy suburbs that lacked tolerance for apartments and high-density living, notably Camberwell,

where the prominent objectors Barry Humphries and Geoffrey Rush have ensured publicity. However, the most high-profile controversy occurred in the apartment-friendly suburb of St Kilda, where the developer Becton's proposal for a thirty-eight-storey tower at the Esplanade Hotel provoked the ire of thousands of local residents. The furore lasted well over five years with a campaign driven by the Esplanade Alliance community group.

Nonda Katsalidis is the architect most responsible for the renewed respectability of apartment living in Melbourne. During the 1990s he

SAVE OUR SUBURB

DEADLINE IS THIS THURSDAY
YOUR INPUT IS VITAL

SAY **NO** TO URBAN CITY

HIGH RISE DEVELOPMENT

WRITE TO THE WALKERVILLE COUNCIL
BY THE 15TH OF DECEMBER 2005

⬆ 'Towering apartments, acres of car parks ... is this where you want to live?' So read a poster in Adelaide's exclusive suburb of Walkerville in 2005, pasted alongside the one pictured above. These public notices are representative of anti-high-rise sentiments in Australia's more affluent suburbs.

⬅ Republic Tower in Queen Street, Melbourne, epitomises the urban and aesthetic impact of contemporary city apartment developments.

designed a series of landmark apartment blocks, including St Leonards apartments in St Kilda. Despite these credentials and an area comfortable with flat-dwelling as a normal way of life, the locals bucked at his design for the development and galvanised a record 11,500 objections. Apart from the size of the planned building, the inspiration for objection was the fate of the 'Espy' Hotel, a centre of Melbourne social life since 1878 and more recently the focus of the city's music scene. Although a much smaller apartment block gained council approval in 2003, the controversy continues.[77]

Save Our Suburbs claimed a major victory in 2004 when a three-storey limit was imposed on apartment developments in most residential areas of Melbourne.[78] The Sydney equivalent of Save Our Suburbs has struggled to generate a substantial public profile, although campaigns against urban consolidation have been prominent in several localities, notably the Ku-ring-gai municipality on Sydney's leafy North Shore. Kathy Cowley, secretary of Friends of Lindfield, argued that 'Ku-ring-gai is not the place for apartment buildings ... Her back garden has old eucalypt trees, lily pillies and maples and 10 species of bird visitors, the kind of place where families relax and "a quiet place for reflection and relaxation in this world of hustle and bustle" '.[79]

Ku-ring-gai is typical of several North Shore suburbs with an ageing, declining population. Yet its protectors see no virtue in urban consolidation and apartment development. Sandy Bathgate, convenor of the Ku-ring-gai Rally Committee, described 'the prospect of an eight-kilometre swathe of apartment development along the North Shore railway line as the equivalent of taking your car keys and scraping them along the side of your new Mercedes'.[80]

After a century and more, the debates between apartment and cottage living continue to rage. If the arguments today concern environment and heritage rather than the birthrate and family morality, they are hardly less vehement for that.

2

In 1912 Professor Robert Irvine of Sydney University was sent by the New South Wales Government to investigate housing in Europe and the USA. He reported:

New Yorkers, it seemed to me, have grown to love the life of the city, its brilliancy, its crowds, its pleasure-houses … They have suffered the tenement-house system to grow to its present proportions because, on the whole, they preferred it; and I should imagine they would be rather unhappy in our sparsely peopled suburbs where life is quiet and beautiful enough, but extremely dull and petty … For the same reason, many people in Sydney are now crowding into boarding and apartment houses.[1]

Sydney's flirtation with city living created Australia's first precinct of apartment buildings, built in and near Macquarie Street after 1900. The precinct reached its social and architectural pinnacle in 1923, with the completion of The Astor apartment building in Macquarie Street. The Astor was declared open by Sir George Fuller, Premier of New South Wales: 'The opening ceremony took place on the roof garden, commanding a magnificent view of the harbour, the Botanic Gardens, and the city. The statement that the roof is on a level with Killara affords an idea of the towering height of the building, which has been erected in Renaissance style, and comprises 13 floors and a basement, with four homes on each floor.'[2]

Despite the continuing apartment debate, The Astor inspired admiration and envy from the start. Apart from its size and prominent location, the social eminence of The Astor's residents ensured a high profile. In 1923 these included the philanthropist Eadith Walker and the entertainment impresario Hugh D. McIntosh, owner of the Sydney Stadium and the Tivoli theatre chain. Another original resident was John O'Brien, grazier turned city property developer, responsible for The Astor's construction. The Astor has since been home to many of Sydney's best-known citizens, including several of artistic note such as Portia Geach and Barry Humphries.[3] Arthur Streeton, Will Ashton and Harold Cazneaux were among those to depict the view from the roof garden.[4]

Macquarie Street

Macquarie Street, which features substantial terrace housing adjacent to major public institutions including the New South Wales Parliament, Sydney Hospital and the Supreme Court, had for decades been one of Sydney's sought-after residential streets. By 1900 the precinct also featured the chambers of legal and medical professionals, as well as numerous gentlemen's clubs. Residential chambers and boarding houses, purpose-built or converted from houses, flourished yet these did not feature self-contained kitchens and bathrooms. However, some professional chambers and clubs were transformed into apartments for residential use. Cromer at 91 Phillip Street, parallel to Macquarie Street, was an example. Built about 1890 as Club Cromer, it became Cromer Flats by 1900, and its function changed accordingly.[5] Chambers and offices were also converted, including Phillip Court in Phillip Street, 'a nest of inconvenient and badly lighted offices, now transformed into commodious and comfortable flats'.[6]

The first purpose-built mansion flats in Sydney combined residential dwellings with professional chambers. The first to be completed was The Albany in 1905. *Art and Architecture*, journal of the Institute of Architects, underlined its novelty: 'the block just erected at considerable cost is situated opposite the Houses of Parliament … it is the first of its kind erected in the city. The building is one of seven storeys. The ground and first floors provide accommodation for twelve suites of medical and dental chambers; the remaining stories include seven suites of flats …'[7]

The Albany was named after a well-known London block of bachelor apartments, whose tenants included leading politicians

➡ No longer Macquarie Street's tallest building, The Astor retains its status as one of Sydney's 'high-class and fashionable city flats'. The *National Times* once drolly observed: 'The Astor is especially difficult to buy into because most of its occupants leave via their deathbeds.'
Overleaf: The Albany, Australia's first high-class city apartment building, with its neighbour the 1840s mansion Burdekin House. Both buildings were demolished during the 1930s for the extension of Martin Place to Macquarie Street, Sydney.

The wool broker Sir James McGregor lived at Strathkyle during 1925 while his Darling Point residence Neidpath was built. Harold Cazneaux photographed McGregor's flat, highlighting his collection of artworks by Will Ashton, George Lambert and Norman Lindsay.

'Of recent years a new factor has entered into Australian construction … the building of residential flats, which are really a series of houses super-imposed' (*Building*, January 1910). Strathkyle in Sydney was one of these.

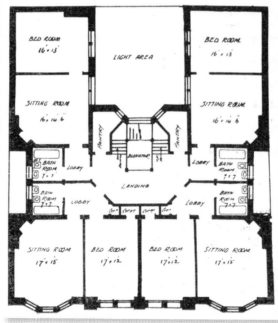

and writers. Sydney's Albany also attracted prestigious clientele; its first residents included Sir Samuel Griffith, Chief Justice of the newly formed Supreme Court of Australia. The professional tenants were primarily dental surgeons. A similar mix of tenants and residents occupied Craignish, which was completed in 1907 in Macquarie Street, and Strathkyle, completed in 1909 in nearby Bligh Street. *Building* marvelled at the skill of Strathkyle's architects in creating 'twenty-four suites of compartments [sic], each complete in itself. The building is eight storeys high, and in addition to the suites contain offices for managers, servants' accommodation, and other accessories.'[8]

Stylistically these first flats found inspiration in the contemporary commercial popularity of Romanesque Revival: heavy rusticated masonry, narrow arched windows and bold 'Roman' arched openings. By the 1920s, the Classical Palazzo style was more in favour for city buildings, and The Astor followed suit, adding prominent windows and concrete construction to the revivalist mix. 'Mr O'Brien's idea is that you can hardly have windows that are too big ... particularly where the view is so magnificant.'[9]

The sole survivor of this first decade of construction is Wyoming, John O'Brien's first apartment venture, completed in 1909. Wyoming was a sought-after address even before construction. According to *Building*, 'Wyoming Chambers ... built for professional chambers and residential flats ... is one of the most satisfactory real estate speculations in Sydney. When originally designed it was considered six storeys would give good return, but as all space was taken prior to the work being commenced, two additional storeys were added.'[10]

A 'self-contained home in miniature'

Apartments came to Australia some decades after apartment living had been established in Europe and North America. After the reconstruction of Paris between 1850 and 1870 perimeter blocks of apartment housing and shops lined broad boulevards, creating a form of housing and streetscape that quickly defined planned European cities, such as Vienna. Urban reconstruction designed by H. P. Berlage in South

⬆ Arthur Streeton painted *The Harbour from Wyoming* in 1926 for Oscar Paul, dentist and resident of Wyoming. Streeton had already produced a similar view from the Wyoming rooftop as well as one from The Astor.

⬆ '... one of the most satisfactory real estate speculations in Sydney ...' Situated opposite the State Library of New South Wales, Wyoming has survived city office tower construction booms.

Amsterdam and Ildefons Cerdá in Barcelona also employed apartments as the basic unit for perimeters of city blocks.

In England and the USA 'French flats' was the term popularly used to distinguish European-style multiple dwellings built for middle-class residents from workers' crowded tenements. However, even this expression became unfashionable in the late nineteenth century because of its link with Continental permissiveness. Nonetheless apartments quickly found favour with the wealthy. New York especially witnessed a rapid change from the 1880s as affluent New Yorkers abandoned private houses in favour of multiple dwellings. The Stuyvescent and the Dakota were among the first mansion flats to be serviced by the recently developed passenger elevator. By 1920 Fifth Avenue and Park Avenue, New York's best addresses, were lined with tall apartment buildings.[11]

European and North American flat-dwellers were drawn from the social extremes of wealth and poverty, and many Australians assumed that a similar pattern would be repeated here: 'Sydney … will in time follow the fashion of the old world cities. The workman will have the modern tenement flat in order to be near to his work … The rich, too, are everywhere swinging back into the flat …'[12]

Although workers' flats inspired controversy, they were quickly outnumbered by apartments for professionals, the middle class and the wealthy, more readily integrated in the status quo. Most press commentary on Australia's first mansion flats was positive: 'the "flat" is a self-contained home in miniature, where the tenants share only the lift and stairs in common. Once inside his own entrance door each is shut off from his neighbour as much as he could possibly be in any house that is not quite detached.'[13] The Macquarie Street cluster of apartments emerged with surprisingly little debate.

The servant problem

Although 1900s Melbourne lacked an apartment precinct, by the end of 1906 it featured a grander apartment building than any in Sydney. Situated at the fashionable end of Collins Street, Melbourne Mansions offered two floors of doctors' rooms at ground and basement level beneath five floors of apartment suites. So novel to the antipodes was the apartment genre that the building's owner, David Syme, researched the design of London apartments as well as the few Sydney counterparts. Syme's informant found that The Albany's tenants were charged for meals in addition to their rental of £150 to £200 per year. The building's manager observed that 'if each flat has its own kitchen the building is charged with the different smells of ingredients, cooking, etc, and causes each Flat owner to engage an attendant to obviate which is the prime reason for going into flats … A lift specially designed for carrying food, etc runs from the kitchen, which is on the roof, through each suite of rooms.'[14]

⬆ For almost two decades, Melbourne Mansions, dominating the top end of Collins Street, was the grandest apartment building in Australia. Like most early city blocks, it offered professional suites and a dining room as well as apartments.

Syme's architects Walter Butler and George Inskip did not follow The Albany's template, and most of Melbourne Mansions' twenty-seven suites featured kitchens, although residents could also be served with meals supplied by the Mansions' chefs or eat at the ground floor dining room. Syme was publisher of the *Age* and other papers, one of which described Melbourne Mansions' tenants as those who 'keep the necessary servants, provide the required food and [are] as entirely independent of the administrative part of the establishment as if resident in a country villa'.[15]

Shared catering, cleaning and other servants' services was also a feature of Cliveden Mansions, a 1911 conversion of a palatial 1880s mansion facing Fitzroy Gardens in East Melbourne. Financed by the Baillieu family, Cliveden Mansions featured similar social distinction

⬆ Cliveden Mansions housed many of Melbourne's 'best people' until it was demolished to make way for the Hilton Hotel. Cliveden retained many interior features of the original mansion, including the main staircase, oak panelling and electroliers.

among its tenants, who included Sir John Madden, the Chief Justice of Victoria. None of the fifty apartments included kitchens, and meals were supplied from a communal kitchen. Unlike most early mansion flats, no accommodation was provided for servants.

Cliveden was one of numerous 1880s mansions converted to flats, boarding houses, private hospitals and other uses during the first decades of the twentieth century. In 1891 Victoria had more than 1200 houses with twenty or more rooms. By 1921 there just 569 such mansions in all of Australia.[16] Scarcity of servants was a major reason, as working women could now find jobs in shops and factories. One consequence was smaller, more efficiently designed suburban homes. Another was the 'luxury flat' with shared domestic assistance to house refugees from larger homes.

⬆ 'The Misses Mary and June Winter-Irving ... in their flat at "Cliveden", East Melbourne', *The Home*, May 1934.

Completed in 1914, Strickland is a contemporary of Kingsclere. Tenants of Strickland, as the first large public apartment building in Australia, could hardly have been more different from those enjoying harbour views from Potts Point. Nonetheless, comparisons were made: ' "The flats are palatial enough for Potts Point," remarked one of the council officials …'[1]

In 1914 Sydney City Council had only recently gained the power to build public housing, and was anxious to provide affordable, quality housing for city workers in Chippendale's 'mean dilapidated houses in mean little streets'. The council's 'original idea was to build cottages', but the price of land a short walk from Central railway station rendered this plan impractical.[2]

Comprising seventy-one family flats in a three-storey building occupying an entire block, Strickland Flats was designed by City Architect Robert Broderick. Including eight shops at street level as well as rooftop laundries and garden, Strickland was a sophisticated response to the problems of cheap urban housing. All flats are self-contained and have balconies and individual entrances, avoiding some of the standard failings of tenement blocks. However, this achievement produced several space-saving compromises, notably bedroom access via other bedrooms and small external windows. Strickland gained integration with its surroundings through the division of the building into seven distinct clusters. A variety of finishes and details have a similar effect of reducing the building's apparent scale.

A second block was planned but not built, partly owing to wartime budgetary restraints, although criticism of the project may also have been a factor.[3] While the architect and planner John Sulman recognised that workers' flats were a necessity 'where people must be housed cheaply in or near the heart of a city', he was disappointed by Strickland: 'The experiment made by the City Council at Chippendale, where the buildings are not too well lighted, balconies too small and rents too high, has prejudiced the consideration of this class of housing.'[4]

Despite moments of disapproval, Strickland attracted many more tenancy applications than it could house. It has provided ninety years of serviceable public housing for working people. Its recent refurbishment to contemporary standards has not required major alterations.[5]

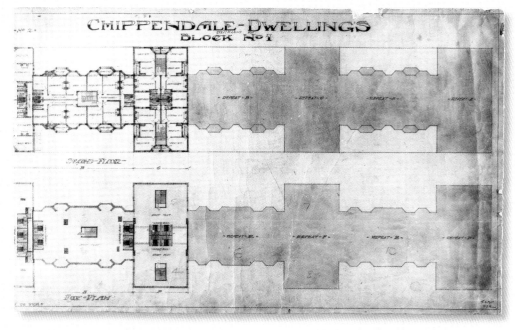

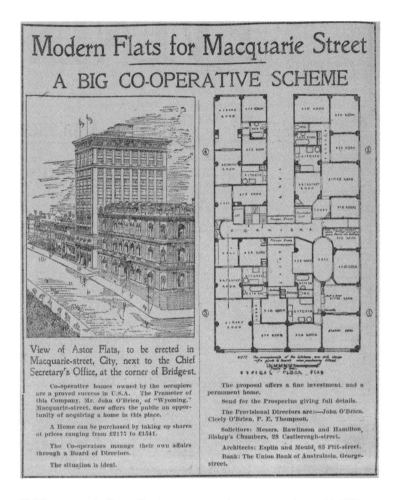

Modern Flats for Macquarie Street

A BIG CO-OPERATIVE SCHEME

View of Astor Flats, to be erected in Macquarie-street, City, next to the Chief Secretary's Office, at the corner of Bridge-st.

Co-operative homes owned by the occupiers are a proved success in U.S.A. The Promoter of this Company, Mr. John O'Brien, of "Wyoming," Macquarie-street, now offers the public an opportunity of acquiring a home in this place.

A Home can be purchased by taking up shares at prices ranging from £2177 to £1541.

The Co-operators manage their own affairs through a Board of Directors.

The situation is ideal.

The proposal offers a fine investment, and a permanent home.

Send for the Prospectus giving full details.

The Provisional Directors are:—John O'Brien, Cleely O'Brien, P. E. Thompson.

Solicitors: Messrs. Rawlinson and Hamilton, Bishop's Chambers, 28 Castlereagh-street.

Architects: Esplin and Mould, 85 Pitt-street.

Bank: The Union Bank of Australasia, George-street.

NOTE: The arrangements of the kitchens are only where the gas and plants when preparing being partly TYPICAL FLOOR PLAN

'The proposal offers a fine investment and a permanent home.' A 1921 *Evening News* advertisement sought investors for The Astor's company title scheme.

In 1919 the *Sydney Morning Herald* argued that servant scarcity was the 'most outstanding' cause of flat construction. According to the *Herald*, the 'privilege of entertaining his friends' was denied the home-owner 'owing to the uncertainty occasioned by the servant problem. It is, therefore, not surprising that many prefer to leave the suburban home for the residential flat …'[17]

Melbourne's *Australian Home Beautiful* agreed: 'Cities and factories offer such advantages to maids that they refuse to take up work of a domestic nature. A roomy flat of from six to 10 rooms, with up-to-date fittings, can be run with the assistance of one, or at most, two maids. Indeed, when the pros and cons are considered, many advantages are to be found on the side of flat life.'[18] By 1937 *Building* attributed an apartment boom in fashionable Point Piper to the fact that individual homes 'are not so popular with women as they were; there is always a feeling of responsibility of a staff and insecurity, as one locks up the myriad of windows and doors at night'.[19]

The debate about servants was irrelevant to most middle-income earners, who preferred suburban cottages to apartments.[20] House ownership was encouraged by improved public transport as well as new forms of government financial assistance. In 1913 the New South Wales Government legislated for the Government Savings Bank to make finance available at low interest, and after the 1914–18 war the Commonwealth Government's War Service Homes Scheme provided similar finance to ex-servicemen. However, many flats were tenanted by the middle class, generally office workers, often bachelors and single women, and those not able to save for a deposit for a block of land.[21]

City investments

George Sydney Jones, president of the New South Wales Institute of Architects, acknowledged as early as 1912 that the era of the city flat had not only arrived but was also here to stay in the private market.[22] *Real Property Annual* of 1913 pointed out the attractiveness of flats to investors as they provided a good return. Two types of flats were suggested as good investment prospects: first, high-class and fashionable city flats with a common dining room and, second, suburban flats to 'meet the needs of the man of middling income and the artisan'.[23]

The Astor was aimed at the first of these markets. Whereas John O'Brien's first project Wyoming targetted the established Macquarie Street demographic of medical professionals, The Astor sought a broader clientele of wealthy residents. Many were from the country, their wealth gained from sheep and wheat stations.

The Astor was the first Australian apartment building to be owned under company title. Each occupier took shares in The Astor Ltd for a sum ranging from £2700 to £4000 depending on their stake in the development. The only extra charge was about £2 per week for rates, taxes, cleaning of lifts and other maintenance services. O'Brien was anxious to raise the social respectability of apartment living and believed that The Astor's company title scheme permitted 'a number of people co-operating to build themselves modern homes, free from landlordism, objectionable neighbours and other flat-life troubles'.[24]

Company title quickly became a crucial intermediary of the marriage of wealth and apartment living. Company title allowed the shareholders to pick and choose the other residents, maintaining the exclusivity of flat life in the numerous buildings financed through company title in succeeding decades. Wealthy widows and retired couples were particularly attracted to company title apartments.[25]

The Astor's catering and service arrangements had also been refined. The Astor had its own basement café and restaurant, which sent food upstairs by dumbwaiters. Many residents also had servants, and the building employed servants as well as a caretaker and a lift attendant. According to John O'Brien, 'In a small house privacy is interfered

The T&G Building, at left, towers over Sydney's Hyde Park in 1923.

Folding wall beds were installed in the T&G Building's bachelor flats. Built-ins were a feature of bachelor flats.

Beulah, at left on the foreshore, was the first of many large Kirribilli and North Shore apartment buildings. The building has had a chequered career. About 1930 it became a private hotel before eventually being restored as flats during the 1970s.

with if you have a girl constantly residing with you.' At The Astor, in contrast, 'if any of the tenants wish the services of a girl, say, half an hour daily in the week … the caretaker will simply make a list and engage a sufficient number of girls to satisfy the demand …'[26]

A similar formula was followed by the T&G Building on the corner of Elizabeth and Park Streets. The Temperance and General insurance company built office blocks in most Australian cities. Completed in 1915, its Sydney offices also housed shops and professional suites, while the upper floors were devoted to flats. The building was a pioneering exercise in adaptive reuse as it converted the three floors of a former tobacco warehouse and added a further three floors above. 'There are, in all, ninety suites, comprising six hundred and eighty rooms, and each apartment is self-contained.' Many of the smaller flats featured folding wall beds. 'With this type of bed the bedroom-sitting room is possible. This is most essential in flat life.' As well as a café and laundry, the T&G Building featured a roof garden and promenade: 'In the perfect serenity of its seclusion and the aerial effect of its environment the premises as a place of residence should be among the most sought in the city.'[27]

Mansion flats neighbour terraces in Edward Warner's 1927 etching *Macquarie Street*.
The 1928 prospectus for Rockcliff Mansions imagined a Venetian setting for the Neutral Bay luxury block, with the Harbour Bridge looming.

Kingsclere was the first of many apartment towers to be built in Macleay Street, which runs along the Potts Point ridge and establishes Kings Cross as Sydney's main apartment precinct. Among the advantages provided by this location was 'a panoramic view of the harbour, Botany, Cronulla, Manly and as far as the Blue Mountains …'.[1] Also significant were the 'Profit Possibilities of Tall Buildings'. Kingsclere 'was let with a guaranteed return of 10 per cent, almost from its beginning. All its floors cover the same rental value.'[2]

At nine floors, Kingsclere was the first multistorey apartment block built in Sydney, and it featured two vast (250 square metre) four-bedroom apartments on each floor, with two balconies and two bathrooms. The building introduced the US style of apartment block built almost to site boundaries, with an internal light well running the height of the building, complete with steel fire escape. In the few decades following its completion in 1912, Macleay Street would see the same design formula used for Kingsclere's progeny including Byron Hall and Selsdon, culminating in 1940 with Cahors and the Macleay Regis.

Maurice Halligan and Frederick Wilton were favourite architects of Sydney's establishment having recently designed the club house of Royal Sydney Golf Club. In later years their work included the Dymocks Building on George Street and the British American Tobacco Company at Kensington. Despite the novelty of Kingsclere, Halligan and Wilton clothed the building in the sober brick and sandstone of many Edwardian buildings.

Kingsclere was built on the estate created by the demolition of the 1840s mansion Greenknowe. Herbert Binnie, a Point Piper merchant and pastoralist, purchased part of the Greenknowe subdivision in 1910, including a narrow strip of land to north of Kingsclere's site. As a result Kingsclere's sunny northern aspect was protected; when the building was completed, unused land to its south was sold. Binnie, who was already the owner of Strathkyle apartments in Sydney's Bligh Street (also designed by Halligan and Wilton), could claim to be Sydney's first promoter of luxury apartments.[3]

Kingsclere was owned for most of its life by the Albert family of music publishers and promoters, for whom the Hollywoodesque mansion Boomerang was built during the

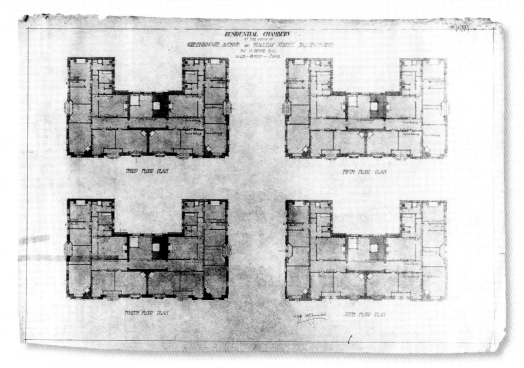

1920s nearby in Elizabeth Bay. The Alberts rented Kingsclere's apartments for seventy years, often accommodating visiting singers and music hall performers. In 1995 the building was strata-titled and its seventeen apartments sold individually, with the result that the wood-panelling and other original features of most were replaced with a variety of designer fit-outs.

'Residential flats and other buildings in Italian renaissance to harmonise with the gardens below could be constructed here.' Construction of the Harbour Bridge boosted flat construction on the lower North Shore. Bridge engineer J. J. C. Bradfield had this vision for Lavender Bay.
Designed in the USA, Kernerator incinerators began to appear in Australian apartment blocks from the 1920s, providing rubbish chutes from each flat to a basement incinerator.

After The Astor and the T&G flats, few major apartment buildings were constructed in the city of Sydney. Retail and office development increased the price of city property, forcing residential development elsewhere. J. J. C. Bradfield supported this process: 'Land near the heart of the city will rapidly become far too valuable to retain the wretched tenements now existing, and the people will either have to erect the lofty apartment buildings such as they have in New York, or move outwards to the surrounding lands.'[28] In fact, apartment development was priced out of the city, along with workers' housing.

The social status of city apartments also declined somewhat. During the early 1930s the novelist Dymphna Cusack lived in a

Macquarie Street flat and included impressions of the night-time city in her novel *Jungfrau*: 'She listened to the faint roar of the trams in King Street. Like a jungle, the city with its dark, stolid buildings all cramped together. Hiding what? You could imagine strange, secret vices, turbulent dreams, mad passions. She laughed ruefully. She was always dramatising things. Probably they hid only frivolling and boredom; at the worst a querulous irritation with life.'[29]

Between 1911 and 1921, the number of private houses in Australia increased by a fifth from 888,045 to 1,068,607. At the same time, the number of tenements and flat dwellings increased by 545 per cent from 6344 to 38,403. This increase was primarily among boarding houses and conversions of private houses to flats, but construction of purpose-built apartments was also booming.[30] Apartment buildings in the inner suburbs became a major new source of urban profit.[31]

Beulah, built in 1908 at Kirribilli, a short ferry ride from Circular Quay, was the first Sydney mansion flat to be built adjacent to the city. It offered renters all 'the attributes of a private residence without the attendant worries'. Meals could be taken in the dining room, which provided a luxurious range of food including smoked blue cod for breakfast, grilled rump steak for a main meal and strawberries and cream for dessert. Beulah was designed by Roscoe Collins for Mary Helene White, widow of a wealthy Mudgee grazier. Its roof garden combined with a billiard room and harbour sea baths to provide an enviable lifestyle at £2.2 per week for a two-bedroom flat and up to £5 for a four-bedroom flat.[32]

Beulah inspired a concentration of apartments in Kirribilli and the lower North Shore. According to the 1917 property guide *Where to Live: ABC Guide to Sydney and Suburbs*, 'One of the best investments

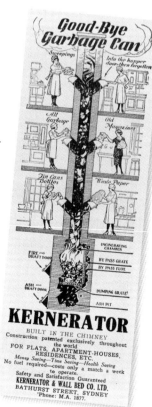

offering is the erection of modern buildings of flats in and around Sydney. Although a number have been erected, especially at Darlinghurst, Cremorne and North Sydney, there is any amount of scope for … a modern building, with every convenience, is sought after by the better class of tenant.'[33] Most of the blocks built in the lower North Shore during the 1920s and 1930s targeted 'the better class of tenant'.

The prospectus for the six-storey Rockcliff Mansions at Neutral Bay called its harbourside location the 'New Potts Point', claiming that the 'Bridge makes this district a new Potts Point for convenience of access to the City'.[34] Even before the opening of the Harbour Bridge in 1932, Kirribilli, Neutral Bay and Cremorne were quickly accessible from the city by ferry. Rockcliff's prospectus stated that the apartments would be

much better appointed than The Astor, architect Stuart Mould's earlier triumph on Macquarie Street.

In 1921 J. J. C. Bradfield too had a vision of what apartments built for the private market could be like along the lower North Shore from Lavender Bay to Milsons Point when the Harbour Bridge was built and land used for railways was redeveloped.[35] This land would be transformed into 'grassed lawns, with a little statuary on the water front, the cliffs covered with creepers, bouganvillia [sic], and shrubs, to provide masses of colour as a background'.[36] Bradfield further envisaged: 'The area above the ornamented cliffs made rich by masses of green and garden bloom, could also be entirely remodelled. Residential flats and other buildings in Italian renaissance to harmonise with the gardens below could be constructed here in charming surroundings, with fine

⬆ In 1928 Kingsclere was about to share its dominance of the Macleay Street ridge with Byron Hall, under construction across the street.

arcaded walks on the edge of the cliffs overlooking the waters of the harbour. Treated broadly, these walks could be made picturesque spots and most delightful resorts for the residents during the long summer evenings ...'[37]

However, the future in luxury apartments had already been announced in 1912 with the completion of Kingsclere in Potts Point. Kingclere's tenants were served by the latest technology, including passenger and goods lifts. 'Each lift is provided with a telephonette, so that tenants may be informed by tradesmen that goods are in the lifts.' Kingsclere was one of the first apartment buildings to feature

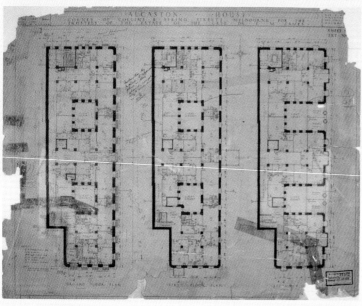

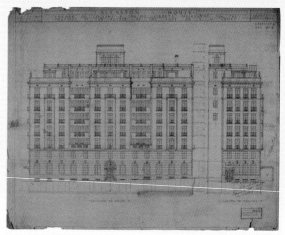

'... the nearest approach to a flat skyscraper Melbourne possesses.'
Alcaston House today and as envisaged by its architect, Rupert
Henderson. 'Light courts' run the height of the three residential towers.

Shops and Residential Flats
Pulteney St. Adelaide—
for R.F. Ruthven Smith Esq.

Mess.rs Black & Fuller, FSAIA
Architects.

Nov 1910.

electric light and power throughout. 'The current is also utilised for vacuum cleaners, which are provided by the owners and sublet to the tenants.'[38]

Apartments with shared domestic services became a minority response to the servant shortage. Kingsclere included a small number of rooms for a caretaker and servants, obviating the need for maids' quarters within apartments, and the provision of a goods lift removed tradesmen from common areas.[39] These interior class divisions became standard practice in the elite apartment blocks built at Kings Cross during the 1920s and 1930s.

⬆ The first stage of Adelaide's Ruthven Mansions on Pulteney Street, as designed in 1910.

Melbourne and elsewhere

Melbourne's 1920s saw a noteworthy exception to the trend to near-city flat living. Alcaston House was built at the expensive end of Collins Street in 1929 and offered medical specialist rooms on its lower floors beneath five floors of apartments. The apartment floors were broken into three towers, creating light access and a resemblance to contemporary American buildings, such as the Beverly Wilshire Hotel in Los

Angeles. According to the art critic Basil Burdett, Alcaston House is 'the nearest approach to a flat skyscraper Melbourne possesses'.[40] However, Victorian building laws requiring 30 per cent of sites to be open space made similar projects uneconomic. No major apartments were built in the city of Melbourne for decades.

The smaller Australian capitals saw fewer apartments built, although all boasted prominent blocks to provide a city domicile for the wealthy. In Adelaide this role was filled by Ruthven Mansions in Pulteney Street, which was built in two stages between 1912 and 1920. Designed by leading local practice Black & Fuller for the investor Frederic Ruthven-Smith, the first building comprised twelve large apartments complete with maids' quarters. The second stage added twenty-eight somewhat less opulent spaces. As well as the upmarket novelties of electric lifts and built-in vacuum cleaners, Ruthven's decorative Arts and Crafts detailing is a rarity among large apartment blocks.

In Brisbane, Craigston in Wickham Terrace introduced urban apartment living. Built in 1927 by the engineer and builder Walter Taylor, Craigston also pioneered reinforced concrete construction and multistorey design in the northern capital. The lower of its seven floors were devoted to professional suites, and doctors and other medical specialists enjoyed the silky oak panelling and other luxuries of the apartments above.

Perth had to wait until 1937 for a major city apartment building, although Lawson Flats is among the most handsome of the genre.

◀ Although unconventional in design and construction, Craigston has remained a sought-after address in Brisbane.

⬆ *View from the Summit of Mount Ainslie* (detail). Although Canberra has become a synonym for low-rise suburbia, Marion Mahony and Walter Burley Griffin's founding vision proposed a dense urbanity of courtyard housing for the Australian capital.

Built by the Colonial Mutual insurance company as a companion to its neighbouring office building, Lawson was designed by the Melbourne architects Hennessy & Hennessy. Like Alcaston House, Lawson Flats' apartments are grouped into separate towers above a podium. Most of the eleven floors contain four flats, arranged in pairs in the matching towers. Home for most of its life to the Perth Club as well as, more recently, the women's Karrakatta Club, Lawson Flats was as central to Perth's monied society as The Astor was to Sydney.[41]

One notable apartment vision went unfulfilled. Walter Burley Griffin and Marion Mahony's successful Canberra plan of 1912 was founded on the vast scale of the Australian landscape. However, Griffin and Mahony's vision was of a more intimate, urban capital than the far-flung suburbs and rambling road system that later evolved. Notably, the commercial, retail and residential heart of the city was to adjoin apartment blocks built around courtyards, providing the city centre with social density, interaction and pleasure appropriate to the capital of a new democracy. The abandonment of this vision was one of many to compromise the metropolitan character of the Australian capital.[42]

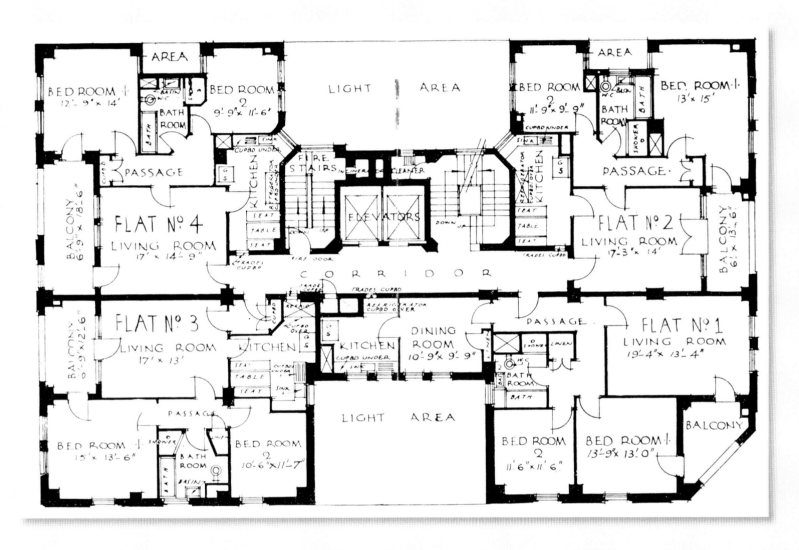

James Russell's 1936 rendering of Lawson Flats in Perth is a fantasy in Hollywoodesque glamour. Lawson's H-shaped floor plan and 'light areas' was typical of the first generation of large apartment buildings.

Apartments are a leading symbol of big city life. For much of the twentieth century they were at odds with the Australian self-image, which, despite our highly urbanised society, remained focused on rural and suburban symbols. Flight to the suburbs was encouraged as a solution to urban social problems. In contrast, apartments celebrated the romance of cities.

In 1921 an *Evening News* editorial suggested that 'people pay very high rates' to live in 'gigantic modern "flat" buildings': 'They do so, not because they suffer from the pressure of economic necessity, but because they have the hotel or flat temperament. It is reasonable to suppose that the same temperament exists in other classes of the community than the well-to-do, and that a not inconsiderable number of families prefer a reasonable amount of congestion near the pulsing heart of city life to the more hygienic life in an idyllic but more distant and duller suburb.'[1]

Florence Taylor of *Building* disagreed vehemently: 'Why encourage the pernicious practice of living in the city in homes that must be cramped because of the cost of land; that must be shorn of beauty and decoration because they must be cheap enough to let at rents within the compass of the earners' pockets; homes that are gardenless, in streets that are hemmed in and crushing in their outlook.'[2]

Flats appeared at a moment of ferment in thinking about the city. Within the space of a few decades the compact classical city was irretrievably changed by the advent of industrialisation and unprecedented population growth. Sydney's population doubled from 480,000 at the 1901 census to 1,025,000 by 1921. The urban squalor and discord of nineteenth-century cities produced a flurry of new urban ideas and a town planning movement, as well as new urban ideologies such as the Garden City Movement, the City Beautiful Movement and, shortly after, Modernism.

Mass transit systems, tall buildings and suburbs of detached cottages were only the most obvious urban changes to occur around the beginning of the twentieth century. Another was the increased specialisation of urban districts. In 1900 the cities of Melbourne and Sydney were jumbled agglomerations of residential, retail, industrial, commercial and transport functions. However, retail and office buildings were becoming the main features of the city, raising land prices and pushing housing, factories and warehouses to the suburbs.

During the 1920s town planners and city governments began to formalise this change with the introduction of zoning regulations that separated urban functions into distinct districts. Protection of the residential character of suburbs was a prime reason for zoning regulations.

Kings Cross

Although Potts Point, Darlinghurst and Elizabeth Bay are distinct addresses, to Sydneysiders they are largely incorporated into 'the Cross', an area so associated with apartment living that it demands specific attention. Melbourne's inner-city flat precincts, South Yarra and Toorak, provide an instructive comparison.

A short tram journey east of the city, Kings Cross was one of Sydney's oldest and wealthiest suburbs when Kingsclere was built in 1912. In 1917 *Where to Live* warned that building land for houses in Potts Point 'is practically unobtainable, and there is not very much to be had at Elizabeth Bay or Rushcutters Bay either'. Even if a house was available, 'the owner or owners are waiting a favourable opportunity to erect flats or residentials'.[3]

The *Sydney Morning Herald* observed in 1927 that 'It is something rare to find a "To Let" notice in the window of a cottage these days', because the rent controls imposed by the New South Wales Fair Rents Act made flats a more attractive investment proposition than cottages. For forty years from 1916, the Fair Rents Act restricted returns on rental property to 5 per cent per year. 'Builders and others reason to themselves that the building which pays best today is a block of flats. Under the one roof can be provided a residence for several families, each of whom pay as much rent for a little flat of two rooms and a small kitchenette as they would for a four-roomed cottage.'[4] A quarter of the flats built in Sydney during the 1920s were built in the Kings Cross area.[5]

➡ 'Darlinghurst is and must ever remain the supreme position for flats. Its height, centrality and accessibility places it in an altogether unique position.' This 1922 subdivision prospectus for the grounds of the colonial mansion Craigend illustrates the creation of Kings Cross flatland.

DARLINGHURST is and must ever remain the supreme position for flats. Its height, centrality, and accessibility places it in an altogether unique position. The CRAIGEND ESTATE is absolutely the last opportunity to secure a position at the very heart of things. Who can estimate the value of this land within the next few years, remembering the continued progressive growth of Sydney, the premier City of the Commonwealth?

THE WISE WILL NOT MISS THIS FINAL OPPORTUNITY

PRODUCED BY E.B. STUDIOS.

CRAIGEND ESTATE.—This splendid Estate, situated on the heights of Darlinghurst, on the exact site chosen by Sir Thomas Mitchell for his family residence, will be offered for Public Auction on Tuesday, the 12th of September, 1922, at 11.30 a.m., at the Real Estate Auction Rooms, 15 Martin Place, Sydney. TERMS—10 per cent. deposit and the balance in 36 monthly instalments with interest at 6 per cent. Title Torrens.

H. W. HORNING & CO., LTD., AUCTIONEERS, 30 MARTIN PLACE, SYDNEY

'The "flatiron" building at the extreme left is "Meudon", the road below is Billyard Avenue, leading to "Del Rio" and "Edgewater" (on the point).' Published in 1947, *The Sydney Book* by Marjorie Barnard and Sydney Ure Smith is notable for its views of and from Sydney flats. It is perhaps the first time this distinctive viewpoint was recognised in a Sydney travelogue.
Rah Fizelle's *Elizabeth Bay* shared its subject with Sydney Ure Smith's sketch, but Fizelle's Modernist colour planes were more suitable to apartment size and symmetry.

Kings Cross flats were primarily built on sites created by the demolition of colonial and Victorian terraces and mansions, or by subdivision of their grounds. 'Famous families had their homes there, usually in spacious grounds. Some of the old homes are left. But many have gone and the land, now subdivided, is occupied by flats.'[6] Instead of the perimeter block apartments that formed city streets in Europe and England, the Kings Cross apartment boom of the 1920s and 1930s was shaped by the existing townscape and available building sites.

The 22 hectares surrounding Elizabeth Bay House were among the estates subdivided during the 1920s. The estate agents managing the sale declared Kings Cross an apartment area: 'this centre of Sydney … compares more than favourably with other centres in London and New York adapted for apartment localities.'[7] The 1830s mansion was itself divided into fifteen bedsitters during the 1940s. The subdivision of Tusculum House and Grounds Estate also produced advertisements proclaiming Kings Cross as the 'Great Apartment District, suitable for Flats, Boarding Houses etc where the upper floors will have Unsurpassed Views of the City and Harbour, and in the immediate vicinity of Palatial Flat & Apartment Buildings, such as KINGSCLERE'.[8]

To achieve the required investment and rental returns on this expensive real estate, building regulations were usually exploited to the limit, producing tall apartment blocks with minimum boundary setbacks. One of the apartments built on the Elizabeth Bay House estate was Meudon, the 'flat-iron' floor plan of which was dictated by its triangular site between Onslow and Greenknowe Avenues. This eight-storey block had to take full economic advantage of its site, given that 'anything between £200 and £300 per foot is now being paid … for land upon which to erect extensive and modernly equipped blocks of flats'.[9]

What could have been a social and aesthetic disaster was ameliorated by the urban character of Kings Cross and its layering of new and old buildings of different functions and styles, both architecturally and socially. Out of this diversity came the social legend of Kings Cross, created primarily by the numerous artists and writers who made the district their home. Often cited is the poet and journalist Kenneth Slessor:

> Kings Cross, indeed, is not Sydney … Yet it gives its own savour to the city. Its plan of living represents a cut across the organic structure of the Sydney ant-heap. Hovels are wedged between palaces. Millionaires look out of their 'luxury apartments', their silver and velvet suites, at the slum-world looking at them from the tenement next door or across the street. Among the termites of the yelling flat-blocks, ladies of unimpeachable virtue lend aspirin to ladies who come home barefoot … Cheeks blush at jowls as they squeeze together in the most thickly populated, and certainly the most noisily infested, square mile of the metropolis.[10]

Slessor lived in Kings Cross flats, including Cavendish Hall, for decades and was perhaps the most assiduous literary creator of its 'bohemian' reputation. Kings Cross gave Sydney's artists and intellectuals a distinctive address, uniting their social and domestic lives in an enclave removed from both the suburbs and the commercial city centre.[11]

Although Kings Cross by 1930 was famous for its apartment towers, smaller blocks jostled for space between them. While the shift from investment in houses to flats ensured the popularity of flats with

🔾 *Sydney Ure Smith's Flat in Manar*, oil painting by Norman Carter, 1939. Smith's Potts Point apartment was also illustrated as an example of 'modernity' in his magazine *The Home*.

🔼 Harold Cazneaux's photo of Molly Grey for *The Home*, 1935: 'The photograph was taken in her flat in Greenknowe Avenue, which is decorated by her.'

🔽 *View from Manar*, watercolour painting by Sydney Ure Smith, 1948.

investors and builders, it also increased rental prices. Most purpose-built Kings Cross flats of the 1920s and 1930s rented for more than a suburban cottage.[12] Critics of apartment living often assumed that a shortage of cottages was forcing tenants into flats. One who did not make this mistake was opposition leader (and later New South Wales Premier) William McKell, who 'disagreed with the claim that people lived in flats and terraces because they could not get cottages. Flats on the waterfront rented for up to £20 a week and anybody who is able to afford such a rental could obviously well afford to construct a home for himself if he were so inclined.'[13]

But a marked variety of rents existed, with a rental premium being paid for the mansion flats springing up along the heights of Macleay Street and the waterfront of Elizabeth Bay. Behind these more afford-able rents were offered by conversions of terrace houses and man-sions to flats, one-room 'bedsits' and 'bachelor flats', and small blocks overshadowed by the towers. As *Decoration and Glass* pointed out: 'Flats of all sizes are being built, and it is possible to obtain luxury fam-ily homes in one building and minimum bachelor flats in the building next door.'[14]

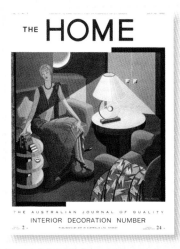

Interiors from Kings Cross and South Yarra—Sydney's and Melbourne's centres of flat living and interior design—featured in *The Home*, 1934.

⬆ Hera Roberts' 1930 cover for *The Home*'s 'interior decoration number' assembled the graphic signifiers for numerous similar images.

Even expensive waterside flats contained a diversity of humanity, according to a *Sydney Morning Herald* contributor: 'Here we are very cosmopolitan. The manager bears a Scottish name, but his Scotch has a decided Teutonic accent. The maid … is from Czecho-Slovakia, while my table wants are ministered to by François, who amid the sultry heat of Sydney, pines for his native valley in the Alps.' Other tenants included 'two very modern flappers … the golf girl … and the tennis star, while at least two prominent rowing men shed a lustre upon the ménage'.[15]

The link between the bohemian and the wealthy apartment dwellers of Kings Cross was Sydney Ure Smith, publisher of *The Home* and *Art in Australia*. Artist, promoter, networker extraordinaire and resident of the Manar flats on Macleay Street, Smith was the linchpin of Sydney's art and society worlds of the 1920s and 1930s. His publications celebrated a 'modern' urban lifestyle, of which apartment living was a central element. Apartment dwellers were educated in the resources and styles of urban life, including interior design, fashion, architecture and art.

'Miss Molly Grey has designed her own flat at Greenknowe, Pott's Point', enthused *The Home* in 1934, illustrating the work of one of

'A delightful environment', according to *Building*, 1942. Built to the design of Arthur Plaisted, Castle Villa in Toorak's Kensington Road epitomised the Melbourne compromise between low-rise suburbia and flat-living. Flats disguised as Georgian villas are grouped around a landscaped garden.

Ruby Rich, photographed 1926 in her Astor flat by Harold Cazneaux. A leading feminist, Rich formed the Federation of Women Voters and the League of Women Voters. She was also a founding member of the Family Planning Foundation. Her mother occupied another, larger, flat at The Astor.

the pioneers of the new profession of interior designer.[16] Sydney's first 'interior decorator' store was opened in 1925 by Margaret Jaye, who chose Darlinghurst Road, Kings Cross, as the appropriate address for her venture. The city department stores also promoted interior modernity to apartment-dwellers. Molly Grey worked for David Jones department store, which was joined in this fusion of commerce, art and modernity by such artists as Thea Proctor, Roy de Maistre and Hera Roberts, who worked in interior and furniture design as well as fine and commercial art.[17] Before becoming Sydney Ure Smith's lover,

Roberts had established a reputation with her covers and artwork for *The Home*, which also featured her interior designs for Elizabeth Bay flats at Cavendish Hall and Cheddington.[18]

Women in fashionable flats were a central element of the city lifestyle chronicled by *The Home*. Photographic essays of notable citizens and their apartment interiors were produced for the journal by the society photographer Harold Cazneaux; his photo essay of the furniture store heiress Ruby Rich at The Astor defined the genre.[19] The Women's Section of the *Sydney Morning Herald* ran similar features.

South Yarra and Toorak

Like Kings Cross, South Yarra and Toorak were well established as Melbourne's most desirable addresses by the beginning of the twentieth century. They also offered the extensive land of redundant colonial mansions, ripe for subdivision. Situated between the transport arteries of Toorak and St Kilda Roads, their northern parts were sufficiently elevated to offer views of the city, gardens and bay, a rarity in inner Melbourne.

During this period, Sydney and Melbourne shared similar economic and occupational structures and a relatively high standard of

⬆ Designed for property investor Mary Williams, Langi was Walter Burley and Marion Mahony Griffin's only completed apartment project in Australia. Langi consists of a four-flat block built behind a house on Toorak Road, which the Griffins then converted into another two-storey block of four flats. Mary Williams lived in one of the new flats.

⬅ Amesbury House was designed by Walter Butler, architect of Melbourne's first prominent apartment buildings. As well as Melbourne Mansions, these included Studley, built 1918 on Toorak Road. Architect of homes for Clive Baillieu and Nellie Melba among other notables, Butler was well placed to accommodate flats to the taste of Melbourne's elite.

living. There were differences, however. Unlike its sprawling counterpart to the south, Sydney was already a more compact city.[20] Indeed, it was argued by the *Australian Home Builder* that time wasted commuting from the Melbourne suburbs was promoting the building of near-city flats for those who 'desire to live near to Collins Street'.[21] With the Melbourne City Council maintaining a harder line on building regulations and open space requirements than its Sydney counterpart, it was difficult to make investment returns from increasingly

⬆ Another of Plaisted's numerous apartment designs, Elvada at Malvern was praised by *Building* for its 'modern Georgian treatment'.
⮑ The largest flat complex of 1930s Melbourne, Howard Lawson's Beverley Hills evoked flamboyance and cosmopolitanism, a contrast to the respectable revivalism of most South Yarra flats.

expensive city real estate. Apartment development focused on adjacent municipalities.

Although Fawkner Mansions, built in nearby Prahran in 1912, was Melbourne's near-city forerunner, the reputation of South Yarra and Toorak was cemented during the 1920s. According to the *Australian Home Builder* in 1924, 'Melbourne's first definite community of high-grade residential flats … might have been developed some years ago in Toorak, but a belief that flat buildings would not be sanctioned in that exclusive neighbourhood was prevalent among investors … Latterly, however, the council has allowed flats to be …'[22]

In 1921 Walter Butler, architect of Melbourne Mansions, completed work on Amesbury House on Domain Road. Butler's decades of work producing English Arts and Crafts-styled houses, churches and flats made him a favourite of Melbourne's establishment. Amesbury House presented the appearance of an extensive house rather than six large apartments and their balconies. Another favourite of the elite, Harold Desbrowe-Annear, designed a portico for Amesbury, which heightened the respectable impression created by Butler's marriage of decorative charm and Georgian symmetry.

A similar outcome was produced by Walter Burley Griffin and Marion Mahony at Langi Flats, built on Toorak Road in 1925. On this occasion a set of walk-up flats was disguised by the sprawling plan and irregular massing of the Chicago domestic style. The respectability of near-city apartment living was enhanced by the involvement of these high-profile architects. 'Within the past few years there has sprung up an increasing demand for a better class of flat, and in the near suburbs of Melbourne, such as St Kilda, South Yarra and Toorak, it is found that flats of a luxurious order are being built, flats that are designed on expensive lines, and that have all the privacy and individuality of a home.'[23]

The art critic Basil Burdett noted that although 'Melbourne, as yet, has no Darlinghurst and no Kings Cross', flats were numerous in South Yarra,

and their advent in Toorak has, I understand, been responsible for quite an exodus to Frankston among our best people. Not only have bright new buildings in brick and stucco arisen in the midst of the grandiose towered and balconied mansions of the 'eighties but the grandiose mansions themselves, in many cases, have—oh! Horror of defilement—been converted to modern and sacrilegious fashions and imagined needs … Melbourne has taken to flats with some of the feverish eagerness of a teetotaller converted to liquor.[24]

Although several large estates were subdivided and built primarily with flats, the result was decidedly more suburban than the intense urbanity of Kings Cross. Subdivision of the Maritimo estate facing Domain Road created Marne Street, one of South Yarra's most concentrated apartment precincts. During the twenty years from 1919 nineteen apartment blocks and two houses were built along Marne Street. Most of the new buildings were of two or three storeys and had extensive landscaped grounds.[25] *Building* observed: 'In Sydney, the tendency in the recognised flat areas is to erect multi-storeyed blocks, complete with elevators and all modern conveniences … In Melbourne, on the other hand, we find the question approached in a somewhat different fashion, the blocks seldom being more than two storeys in height, and stretched horizontally rather than vertically …'[26]

That flats in South Yarra and Toorak blended almost anonymously into respectable streetscapes was in part a response to the strength of anti-flat opinion in Melbourne, which was reflected in council by-laws that limited apartments to two or three storeys throughout most of the affluent inner eastern suburbs. *Australian Home Beautiful* noted that although 'prejudice still lingers in the minds of many people … changing conditions have revolutionised the whole meaning of the word "flat" as understood a generation or so ago'. Among these changes was architecture that 'seems to belong to some old-world cathedral square than to a street in modern flat-dom'.[27] Garden flats with separate entrances were Melbourne's contribution to the apartment genre, and were all but unknown in Sydney.

Victoria's absence of rent controls meant that tenanted cottages remained the investors' preference and supplied the majority of rental

⬆➡ Arthur Plaisted's Castle Towers and Park Towers (at Adam Street, South Yarra) brought the Sydney combination of curves and banded brickwork to Melbourne.

housing for working Melburnians. As a residential option, apartments remained the province of the relatively affluent. In 1933 the average rentals for flats were higher than for houses in both Sydney and Melbourne, but by the 1947 Census Melbourne flats were dearer than Sydney's (42 s. 6 d. per week against 37 s. 4 d.) and much dearer than Melbourne cottage rentals (26 s. 7 d.).[28] By this time Toorak had almost as many flat dwellings as house dwellings.

In contrast to Kings Cross and Potts Point, South Yarra and Toorak retained their identity as exclusive suburbs. Even Melbourne's most active and flamboyant flat promoter was careful to blend his buildings with the neighbourhood. By 1935 Howard Lawson had designed and built 175 flats within several increasingly ostentatious blocks on a large tract of land bounded by Domain Road and Alexandra Avenue.

Denied registration as an architect owing to his entrepreneurial activities, Lawson billed himself as 'the Architect who builds'. Two blocks named Beverley Hills, built in the mid-1930s, are expressions of Hollywoodesque glamour. They were also integrated into the landscaped grounds of the estate, although this did not stop nearby residents protesting further development. After the five-floor Beverley Hills blocks, Lawson restricted the Maritimo and Stratton Heights buildings to three storeys.

The exotic architecture of Beverley Hills and many other 1920s and 1930s apartment buildings was often criticised by the architectural and mainstream press. 'The fine old Spanish architects would not only turn in their graves but jump out of them with fright if they were confronted with our "Spanish".'[29] These architectural imports were one of the many fashions and fads of city life popularised by movies, magazines and other forms of popular media during the between-wars decades. Flats were central to this new appreciation of urban life, which is reflected in a 1937 spoof by the architect W. Watson Sharp: 'There are, of course, several advantages to this way of living. It is not necessary to buy a

clock, for instance. One just listens for the people across the landing to come home from the party and one knows it is time to get up.'[30]

In 1941 South Yarra's Marne Street hosted a challenge to its low-rise character. Castle Towers had '40 units distributed over its five floors. The erection of the building caused considerable controversy and the result was that the City Building Regulations were altered lowering the height limit of buildings in the locality.'[31] In 1945 the Victorian Government introduced new uniform building regulations for Melbourne, which set out height limits and street setbacks for apartment buildings and granted powers to local governments to apply further restrictions.

Among the critics was the young Robin Boyd, then editor of *Smudges*, journal of the student chapter of the Royal Victorian Institute of Architects. Training for his later career as crusader for Modernism, Boyd attacked 'the inglorious reign of the luxury flat' in general, and Castle Towers in particular, 'as bad from a social viewpoint as it is ridiculous from an aesthetic viewpoint'.[32] With its decorative cornice and luxury features (including separate service entrances to each flat), Castle Towers did not conform with the Modernist rigour espoused by Boyd.

Castle Towers was designed by Arthur W. Plaisted, who issued a £3000 writ for defamation against Boyd and the RVIA, before being persuaded to accept a published apology. Melbourne's most prolific architect of the 1930s, Plaisted designed numerous South Yarra and Toorak apartments that incorporated an extraordinary variety of revivalist styles, including 'French', 'modern Georgian' and 'Norman'.[33] For Castle Towers and his nearby Park Towers, Plaisted adopted the mixture of 'streamlined' windows and plain brickwork that was popular in Sydney.[34]

The controversy was further evidence of the different character and role of apartment living developing in the inner suburbs of Sydney and Melbourne. Architectural differences between the two cities reflected the more uniformly affluent status of Melbourne flat-dwellers.

'This revolutionist style'

Architects have a closer relationship with apartment design than with that of the suburban cottage. For better or worse, more apartment buildings are the work of professional designers than are suburban cottages. Architects have long argued that improved design would mollify apartment critics. In 1917 *Architecture* editorialised that 'to many people in Australia the idea of flat life is objectionable. But this is to a large extent due to the fact that we have not so far had proper flats, or very few of them, installed in Sydney …'[35]

Architects were generally—although far from universally—sympathetic to the new building type. George Sydney Jones, president of the New South Wales Institute of Architects, acknowledged that while 'To many in Australia the idea of residential flats may seem reprehensible', the apartment 'also brings a new side of living conditions into constructional design, and allows of still further triumphs for the

⬆ Workers flats at Siemensstadt, Berlin. Designed by Walter Gropius, this seminal building was illustrated in *The Modern Flat* by London architects F. R. S. Yorke and Frederick Gibberd. Published in 1937, this compendium of contemporary apartment design was influential among Australian architects.

profession, because construction shows its progress in nothing so much as the overcoming of the difficulties it creates'.[36]

The association of architects and apartments became more pronounced after the economic depression of the early 1930s. With building activity in Australia all but ceased numerous young architects visited and worked in the USA, Europe and England. Others were granted travelling scholarships by the architects' institutes. Many returned home fired with enthusiasm for Modernism in general and modern apartment design in particular. Notably, the large public housing developments built in Germany, the Netherlands, Sweden and other European societies during the 1920s and 1930s offered a new

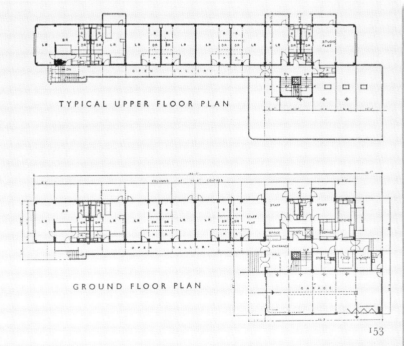

'The block consists mainly of a standard minimum flat.' Lawn Road bachelor flats, Hampstead, London, as illustrated in *The Modern Flat.*

TYPICAL UPPER FLOOR PLAN

GROUND FLOOR PLAN

153

↑ Best Overend's Cairo brought the minimum flat concept to Melbourne.

model of apartment design that lacked many of the social and physical failings of tenement blocks.

During the late 1920s, apartment developments in Berlin, Moscow, Stuttgart, Rotterdam, Vienna and New York established the design language later named the International Style. Such architects as William Lescaze, Ludwig Mies van der Rohe, Le Corbusier, Ernst May and Walter Gropius produced a new type of economical yet aesthetically pleasing apartment design, distinguished by features such as park-like settings, generous glazing and balconies and rigorous open-plan interior design.

Exposure to Modernism at its peak of achievement and credibility telescoped the interval between international developments and local practice. The pillars of the architectural establishment were often unimpressed. In 1936 Jack Hennessy of the leading practice Hennessy & Hennessy attacked the 'international style copied from European revolutionists … there are some young architects without proper training or the knowledge of history who are trying to foist it on us by slavishly copying and calling it modern architecture.' Hennessy scorned Modernism's claims to international status: 'It is an utter absurdity … Hitler has seen ahead, and by law has forbidden any more of this revolutionist style being erected in Germany, as it in no way reflects the ideals of the German people. When will the lovers of art and architecture take such steps here?'[37]

The apartment building was a primary point of entry for Modernism in Australia. The most influential format was the *zeilenbau*, or linear housing. Arrangement of apartments into horizontal rows could provide equal access of light, air and views to each apartment; other forms of open planning could have a similar benefit. As the young Modernist Peter Kaad put it, in Europe 'the erection of higher buildings gives larger and wider areas of ground per unit of flat between buildings, thus enabling light and air to reach the lowest rooms and ensuring that from each there will be a pleasant prospect'.[38]

It was difficult to reproduce the *zeilenbau* model in Australia, however. Before he designed the controversial Erskineville public housing, Morton Herman was among the architectural tourists, concluding that Australian apartments compared poorly to those he visited in Europe: 'In Sydney, the usual cry is that there is no privacy in flats, and what else can be expected when the blocks are jammed together with the windows staring at each other across a few feet of alleyway?' Herman blamed these failings on Australian building regulations, noting that England planned for 'a community of dwellings … not as a series of pocket-handkerchief sites' as happened in Australia.[39]

Among the first buildings to transcend this problem was Cairo Flats, completed in 1936 at Fitzroy. During the early 1930s Cairo's designer Best Overend worked for the London architect Wells Coates, famous for the Lawn Road bachelor flats, Hampstead. A few years after helping to bring the European concept of the 'minimum flat' to England, Overend introduced it to Australia. Upon his return to Melbourne in 1933, Overend began publicising Modern architecture in general and minimum flats in particular via a weekly column in the *Argus* newspaper.[40] In *Australian Home Beautiful*, Overend argued: 'The vast floating population here is requiring a distinctive type of accommodation, and this may be termed the "the minimum flat" … Each will house in a degree of comfort and privacy unfortunately rare in Melbourne, either one or two people. So economical a plan necessarily reduces the rental to the absolute minimum …'[41]

In most respects, Cairo could hardly have been more different from the luxury flats of South Yarra in size and appearance. Its flat roof, curved concrete balconies and stairs made a public statement of modernity, albeit slightly compromised by homely brick walls (Lawn Road was constructed of sheer concrete). However, Cairo's common central garden followed the Melbourne tradition, as well as achieving the Modernist ideal of equal access to views and light.

Cairo was the forerunner of several minimum flats built in Melbourne after 1935. Two other architect tourists, Geoffrey Mewton and Roy Grounds, were responsible for most of these, notably Mewton's Woy Woy at Elwood and Grounds' Quamby and Clendon at Toorak: 'The eight flat units, which are planned around a courtyard, provide complete "walk-in" living facilities for one or two people. There are twenty-five built-in cupboards and fitments to each flat, including a [folding] wall bed.'[42]

However, the small size and mostly polite exteriors of these early Modernist blocks limited their urban and social impact, despite vigorous publicity by Robin Boyd and others.[43] Melbourne's restrictive building laws ensured that in most suburbs Modernism was blended with the scale and garden setting of low-rise suburbia, denying them the advantages of height, views and breezes.

A less compromised statement was made by Frederick Romberg, a recently graduated student who arrived in Melbourne from Zurich in 1938. Despite his inexperience, Romberg's European background and entrepreneurial flair saw him designing innovative apartment buildings within two years.[44] His Glenunga apartments confused local aesthetes with its mixture of modernisms, including rubble-rock feature walls. In contrast, his Newburn and Stanhill apartments, both on Queens Road, South Melbourne, featured concrete construction of severe yet expressive character. More significantly, these structures used height, generous galleries, balconies and glazing to create aspect and access to the elements.

Designed for the industrialist and property speculator Stanley Korman, Stanhill is the most expansive of Romberg's creations. Designed in 1943 but not completed until 1950 owing to war-time shortages of labour and materials, Stanhill was the first multistorey apartment block built in Melbourne for two decades. It challenged the city both aesthetically and socially, and triumphantly demonstrated the compatibility of Modernism and comfort. The architect Neil Clerehan observed: ' "Stanhill" … is the city's most glamorous post-war building. At night

⬆ Completed in 1936, Geoffrey Mewton's Woy Woy is one of Australia's first International Style apartment buildings. Its combination of geometric shapes and rendered walls still stands out along Elwood's Marine Parade, where it remains one of the tallest buildings. Larger windows have altered the original, carefully harmonised exterior.

its enormous windows blaze with light … In any city overseas, blocks of the standard of Stanhill would be taken as a matter of course. In Melbourne we have come to regard anything better than or different from the brick veneer cottage on a fifty-foot lot as "luxury".'[45]

With shops at ground level, Stanhill's size and ten-floor height was made possible by its long gestation and exemption from the 1945 uniform building regulations. Partly for this reason, Romberg's urban Modernism produced few imitations in Melbourne, with the notable exception of J. W. Rivett's Caringal at Toorak. Combining a curved three-floor block and a six-storey tower, Caringal joined Stanhill in expressing the idealism of the 1930s: 'Special features are a children's playground on the roof, surrounded by an unscaleable wire fence and equipped with swings, slippery slides and sandpits.'[46]

In 1934 *Australian Home Beautiful* noted 'a definite demand existing for small, but well-fitted, living quarters in a good part of the city', claiming that 'this type of flat is becoming an established fact, and its inclusion in most of the large good-type flat buildings will soon become a matter of course'.[1] The young and childless were always a major component of the flat-dwelling demographic, although most could not afford independent living until the booming economic times of the 1950s and 1960s.

In his ambivalent paean to suburban living, the architect and writer Robin Boyd noted the appeal of flat living to young people who 'eagerly welcomed the escape from suburbia, the low rents, the short-lived glamour of elevated living, the compact economy of furniture and the harbour views which lasted until the neighbouring block reared up'.[2]

Although plenty of 'bedsits' and small flats were already in existence, the first of a new generation of 'minimum flats' was Cairo, built in 1936 opposite Melbourne's Carlton Gardens. Cairo combined 'what are so often incompatibles—space-economy, comfort, absolute modernity, and minimum rentals'. As well, 'each one-room flat has an array of luxury features normally seen only in a more ambitious setting than a bachelor apartment'.[3] Aimed at young professionals lacking the time, finances or inclination for domestic work, its twenty-eight bedsit or one-bedroom apartments were shorn of decoration or superfluity; its integral furniture, fittings and appliances requiring only the addition of a bed.

The 'minimum flat' was developed in Europe during the 1920s as the basic liveable standard of space and amenity for public housing, allowing architects to maximise the number of workers rehoused in new apartments. It was a key element of the early marriage between Modernism and left-wing politics, with its preference for collective living arrangements.[4] However, the minimum flat quickly found favour in the private market, offering a new generation of stylish and economical apartments to middle-class couples and single people. The minimum flat concept was brought to Melbourne by Cairo's architect Best Overend, one of many Australian architects to work in England and Europe during the depression years of the early 1930s. Overend publicised the building's concept for a couple of years before the project eventuated.

The modern labour-saving kitchen had also been pioneered during the 1920s by Margarete Schütte-Lihotzky, who designed standardised, prefabricated apartment kitchens for public housing in Frankfurt (top right). Easy to clean surfaces and built-in storage were hallmarks of these kitchens, which were forerunners of modern kitchens throughout the world. Cairo included some of the first Australian examples. For those lacking the time for cooking, the complex imitated luxury flats like Alcaston House in

including a restaurant and dining room. A flat roof provided space for sunbathing and clothes drying, while the arrangement of flats in two floors around a common garden guaranteed light and aspect.

Its common garden now lushly green, Cairo continues the role it has played since 1936, a home to those wishing to live the life of urban modernity in appropriate surroundings.

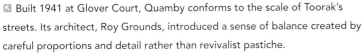

↘ Built 1941 at Glover Court, Quamby conforms to the scale of Toorak's streets. Its architect, Roy Grounds, introduced a sense of balance created by careful proportions and detail rather than revivalist pastiche.

↙ Clendon at Clendon Road, Armadale, contains eight flats on two floors, built around a courtyard. Roy Grounds' design focuses on these enclosed spaces, including this typical interior, in response to the height and space restrictions imposed on most Melbourne flats.

⬆ Frederick Romberg was twenty-five when he arrived in Melbourne from Switzerland in 1938. Within a year he had founded his own practice and began work on Glenunga at Horsburgh Grove, South Yarra. Like Grounds and Mewton, Romberg reworked the walk-up flat to combine elements of suburban architecture with European functionalism.

'Modern Continental principles'

Sydney was more accepting of the combination of Modernism and urbanity. However, this was a difficult combination to achieve when flats were permitted to dominate their sites, often denying light and views to neighbouring apartments. The writer and critic Leslie Rees commented in 1936: 'It is necessary to go on to the Bridge ... or to rent a top chimney flat to see the harbour at all ... Individuals, not the public, come first in Sydney. Grab what you can because it won't last long. Big, restless, sky-tearing blocks of flats are allowed to jostle ...'[47]

⬆ Frederick Romberg lived in Cairo, Fitzroy, while designing Newburn with his associate, Mary Turner Shaw. The first Australian combination of Modernism and its favoured material of reinforced concrete, Newburn was also a bold departure from Melbourne architecture, which was dismissed by Romberg as notable for flats 'desperately trying to imitate English mansions'.

Many Kings Cross apartment buildings were designed with an 'H'-shaped floor plan or variations; the indentations at each side created a 'light area' for the flats facing the neighbouring buildings. This policy was adopted even when, as with Selsdon built on Macleay Street in 1934, the building was initially free of tall neighbours. Selsdon's light areas eventually sank into gloom as neighbouring apartment buildings sprang up. A more expansive and successful use of the 'H' plan was the Macleay Regis, the last prestigious apartment tower built in Kings Cross before war brought building activity to a standstill. The Macleay Regis was also the last major apartment building to use light areas, as the new 1940 building regulations introduced Sydney's first open space and floor space ratio requirements for flat buildings.

The first Sydney apartment block to adopt the contemporary European model was Rutland Gate, a pair of buildings built in 1935 and 1936 on a sloping site above Double Bay. According to *Decoration and Glass*, Rutland Gate 'must not be confused with an ordinary block of flats because it has something far more valuable to offer',

Like Glenunga, Stanhill combined the rationality and regularity of the International Style with diverse aesthetics and responses to its setting. Stanhill's four elevations are distinct, creating a variety of experiences for viewers and residents. Decades later, Stanhill remains one of Australia's most spectacular buildings.

Stanhill's developer Stanley Korman and wife, photographed in Stanhill by Wolfgang Sievers, 1959. Korman arrived from Poland during the 1920s, established the Holeproof hosiery company and became a flamboyant property developer in Melbourne and the Gold Coast. His Modernist architectural tastes did not, apparently, extend to his furniture.

A Modernist apparition in the streets of Toorak, Caringal appears to have parachuted in from another aesthetic realm. The inventiveness of its architect, John William Rivett, extended to steel reinforcing that doubled as heating and cooling pipes.

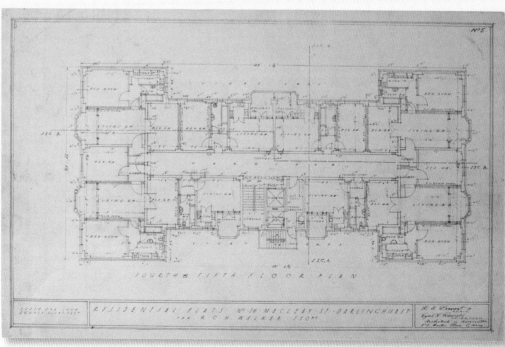

Completed in 1934, Selsdon was one of the first apartment towers built at the Potts Point end of Macleay Street. Designed by the prolific architects Reg Provost and Cyril Ruwald, its six floors and fifty-two flats are clothed in an uncertain combination of 'old English' and Romanesque styles.

'… the modern trend in architecture': Dudley Ward's Rutland Gate.

The last luxury tower built at Macleay Street, Kings Cross, before the 1990s, the Macleay Regis' ten floors house eighty-seven one- and two-bedroom flats, in contrast to the ample spaces offered by Kingsclere and similar prestige addresses. The Macleay Regis compensated with lavish materials and style, as well as a range of conveniences including a restaurant, dumb-waiters and telephonettes.

specifically 'a group of buildings composed of home units, each one enjoying exactly the same amenities and outlook'. This occurred through careful use of a generous site and the adoption of 'modern Continental principles': 'a remarkable simplicity … plain wall areas broken by sun porches, either curved or straight, corner balconies or large areas of glazing … The style requires very little adaptation, for it has proved suitable to our climactic conditions. It allows for large lighting units and the admission into the building of the maximum of sunlight and its functional designing, which permits large areas of plain wall surfaces, makes for economy of construction.'[48] The *Sydney Morning*

Herald enthused that even the bottom flats 'have such a lovely view, and almost too much sun'.[49]

Rutland Gate's architect Dudley Ward graduated from Sydney University in 1929 before spending five years in England, Europe and the USA. *Building* noted: 'The architect for these flats was a travelling scholar … and the designs of buildings erected by him since his return show undoubtedly that he has been influenced by the modern trend in architecture that has found favour in Europe and which originated in Germany. Mr Ward has shown courage in introducing this type of architecture into the better-class residential districts of Sydney in the form of flat buildings.'[50]

There is an element of irony that a genre originally developed with an economy of construction and repetition suitable for workers' and public housing should be transformed in Sydney into expensive eastern suburbs real estate. One of Rutland Gate's first tenants was the American movie star Helen Twelvetrees, who was in Sydney to shoot Ken G. Hall's *Thoroughbred*.

Dudley Ward went on to design several similar projects during the 1930s. The best known is Gowrie Gate, a six-storey block at Macleay Street, Kings Cross. The ground floor is devoted to shops, professional suites and a restaurant, which exploits its urban situation and gains elevation for all apartments. Occupying a corner site, Gowrie Gate is one of the few Macleay Street apartment blocks with an unobstructed northern frontage (Kingsclere and Byron Hall are others), permitting views and light to most of its fifty-eight flats.

Only a small number of Kings Cross apartments occupied generous sites. A notable example is Wyldefel Gardens, which was built in 1936 at Potts Point. Wyldefel was the brainchild of William Crowle, car importer, philanthropist, art collector and traveller. Crowle told *Decoration and Glass* that 'the entire scheme is practically a faithful adoption of a similar scheme on a similar site which Mr Crowle saw carried out with great success near Herr Hitler's house … right in the heart of the hills near Oberammergau, in Germany'.[51] Architect John R. Brogan was contracted to design, using Crowle's travel snaps, an apartment complex on the sloping harbourside site below Crowle's mansion Wyldefel. Brogan spent most of his career fulfilling his clients' desires, creating large houses in 'stockbroker Tudor' and other revivalist styles, but through his collaboration with Crowle his name has a lasting connection with a Modernist landmark.

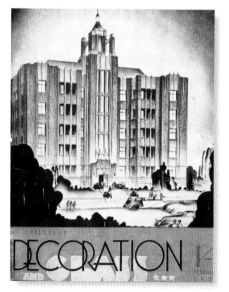

Wyldefel Gardens consists of twenty apartments, with the flat roof of each apartment forming the terrace of the next highest apartment. Each apartment gains a similar aspect and private and public spaces: 'two lines of building are served by a common space of garden, tennis court and swimming bath, thereby promoting a community spirit which is one of the best aims of modern civic planning'.[52] Despite their harbourside dress circle address, the units are simple and economical in construction, with curved concrete walls broken by curved glass windows and glass brick insets. At the water's edge was 'a two storied maisonette which Mr Crowle has built for his own use', although this building and water access was lost when Garden Island dockyard was expanded during the Pacific War. Nora Cooper of *Home Beautiful* enthused that Wyldefel was 'a little bit of modern Germany transplanted to the shores of Sydney … a scheme of modern building which is a triumphant *fait accompli* and a significant forecast'.[53]

However, few property investors were as generous or as personally involved as William Crowle. In Sydney Ure Smith's view, 'our speculative builders and property owners … are not far-sighted enough to plan permanently' and make 'provision for some communal gardens and trees'.[54] Some luxury apartment towers in wealthy suburbs such as Edgecliff and Double Bay remained the sole occupant of the grounds of demolished mansions. An example is Hillside designed by Aaron Bolot, a sumptuous tower in what the *Sydney Morning Herald* described as 'a modern adaptation of the Gothic' built by Edgecliff Road in 1936.[55]

The only similarly sited Kings Cross tower was Birtley Towers, the largest apartment block in Australia when completed in 1934 and the definitive adaptation of US skyscraper style to

⬆⬆ The urban setting of Gowrie Gate is richly depicted on a 1936 cover of the building journal *Decoration and Glass*. Widely publicised and praised during the 1930s, Dudley Ward's work was ignored by post-war architectural historians, presumably for insufficient conformity to the International Style.
⬆ Aaron Bolot's Hillside is a lavish exercise in skyscraper Gothic. The central tower contains the lifts and stairwell, and three-bedroom apartments form the wings. Hillside's revivalist aesthetic was belied by technological novelties that included car park turntables.

⬆️◀️ Like Hillside, the red texture brick of Birtley Towers in Kings Cross lends the sculpted tower an impression of luxury and solidity. Emil Sodersten designed six flats per floor in a U-shaped plan, maximising light, views and construction cost. The foyer is also a no-expense-spared statement, at odds with the asceticism of the International Style.

Australian apartment design. Built for the Consolidated Real Estate and Investment Co., a private company that financed several Kings Cross apartments, Birtley Towers' uncluttered site heightened its dramatic profile, as did its texture brick exterior, which lightened in colour towards the peak.

Birtley Towers was designed by Emil Sodersten, one of the few Sydney architects of the 1920s and 1930s to build a lasting reputation primarily from apartment architecture. So wedded to brick construction was Sodersten that *Art in Australia* praised his 'delightful essays in brickwork', claiming that 'love of this versatile medium' made him a worthy successor to John Horbury Hunt, colonial Sydney's leading exponent of the masonry aesthetic; Sodersten's 'fine modern piles of flats are surely bold challengers to the many thoughtless and shoddy buildings of this type that unfortunately already exist to spoil our skyline'.[56]

Sodersten's apartments summarise the eclectic character of apartment design in Kings Cross and inner Sydney generally. The combination of multiple storeys and balconies offered a challenge to the historically oriented architectural styles of the early twentieth century, with Spanish, Old English, Arts and Crafts and other picturesque idioms being pressed into decorative service. Around 1930 the sunburst idioms and vertical emphasis of Art Deco became common elements of Kings Cross apartments. Sodersten's Wychbury was among the first; he had earlier produced apartments in Spanish Mission, including the Broadway at Rose Bay, a rare combination of a flat block with a service station.

After Sodersten travelled overseas in 1935, his work adopted the simple forms of European Modernism and Dudley Ward's combination of exposed brick construction and forthright horizontal and vertical articulation. Rather than the trademark Modernism of sheer white walls, this combination proved influential in Sydney, whether expressed in a walk-up block or stand-alone tower.[57] Many Australian architects were impressed by the Dutch architect Willem Dudok's combination of brickwork and powerful massing. Decorative brickwork was a strong tradition in Sydney architecture, and it helped to ease acceptance of the confronting new look.

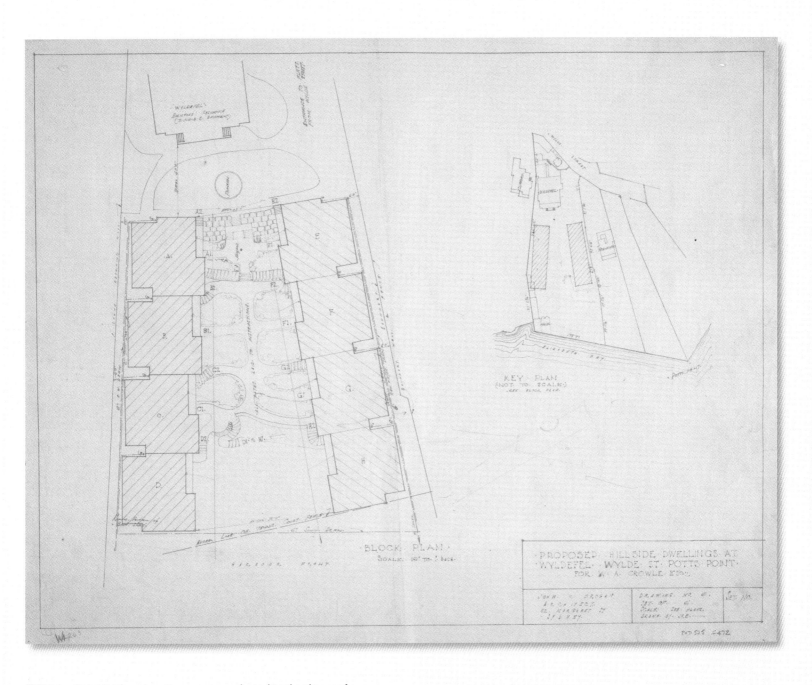

⬆️⬅️ '… a little bit of modern Germany transplanted to the shores of
Sydney.' Wyldefel Gardens through Max Dupain's lens, and John R. Brogan's
site plan.

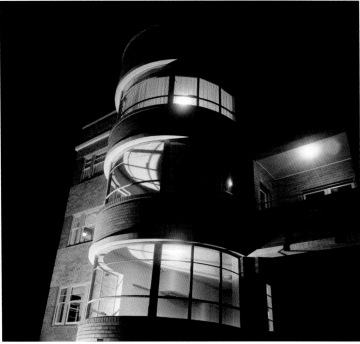

⬆ Dupain's photo of a Darjoa interior featured Mrs Edwards, 'a well-known radio player' according to *The Home*, which also noted that the walls were stippled cream, carpet cigar brown, timber light honey colour, upholstery off-white and beige with chevron design, curtains of transparent marquisette (*The Home*, February 1938).

⬅ Designed by Samuel Lipson, Darjoa at Point Piper was a typical product of the Sydney marriage of European Modernism and conspicuous wealth. Max Dupain's 1938 photos emphasised the former element, focusing on Darjoa's steel-framed windows.

New frontiers

Flats came late to Brisbane. The tropical capital evolved a form of timber and iron bungalow, more appropriate aesthetically and environmentally than the suburban housing of southern cities. Many large houses were divided into flats when Brisbane's population began to increase rapidly at the start of the twentieth century, but purpose-built flats did not appear in numbers until the mid-1920s.

At the same time Brisbane City Council was formed from an amalgamation of twenty small councils, controlling the building activity of a much larger area than the city councils of Sydney, Melbourne or Perth. In 1926 the council introduced building regulations for flats, including a limit of 50 per cent site coverage for flat buildings unless of three floors or less.

Not surprisingly, most Brisbane flats were two- or three-storey walk-ups, similar to those of suburban Sydney. Despite an interruption during the depression, booming flat construction was encouraging speculation that a northern equivalent of Kings Cross would soon appear: 'flats were the first form of building to show activity when the recent building depression began to wane'.[58] Certainly some inner suburbs quickly came to be known for concentrations of apartment buildings, notably New Farm, Fortitude Valley, Hamilton and South Brisbane. Rows of walk-ups appeared in some streets until 1937, when the City Council came up with further building regulations specific to apartments, setting minimum sizes for block frontages and floor space. The council also limited apartment buildings to three floors, unless there were 'special circumstances regarding position or isolation or permanent surrounding vacant space ...'[59]

The Brisbane flats of the 1920s and 1930s were aimed at the usual tenant markets for bachelor flats or bedsits, larger apartments for couples and a small number of luxury flats with servants' quarters. The latter included Craigston at Spring Hill and Cliffside, a five-storey block of seven flats at Kangaroo Point across the river from New Farm. Brisbane flats were almost invariably clothed in a variety of revivalist or exotic styles, including versions of Spanish, Mediterranean or 'Old English'. A notable exception is Coronet Court, an Art Deco block built in Brunswick Street, New Farm, in 1934.[60]

Many Brisbane flats also included the tropical bungalow features of local architecture, such as gabled roofs, shaded windows and sleep-out balconies. Others stood out from their southern counterparts by combining brick construction with timber frames and timber or asbestos-cement (fibro) cladding. A notable example is Green Gables, built 1935 in Julius Street, New Farm. A brick ground floor is surmounted by two fibro-clad floors (later rendered to give a masonry appearance), and sleep-outs are sheltered by timber blinds.[61] *Building* praised a Dornoch Terrace block for showing 'how fibro-cement balconies can be treated effectively to combine with more solid materials ... in the façade of a flat building'.[62]

Green Gables is the work of George Rae, Brisbane's leading apartment architect of the 1920s and 1930s. Rae's work also included Greystaines at Hamilton Road, Hamilton, Highview at Highgate Hill, and Casa Del Mar, also at New Farm. By 1947 almost a tenth of Brisbane's dwellings were flats, a similar proportion to that of Melbourne.

Perth flats were similarly concentrated in and around the city, with apartment living becoming popular during the 1930s. Many 1930s

⬆⬆ Emil Sodersten designed the Broadway at Bellevue Hill, a flat block above a service station and garage, about 1928. With its Californian provenance, the Broadway's 'Spanish' style was a popular look for commercial buildings of the time.

⬆ Built above Newcastle's city centre and port in 1930, Segenhoe was the first of Sodersten's apartments to use a complex floor plan to heighten aspect and create a dramatic elevation.

apartment buildings were designed by Harold Krantz, who almost single-handedly created the apartment industry in the western capital, where he designed almost 90 per cent of Perth's early flats. Krantz's influence extended beyond his architectural activities to vigorous advocacy of apartment living: 'A great number of people demand housing near the city and their work. If adequate flats are not provided they will crowd together in hotels, hostels and pseudo-accommodation. Flats are demanded by a great number of people ...'[63]

⬆ Comprising seven flats, each with their own entrance, Cliffside is one of Brisbane's grandest apartments. Cliffside was designed by R. Martin Wilson for Doris Booth, a successful prospector and miner who, in a landmark legal case, gained control of common property from her former husband. Built near Booth's childhood home, Cliffside was financed with the proceeds of this triumph.

➡ 'The wide overhanging eaves and lower hood will ensure that shade is thrown on the walls during the noonday heat.' The Sydney architects Morrow & Gordon made appropriate adaptations for these South Brisbane bachelor flats.

◪ Completed in 1934, Greystaines is typical of numerous 'Spanish' or 'Mediterranean' flats built for middle-class tenants in Brisbane and other Australian cities. Its exotic details lighten an otherwise stolid grouping of six flats.

Perspective shows a new block of Bachelor Flats to be erected in Appel Street, Brisbane. The building will consist of nine flats and six garages . . . 3 flats on each floor and the garages and boiler room in the basement. Each flat will contain an entrance hall, a living room with cooking recess and a bedroom with conjoined bathroom, and all will be equipped with every modern device for comfortable living. The wide overhanging eaves and lower hood will insure that shade is thrown on the walls during the noonday heat, while full advantage of the prevailing breeze will be taken by the use of a U-shaped plan at the rear and the studied placement of windows. Through the large expanse of glass to the living room tenants will be able to admire an excellent view. The architects are Messrs. D. T. Morrow & Gordon, of Sydney.

Bachelor Flats

ARCHITECTS: D. T. MORROW & GORDON, SYDNEY

TO BE ERECTED AT BRISBANE

Apartment living Geoff Cousins

'Most of my friends, in fact all of my close friends, live in apartments scattered over the eastern suburbs of Sydney. None of them live in houses. Our apartment tends to be a social hub, a meeting place for all our friends, somewhere

to congregate for drinks before heading out into the night.'

Geoff Cousins is describing his home in Ashdown, a much-loved 1930s block of thirty apartments in Elizabeth Bay, which he shares with his partner. He bought into the building only a few years ago but has become a central part of life in the block having established a communal herb garden behind the block, a landscaped area with chillies, basil, parsley and rosemary for all to share, with a worm farm and compost heap. If you asked anyone in the building what they most liked about living there, Geoff said they would identify the pathway to the side of the asymmetrical, white-rendered block, which leads to the apartment

entrance. It provides a transitional space between public and private domains.

Geoff grew up in country South Australia and knew little about apartment living before relocating to Sydney in his twenties. Ever since he has lived in a range of different blocks from Balmain to Petersham to Paddington to Darlinghurst: 'Until I can afford a house, if that's what I want, an apartment is the only option if I want to live in such a great area, which is centrally located. One day I would like a garden, but until then I'm happy pottering about in the shared garden on the weekend … I'm more than happy to spend a whole weekend at home and in the garden without feeling any

need to leave; it's got such a lovely ambience, such a lovely feel.'

The block, designed by well-known Sydney apartment architect Aaron Bolot, is company title and is home mostly to owner-occupiers and only a few renters. This appeals to Geoff, who states that when he is outside at the weekend, he talks to the neighbours. In other blocks he did not always know the other residents. Geoff worries about the potential build-up of new apartments in the area but maintains an active interest, attending council meetings to voice his concern when new developments arise that would compromise the historical integrity of the block and environs.

Seven Elizabeth Street is less complete an expression of apartment Modernism than Marlborough Hall, which was built above Elizabeth Bay in 1938.

This seven-storey block was designed with an L-shaped plan, which opens most of the sixty-two apartments to a north-easterly aspect, capturing view and sea breezes. It also means that the building's considerable garden space (and swimming pool) is blessed with a sunny aspect. The apartments are more generous in size than many of the minimum flat genre, offering separate bedrooms and living rooms as well as an enclosed balcony. Always careful to create striking exteriors, Sodersten used the entry tower to produce a vertical contrast to the horizontal banding of windows and balconies. This European aesthetic was clothed in texture brick, a signature element of Sodersten's work.

The relationship between Australian architects and international apartment design is complex. Some important architects, like Best Overend and Harry Seidler, imported complete elements of the Modernist project, promoting them vigorously in Australia. Others added new elements to their existing practice. In this category was Emil Sodersten, perhaps Sydney's highest-profile architect of the 1930s.

A precocious talent, Sodersten did not travel overseas until he was in his mid-thirties. He had already won the competition to design the Australian War Memorial in Canberra and had also designed office towers, the Hotel Australia and several upmarket apartment buildings, notably the luxurious Birtley Towers.[1]

Sodersten's return produced a new burst of productivity. In 1938 *Decoration and Glass* observed: 'Small flats, known generally as "bachelor flats", and slightly larger than "minimum flats", are very popular in England and on the Continent, and are fast becoming the vogue here in Australia.'[2] The journal was reviewing Marlborough Hall, one of two bachelor flat complexes designed by Sodersten on his return to Australia. The other was Seven Elizabeth Street, Sydney, described by its prospectus as 'luxury flats for moderate incomes'.[3] This ten-floor, fifty-four-flat city complex was also notable for interiors by Marion Hall Best, the designer's first major commission (pictured bottom left). Because of its cramped location between other buildings,

Many notable Sydneysiders have resided in Marlborough Hall. They include architect and designer Douglas Snelling and his wife after their 1948 arrival in Sydney from the USA: 'In the mornings, Snelling does his outdoor work while Nancy cleans the flat. After lunch, the flat is converted into an office for receiving clients … He works late over his board every night, smokes and drinks black coffee to keep awake.'[4]

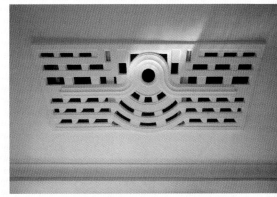

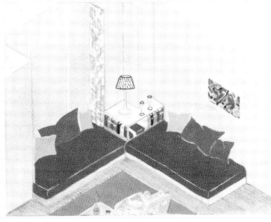

Front Flat, No. 5, facing Elizabeth Street. Note the Venetian blinds.

For people of discriminating taste; in this difficult search for flats, we offer originality and charm in the freshness of our colour schemes.

The curtains have been hand-blocked for us, and our carpets especially hand-hooked in India.

The modern furniture is designed on traditional lines, giving beauty and comfort.

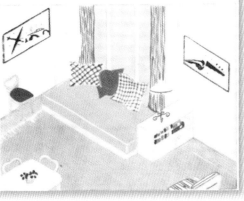

Green Gables and Evelyn Court are two of several flats built at Julius Street, New Farm, after the street was subdivided in 1934. A cul-de-sac overlooking the Brisbane River, Julius Street remains a museum of early Brisbane apartment architecture. Evelyn Court's Art Deco styling stands out from its neighbours, although its six-flat interior was typical until substantially renovated in 1999.

Krantz's best-known 1930s building was Riviera Flats in Mill Street, designed with John Oldham for the entrepreneur Joe Skinner. Like Best Overend, Skinner had been impressed during a London sojourn by the potential of bachelor flats. Krantz had already designed some small suburban flat blocks and some flat conversions of warehouses and other buildings. Riviera gave him the chance to produce a Perth equivalent of Melbourne's Cairo and Sydney's Marlborough Hall. Offering bachelor flats with built-in furniture and kitchenettes, Riviera's Moderne curves, steel windows and roof garden advertised the new type of living.[64]

The *Daily News* wrote of Riviera: 'Young people who live alone and newly married couples want to live under clean, bright, independent circumstances … Ugly, depressing surroundings are a handicap to enjoyment. Neat, clean, well-planned rooms with built-in modern furniture, tastefully chosen floor and window coverings and private

⬆ Coronet Court at New Farm was one of Brisbane's largest apartment buildings when built in 1934. Its decorative brickwork and mannered facade and foyer is more typical of contemporary Sydney blocks than its Brisbane neighbours.

bathrooms and lavatories are available at modest rentals. The competition to rent these apartments in Perth today indicates that they supply a long-felt want.'[65]

So successful was this project that Krantz cooperated with other developers on bachelor flat projects including Arbordale, a six-floor conversion of two semi-detached houses on St George's Terrace. The city location of these flats and the office and retail property boom of the 1970s and 1980s has unfortunately seen many of Perth's city flats demolished, including both Riviera and Arbordale.

⬆ Completed in 1942, Deep Acres in North Adelaide was designed by
Jack McConnell, who went on to become a prolific architect of educational
and commercial buildings. Deep Acres combines ample but unadorned
apartments with an extensive landscaped site, one of the few early
Modernist apartments (with Cairo and Wyldefel) to achieve this combination.

PROPOSED BLOCK OF MINIMUM FLATS
HAROLD A. KRANTZ A·R·A·I·A A·R·I·A·W·A ARCHITECT

'The competition to rent these apartments in Perth today indicates that they supply a long-felt want.' As built, Riviera bachelor flats was somewhat less striking than in Harold Krantz's original concept. However, as depicted in John Oldham's rendering in the prospectus, the interiors were both beguiling and simple.

A new style of living Inner-city apartments 1950–80

According to its architect Robin Boyd,

Domain Park was 'the first example in Melbourne of a genre that has some powerful, sincere opponents: a "high-rise" block'.[1] Domain Park was financed and built by Lend Lease, which stipulated that the building include the maximum number of apartments compatible with Melbourne's uniform building regulations. These restricted overlooking neighbouring properties, but also permitted tall apartment blocks to be built opposite parks.[2]

Domain Park was built in South Yarra opposite the Botanic Gardens, its twenty-floor format dictated by these rules 'and by the magnificent views: to the north the sun and the city seen across a green mile of the Botanic Gardens: to the south Port Phillip Bay'. The building was 'narrow enough for all main rooms to fill its width and have an outlook both ways, so giving these rooms a heightened sense of isolation and suspension in space'.[3] Boyd designed four types of apartment, creating a variation of infill surfaces and spaces between the rigid grid of concrete walls and floors forming the northern face of the structure. According to its prospectus, Domain Park 'provides a home for those who find it desirable to be free of responsibilites, without parting with the essential features of a graceful home and garden'.[4]

Robin Boyd and Harry Seidler performed similar roles in their respective cities. Both were prominent public figures and articulate and tireless advocates of modern architecture and urban planning. However, Boyd's architectural oeuvre was largely confined to houses; Domain Park was his largest commission and sole apartment building. In contrast Seidler was one of Australia's most prolific architects, producing notable structures across the range of building genres, including numerous city office complexes.

Boyd's reputation survives less on the basis of his architectural product than on his writing, notably his polemical classics *Australia's Home* (1952) and *The Australian Ugliness* (1960). Typically he participated in the controversies sparked by Domain Park, which continued for more than a decade after its completion. Answering claims that buildings overlooking the gardens represented 'the selfish demands of a few', Boyd argued that a ban on tall residential buildings 'where they are most needed' near the city would only have the result of 'increasing

↑ '... the city seen across a green mile of the Botanic Gardens.' Low-rise building laws and topography meant that the association of apartments and views was less close in Melbourne than in Sydney. Domain Park was one of the first to make potential vistas a selling point.

'Domain Park provides a home for those who find it desirable to be free of the responsibilities, without parting with the essential features of a graceful home and garden.' The prospectus for Domain Park apartments, about 1960.

the jungle of pink walk-up flats in the inner suburbs and increasing the sprawl'.

However, Boyd had to admit that 'skyscraper flats' in and near the city 'have not so far proved to be a great economic success'.[5] Apartments in Domain Park sold more slowly than Lend Lease expected, and the company did not pursue further apartment plans in Melbourne.

'Home units'

Domain Park was part of a new generation of apartment towers to appear around 1960, which inspired decades of debate. The largest of these was Brisbane's Torbreck, designed by local architects Aubrey Job and Bob Froud. More significantly, Torbreck was financed and marketed by Reid Murray Holdings, one of several ambitious and entrepreneurial property companies to emerge during the 1950s and 1960s, with profound effects on the apartment building industry.

In earlier times, most major apartment buildings were financed by a variety of private and public investors, content to profit from the rental income paid by their tenants. In contrast, Reid Murray and similar companies managed both the finance and construction roles, as well as taking a leading role in the promotion and sale of the new apartments. Formed in 1957 from a merger of retailing companies, Reid Murray expanded aggressively into the property and construction industries. It subdivided and sold land and built houses and flats for sale in Adelaide, Melbourne, Sydney and Brisbane. It also built shopping centres and hotels.

Torbreck was Reid Murray's most ambitious apartment project, its success inspiring plans for further Queensland towers using the Torbreck name. These plans went unfulfilled. In 1961 Reid Murray Holdings was the fourth largest Australian-owned company. Two years later it collapsed with losses of almost $24 million, a victim of the early 1960s credit squeeze as well as the company's recklessly fast expansion. At the time, Reid Murray was Australia's largest corporate failure, and it left numerous contractors, mortgagees and shareholders out of pocket.[6]

Reid Murray was the first of several high-profile property and building companies to collapse during the 1960s and 1970s. Like Mainline, Parkes Developments and Home Units of Australia, its level of indebtedness could be serviced only if property prices and profits continued to soar. Unlike many of its competitors, Reid Murray at least left a notable building. This heyday of property speculation was by and large a festival of the cheap and nasty.

Lend Lease, another new construction company, proved more enduring. In part the expanded role of property and building companies was encouraged by a move towards a new market in individually purchased apartments. Torbreck's apartments were purchased through company title, but Blues Point Tower was the first to take advantage of new strata title laws, which allowed the purchase of individual apartments rather than a share in the entire block as in company title schemes. During

'Congestion and overcrowding can be eliminated by building vertically.' Harry Seidler's plan for a McMahon's Point apartment city remains at odds with Sydney's history of piecemeal development. Perhaps unwisely, Seidler later used this plan to defend its sole completed element, Blues Point Tower.

the 1950s, private ownership of apartments increased markedly in New South Wales, especially after rent control was abolished in 1954. Nonetheless, company titles remained an expensive and complex form of ownership, and forms of cooperative ownership appeared during the 1950s.

Not surprisingly, Lend Lease played a leading role in the introduction of strata title. Lend Lease was founded by Gerard Josef 'Dick' Dusseldorp, who came to Australia from the Netherlands in 1951 to work on the Snowy Mountains Scheme. Within a decade Dusseldorp and his new company were remaking Sydney through high-profile projects including the first stage of the Sydney Opera House and Caltex House,

Blues Point Tower's intricately patterned facade belies its austere outline, demonstrating Harry Seidler's ability to create visual tension out of functional building elements.

Sydney's first office 'skyscraper'. Dusseldorp was also anxious to involve Lend Lease in apartment building, arguing that Sydney's cottage building industry was 'better suited to semi-rural Australia—not a huge metropolitan centre such as Sydney'.[7] While not denying Lend Lease's interest in apartments, Dusseldorp claimed also to be motivated to create 'a better means of accommodation for the "average guy"—who wanted to live close to the city, or on a transport line, but who couldn't afford a house on the proverbial quarter-acre block'.[8]

Dusseldorp argued that the price of flats would fall if strata title legislation was enacted, and in 1959 he engaged a lawyer to expedite the law reform process. The result of Dusseldorp's campaigning was the New South Wales *Conveyancing (Strata Titles) Act 1961*, which allowed, for the first time in Australia, freehold ownership of individual flats. This pioneering legislation was emulated by the other Australian states. The 'home unit' was born.[9]

Tower of controversy

Blues Point Tower was initially conceived by Lend Lease as part of a redevelopment scheme for McMahons Point, just west of the Harbour Bridge. In 1957 North Sydney Council rezoned a major portion of McMahons Point from 'residential' to 'industrial'. The McMahons Point and Lavender Bay Progress Association joined a group of nine architects led by Harry Seidler in a campaign to overturn the rezoning decision, arguing that the site was ideally suited to being a residential area rather than 'factories and smokestacks'.[10] Before developing the plans, residents were surveyed and habits and needs taken into consideration.[11]

The McMahons Point campaigners issued photos of the site, captioned 'A cement factory will enjoy this view'.[12] Their booklet *Urban Redevelopment Concerns You!* argued: 'We need a back to the city movement, one of re-centralization rather than de-centralization. Congestion and overcrowding can be eliminated by building vertically.'[13]

The McMahons Point controversy was the focus of a growing media consensus that Sydney's horizontal sprawl was reaching 'alarming proportions' and that the 'decaying' inner suburbs should be developed in preference to new settlement on the city's fringe.[14] The *Sun-Herald* supported the campaign to 'revitalize the moribund inner city' and allow new residents to enjoy harbour views.[15] Denis Winston, Professor of Planning at Sydney University, chimed in: 'I completely support the idea of redeveloping Glebe and Balmain and other inner suburbs … If comfortable, high density housing can put 15,000 people on McMahon's Point, where there are 3,500 at present, the same thing can be done many times over on the other side of the Harbour.'[16]

Seidler's statement on the issue was the McMahons Point Redevelopment Scheme: a detailed model of an 'ultra-modern' residential suburb with a population of more than 15,000 people, strategically located close to the new office buildings of North Sydney and a five-minute ferry ride away from Sydney's CBD. The architect's proposal was a Modernist vision of twenty-nine apartment blocks (seven high-rise towers; twelve mid-rise blocks; nine low-rise blocks and a hotel) set in gardens with a floating restaurant/nightclub, shops, kindergarten,

Built during the mid-1930s, Berthold Lubetkin's Highpoint at Hampstead, London, was for decades the paradigm of the International Style tower block.
In 1955–56 Harry Seidler made a speedy tour of the major sites of Modernism, including Le Corbusier's Unité d'Habitation at Marseilles, here captured in one of Seidler's travel snaps.
Alton Estate, Roehampton, London, photographed by Harry Seidler, was a leading influence on his McMahon's Point plan. Seidler argued that Australian prejudices against flats could be overcome by the construction of a similar estate in Sydney.

music bowl and offices. Based on social housing principles of communal living, the scheme employed the principles of tiered development, featuring low buildings on the water's edge, medium height on the slopes in staggered groupings, high rise towers on the crest, and a hotel on the point.[17]

In October 1958 the McMahons Point campaigners succeeded in persuading the New South Wales Government to overturn North Sydney Council's zoning decision. However, Seidler's vision for the peninsula never materialised. A series of factors contributed: property prices escalated, council made no effort to promote or enforce the scheme and there was no sign of potential finance for such a large-scale project. Only Blues Point Tower was built on Seidler's ideal site for a high-density residential development.

Following Torbreck's lead, a helicopter was used while the building was under construction during 1960, flying prospective buyers to the proposed building height to hover there and drink in the view that could become theirs. Blues Point Tower gave a boost to advertising and media coverage of apartment living. 'Glamorous Yet Practical is Home Unit living at Blues Point Tower' appeared alongside articles titled 'Smart, thrifty and carefree—that's home unit ownership'.[18]

The promise of strata title laws produced numerous media reports about this 'new style of living': 'All over the metropolitan area ultra-modern blocks of home units are springing up, sparking off a new way of life,' enthused the Sunday Telegraph.[19] Seidler played a leading part in promoting the new lifestyle, assisting in the development of the Home Unit Display Centre, which opened in 1959 at Caltex House in Kent Street. The showroom designed by Seidler included models, photos and plans covering ninety projects, many of which were home units described as providing the same standard of amenities as the suburban home.

The publicity was poorly timed, as the 1961 credit squeeze restrained the home unit boom almost as soon as it had begun. Despite the hype, Blues Point Tower was not completely sold until 1966. Lend Lease closed its display centre and restricted its apartment investments for some years.

The modern material

With its prominent harbourside site, Blues Point Tower has regularly been criticised for epitomising private privilege at the cost of public aesthetics. However, when viewed at close range, Blues Point Tower's prosaic substance looks at odds with its sophisticated composition and its sleek appearance from a distance.

Blues Point Tower's marketing targeted 'the young marrieds who both go to work, the couple in their early fifties who lived in a large home that is now too big … or the people who live on their own'.[20] Seidler transformed the materials of Sydney suburban flatland; the tower's inexpensive components are typical of the post-war housing boom and attendant shortages of materials and labour. During the succeeding decade, dozens of Sydney apartment buildings would feature the same combination of reinforced concrete structure and balconies with brick infill walls and aluminium-framed windows. Few displayed a facade of similarly strong visual contrasts and patterns.

Torbreck, Domain Park and Blues Point Tower took advantage of earlier international developments in apartment design. Residential towers were still a developing genre during the 1930s. European and North American Modernists primarily designed low-rise *zeilenbau* or linear housing. Although some notable apartment towers were built for the private market during the 1930s, notably London's Highpoint, the marriage of height and functionalism was not widely consummated until after 1945.

Among the most influential post-war designs was Le Corbusier's Unité d'Habitation in Marseilles, notable partly for the use of reinforced concrete in both structural and sculptural forms. Reinforced concrete construction had been in use for decades, providing the structure and walls of several Australian apartment blocks including The Astor. Apart from Frederick Romberg's Newburn and Stanhill, the most spectacular concrete apartment building in Australia was Adereham Hall, built at Elizabeth Bay in 1934. Designed by Gordon McKinnon, this nine-storey luxury building is widely known as Gotham City thanks to its lofty stepped parapet and cast concrete sunbursts.

By the 1950s the practical and aesthetic potential of reinforced concrete had been further explored by Le Corbusier and others. Concrete

floor slabs, frames, walls, balconies and sunscreens became elements of both the structure and facade of many apartment buildings, adding a new aesthetic dimension, more integral to building structure than the smooth curves of 1930s concrete balconies and window hoods.

Labour intensive but cheaper than steel framing, concrete broadened both the market and the architectural possibilities of apartment buildings. Prefabricated concrete elements were central parts of a new generation of tall, wide and narrow apartment buildings that appeared in Europe and the USA during the 1950s. Often called 'slabs', these buildings align apartments along continuous corridors, often with interlocking spaces opening the apartments to light and breezes on opposite sides of the building.

Believing that Le Corbusier's Unité d'Habitation was 'a milestone' in housing design, Harry Seidler was keen to apply its principles to Australia.[21] Shortly after his arrival in Sydney, Seidler designed a forty-unit slab block for a site at Elizabeth Bay. Designed for 'comfortable, sophisticated living', Ithaca Gardens combined a concrete framework, balconies and sunshades into a strong elevational pattern.[22] Like Unité d'Habitation, Ithaca Gardens was raised off the ground on pilotis (sculpted concrete columns), creating parking space beneath and maximising the view and breeze potential for all residents. Each access gallery served two floors. This split-level access opened the flats to light and air from north and south.

The expressed concrete frame and brick infill was a feature of many of Seidler's blocks, as were private sun-protected terraces and a communal roof garden. *Building* described Ithaca Gardens as 'Flats of the future. Maximum of light; minimum of housework. Healthful in-and-outdoor living.'[23] Less complimentary was the architect and cartoonist

◄ 'Flats of the future.' Seidler's Ithaca Gardens displayed its concrete elements frankly. Behind it an earlier concrete aesthetic can be seen in Adereham Hall's Art Deco expressions.

▲ Seven Seas introduced the slab block to Sydney's North Shore. Its descendents were numerous.

Apartment living   Marita Leuver and Sylvia Weimer

This couple both grew up in houses, Marita in Turramurra on Sydney's upper North Shore and Sylvia in Wiesbaden, a baroque spa city in Germany. Both places are far removed from their current abode in Harry Seidler's ground-breaking Ithaca Gardens in Sydney's

Elizabeth Bay, 'a home of beauty and functional design that [we] couldn't bear to leave'.

Having lived in the block for fifteen years over two stints, Marita explains: 'We like the era of the block—it goes with the style of furniture we like, and our choice in art doesn't fight with any cornices. I'm not so keen on the outside. I used to think it looked like a hospital, but the minute you walk in it's mind-bending. The apartments are hidden jewels.'

The apartment is very quiet with one lift serving two apartments and an open walkway to the other side when the forty-five-year-old

lift breaks down. With their office in the vicinity, any number of cafés lining the streets, the expansive Rushcutters Bay park and all the little shops up the road, they have little reason to leave the 'hood. Sylvia says in many ways the area is reminiscent of pockets of Berlin, not architecturally or visually, because 'the European capital is more gritty and historical, with Marlene Dietrich-type apartments with five-metre high ceilings, but by the fact that they—all the residents—eat, drink, work, socialise in the area'.

'We love Elizabeth Bay. But the vibe of the area is changing with the arrival of empty-nesters,

the only ones who can now afford to buy in the area. The increasing homogeneity of the residents in this block and others is obvious. While there used to be greater diversity with writers, photographers and designers, many of them have moved out as the area has become expensive and sanitised. The cafés are becoming a bit like Double Bay or Mosman.'

Symptomatic of the change of the area is the new fence and gate, which is not sympathetic to Seidler's pared-back functional aesthetic, but fulfills its job of excluding the area's undesirables, which were never a problem anyway, says Marita.

⬆ This Etham Avenue block was one of three designed by Aaron Bolot for Darling Point during the 1960s as the 'home unit' boom accelerated through Sydney's waterside suburbs.

➡ The Quarterdeck hastened the demise of Kirribilli's exclusive character, replacing the mansion Miendetta, former home of founding Australian prime minister Edmund Barton.

George Molnar: 'The way Ithaca Gardens Apartments (which for some reason reminds me of a biscuit factory) dominates the curving Ithaca Road is victory to the point of total surrender.'[24]

First proposed in 1951, Ithaca Gardens was not completed until 1960 as finance, building materials and construction expertise were in short supply in the decade following the war. Seidler spent most of the 1950s arguing for an 'open domestic architecture' and designing open-plan suburban cottages. Apartment buildings in his adopted country were criticised for a superficial take on Modernist principles: a reduction of 'modern architecture to some superficial design tricks, which similar to other stylistic exterior decorating, deprives the building not only of a logical interior layout, truthfully expressed in its entire form, but of any genuine aesthetic value'.[25]

Harbour views

After Seidler formed an alliance with Dick Dusseldorp and Lend Lease, his career blossomed with the wider apartment building boom. Blues Point Tower was the most publicised product of a new apartment boom on the lower North Shore. The president of the Milsons Point–Kirribilli

Chamber of Commerce claimed in 1961 that Kirribilli 'because of its picturesque location and proximity to the city, will become another Manhattan within a decade'.[26] He was able to point to sixteen apartment projects in progress, all taking advantage of the new strata title laws.

However, Kirribilli's transformation was already underway in 1958, with the completion of Seven Seas, an eight-floor block (with a parking floor beneath the building) designed by Douglas Forsyth Evans, a prolific and entrepreneurial architect who often took the developer role as well as that of designer. Comprising fifty-five bachelor flats, Seven Seas was notable for its staggered facade of individual balconies, extensive glazing—'some of the walls will be completely of glass'—and concrete framing.[27] Despite Seidler's dismissal of local apartment architecture, Seven Seas was one of several apartment blocks to employ the contemporary slab block formula. Another Kirribilli example was the Quarterdeck, 'a 12-storey contemporary styled home unit building containing 48 two and three bedroom units', which also used the slab format.[28]

A Lend Lease project, the Quarterdeck was designed by Aaron Bolot, architect of Wylde Street Cooperative Apartments and several other apartments. Bolot had already designed another 'neat 10-storey slab' for Lend Lease at Darling Point, the first of three he created for this affluent peninsula. The Melbourne University architectural journal

Designed by Theodore Fry, Oceana, centre, was one of the first post-war additions to the Elizabeth Bay skyline.

Cross-section used it to summarise the pros and cons of the slab block in Sydney: 'Its 32 units … face north-east and have magnificent views, and are being sold, not let. Such a tall slab scheme offers its occupiers better breezes, more ground-level garden and a neater, easier-built building. It is also likely to shut off more view from the neighbours, a constant source of irritation around the Harbour (there were stormy Council meetings about an 8-storey block at Potts Point, and angry protests at Rose Bay recently).'[29] In 1961 *Building* reported that 'new home unit projects were sprouting at all points around the Harbour— like asparagus beginning to emerge from its bed'.[30]

Several other large slab-format blocks were built around 1960 for different economic levels of the Sydney apartment market. Oceana was a thirteen-floor slab block by the harbour at Elizabeth Bay designed by Theodore Fry. With expressed concrete frame and individual balconies on the harbour side and access galleries on the opposite side, Oceana shared many features with the Quarterdeck, notably free-standing elevator towers. However, with typically seven one- and two-bedroom flats on each floor, it was less spacious than 'the family type accommodation' offered by the Quarterdeck.[31]

The developers of Glenhurst at Darling Point sought the upper end of the Sydney market. Overlooking Rushcutters Bay, Glenhurst was

heralded for its size—being the largest privately developed block of apartments in Australia—and for being the largest lift-slab constructed building in the world when completed in 1959. This construction method speeded the erection of the large floor spaces of slab blocks by having reinforced concrete floors precast before being lifted into place. Designed by Douglas Forsyth Evans for the established building firm Stuart Bros, Glenhurst was a self-consciously ' "prestige job" … in the nature of a monument to the well-known family of builders'.[32]

Glenhurst followed the tradition of luxury apartments established decades before by Kingsclere. With peerless panoramic views of the harbour and a northern facade of almost uninterrupted glass broken only by generous balconies, ample covered car parking accessed by a specially built private road, state-of-the-art appliances including a TV antenna outlet in each apartment, excellent cross-ventilation, solar access and flexible layouts to suit any 'discerning investor', these apartments bore little resemblance to their public housing contemporaries.[33] Press advertisements for Glenhurst featured a glamorous woman's profile, asking: 'Me complain? Never!'[34]

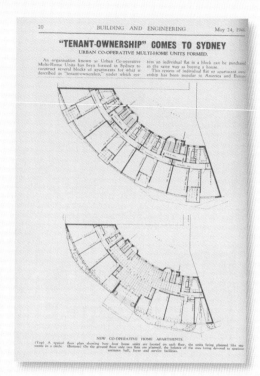

Such Modernist concepts as the minimum flat and repetition of building components were intended to make the new architecture more affordable and accessible. Despite this, apartment living in prime locations remained expensive, and individual apartment ownership was restricted to upmarket company title buildings. In 1945 it became legal for cooperative building societies to finance apartment blocks on a similar model to cottages, and a building society called Urban Cooperative Multi Home Units was formed for this purpose. Aaron Bolot designed cooperative apartments at Kirribilli and Blues Point for the society, but it was the Wylde Street Cooperative Apartments that secured his place in architectural history.

As well as democratising the ownership of apartments, the building was similarly

Wylde Street Cooperative Apartments was completed in 1950, but embodied the best architectural ideals and practices of the 1930s. The building was designed by Aaron Bolot, one of Sydney's most prolific architects. Born in the Crimea in 1900, Bolot emigrated to Australia with his family in 1911. After studying architecture in Brisbane, Bolot moving to Sydney during the 1930s,

where he designed cinemas—including the Randwick Ritz—but was most active in the apartment field. He gained considerable recognition for Ashdown at Elizabeth Bay, described by *Art in Australia* as 'an excellent example of the dignity that comes from well-considered proportions and absolute simplicity. The building is of reinforced concrete construction and is painted pure white …'[1]

egalitarian in offering similar aspect and facilities to all flats. Although the small site offered no possibility of generous common spaces (apart from the rooftop), Bolot created a floor plan that maximised the apartments' aspect and spaciousness while creating a building of unique appearance in the Sydney of 1950.

The curved northern face is almost entirely glazed, broken by balconies of the thirty-eight apartments. Apart from the top floor there are four apartments per floor, with a sense of privacy being created through lift and stair access that services only two apartments on each floor. Kitchens and bathrooms are grouped at the southern side, and the living rooms and bedrooms are on the sunny northern side. Each apartment has a balcony situated between the living area and the two bedrooms, which is accessible from each of these three rooms.

As well as kitchens designed to minimise walking and other movements, Wylde Street included a specially designed carpet because of the lack of straight walls in the building. The exterior pattern of glass, balconies, rendered brick spandrels and reinforced concrete structural elements creates a pleasing visual rhythm to the building's major facade, as do the variations in the radius of its curve. 'Apart from the excellence of the planning, the elevational treatment developed therefrom is most successful, monotony being avoided by the balconies and the projecting of certain elements of façade.'[2] Not until Harry Seidler began designing apartments a decade later would Sydney see such memorable visual expression of an apartment building's floor plan and structure.

Like Blues Point Tower, the Wylde Street apartments are an expression of democratic Modernism. Both took European social housing and transformed it into a desirable harbourside lifestyle for the averagely wealthy. Despite its humble origins, Wylde Street is today among Sydney's most desirable addresses. When first built it gained little publicity, mostly centred on the cooperative ownership scheme. According to the building's developer and long-time resident John Davis, 'It's got more publicity since it's got older, not when it was outstanding ...'[3]

'Designed for young executives.' After Harry Seidler, Hans Peter Oser and Jean Fomberteaux were perhaps the most prolific of Sydney's many émigré architects. This Bayswater Road bachelor flat was typical of their work.
↗ ➔ Taking advantage of the spectacular views afforded along Sydney's eastern suburbs, Broadwaters and Bibaringa contributed to the dramatic rescaling of these suburbs in the early 1960s, offering an alternative to the suburban home.

A diverse market

The apartment market was diversifying. Thanks to strata title and other 'own your own' schemes, ownership was no longer the preserve of the prosperous end of the market. In 1960 *Architecture and Arts* observed that 'the housing shortage in Sydney … has resulted in an apartment boom in this city. The building shown is located near the heart of the downtown district and is designed for young executives who desire to live close to their offices.'[35] The building in question, a Potts Point bachelor flat slab block, was designed by Hans Peter Oser, an Austrian émigré who formed a successful partnership with the French architect Jean Fomberteaux.

Many of the best examples of contemporary apartment thinking were designed by émigrés; as well as Harry Seidler these included Douglas Snelling and Hugo Stossel. The Hungarian Stossel brought extensive experience from Budapest and Vienna. In contrast, despite wide-ranging work experience in the USA, the English-born Snelling had to make three applications before qualifying for registration as an architect.[36] Stossel's most notable project was Broadwaters, a spectacular thirty-five-unit luxury block that cascades down the shore above Darling Point beach. Snelling is today best known for his furniture designs, but he also designed Bibaringa, a twelve-floor block at Double Bay; its concrete balconies and walls are a severe expression of the slab format.

In many respects this cosmopolitan influx represented the wider changes that encouraged apartment construction from the 1950s. In 1955 the physical form of Sydney and Melbourne had barely changed in two decades. A brief post-depression flurry had produced new office buildings, apartments, pubs and cinemas, but the war called a halt. For a decade after 1945 building activity was concentrated in the suburbs rather than the city, reinforcing the cultural effects of restrictions on non-British immigration. Socially and architecturally, the inner suburban apartment precincts were one of Australia's few connections with the wider world. In this stagnant urban context, apartments became a signifier of modernity, progress and cosmopolitan living.

Thanks to the post-war 'baby boom' and an unprecedented influx of immigrants, Australia's population surged in the 1950s and 1960s from less than nine million in 1954 to 10.5 million by 1961. Significantly, households formed at an even faster rate, in turn increasing the demand for new housing. Famously, the 1950s and 1960s saw a rapid growth in the popularity of marriage, although this was only the most obvious part of a wider trend.[37] The fragmentation of families, earlier marriages, affluence and greater life expectancy were all contributing to rapid creation of new households: 'The closely integrated family of the 19th century is giving way to a loose collection of individuals having their own interests, jobs and friends. This change is creating new demands on housing accommodation and causing radical changes in housing concepts.'[38]

Despite the extraordinary fertility rates of the baby boom, the average number of people occupying each private dwelling began to decline slightly but steadily, from 3.54 people per dwelling in 1954 to 3.47 in 1966.[39] From the 1950s, new housing was built at a faster rate than the population increased. This was especially true of flat construction.

⬆ By the late 1960s, much of the Sydney Harbour foreshore had become a solid wall of apartments, as depicted by David Mist at Kirribilli.

⬅ Apartment rooftops were often communal and functional spaces, sometimes providing relaxation space in dense urban areas or, more usually, a place to do the washing. Automatic washing machines were a novelty in 1954 when a news photographer shot this Hydromat machine on the rooftop of the Macleay Regis.

While Sydney's population increased by 17 per cent between 1954 and 1961, apartment dwellings grew in number by an even more spectacular 28.5 per cent.[40]

'Who is buying home units?' asked the *Sydney Morning Herald* in 1959. 'There are three main classes of buyer: single men and women; older people whose families have left home … and young couples.'[41] According to *Australian House and Garden*, home units 'are now being sold to young marrieds, to families with children in some States, and to large and small investors'.[42]

Although married couples remained the majority occupants of flat dwellings, much of the post-1954 increase in flat-dwelling households

◀ ▲ Fairlie Flats, South Yarra, and its view towards Melbourne, photographed by Wolfgang Sievers in 1961. Sievers was one of many refugees from Nazism who enlivened Australia's architectural and artistic life. From his arrival in 1938, Siever's alignment of photography and Modernism created a record of Melbourne that rivals the quality of Max Dupain's Sydney oeuvre.

was found among the young and unmarried. A greater variety of domestic arrangements was reflected in an increased demand for non-traditional housing, and affluence and full employment allowed many more young people to participate in the housing market.[43]

From the late 1950s apartments formed a major share of the growth of new housing in Australia, particularly in Sydney and Melbourne. While 78,000 houses were produced in 1951–52 in Australia, a figure that grew only slightly to 81,000 in 1960–61, the output of apartment buildings increased from 2000 to nearly 14,000 in the same period.[44] From 1961 almost as many flats as houses were being built. The introduction of strata title legislation obviously played a large role in the boom of apartment completions in the 1960s, yet the new ownership laws added momentum to a boom already underway. In 1954 only 14 per cent of flats were occupied by their owner or purchaser. This proportion had reached 21 per cent by 1966, while the percentage of private tenants occupying Sydney flats decreased by 11 per cent in the decade following the introduction of strata title in 1961.[45]

About 65 per cent of Sydney and Melbourne flats were still privately tenanted in 1966, yet this was a dramatic decrease from the 1930s, when almost 90 per cent of flats were occupied by tenants.[46] Flat ownership was becoming more widely dispersed, both socially and geographically.

With strata title flats could become 'homes', an acceptable alternative to the freestanding house and garden for a substantial minority of the population. The term 'home unit' became popular with real estate agents and flat-dwellers, emphasising the new acceptability of this form of housing.

Significantly, the first decade of strata title produced campaigns by the newly established bodies corporate for greater control over the behaviour and character of tenants. The mixture of tenants and owners became a continuous source of tension in numerous home unit blocks.[47] A typical young tenant's complaint was reported by the *Sun-Herald*: 'I'm not allowed to sunbake on the lawn, or wear my bathing costume in the lift. The TV has got to go off at 11 pm ... Even if I use the washing machine twice a week they are on to me for using too much power. It's like living in a boarding house with a mean old lady.'[48]

The combination of flats and young people provoked a new round of prurient moralism from the press, which was fascinated by

⬆ As well as this landscaped pool area, Kilpara Flats featured an internal courtyard and, like Fairlie, balconies formed as colonnades. Built to Yuncken Freeman's design on Orrong Road, Toorak, in 1971, Kilpara was part of a new generation of luxury Melbourne flats.

the likely doings of flat-dwelling 'bachelor girls' and 'swingers'.[49] This trend reached a peak with the 1970s TV series *Number 96*, which fictionalised the spectrum of apartment-living stereotypes, including gay men, in a small breakthrough for television tolerance. Given the popularity of flats with the young and unattached, the stereotype is not unrelated to reality. Robert Drewe is one of many writers to explore it: 'They leave together. There is hardly any conversation or indecision about their destination. Yvonne's flat is only two blocks away. It is small and its walls feature gift shop prints of big-eyed street waifs and sad anthropomorphic kittens. Paul blocks out the cats and waifs and more with a glass of wine and a shared joint …

In bed Yvonne is lithe and passionate and full of grave and graceful tricks.'[50]

Apartment construction remained fundamentally a speculative exercise in which tenant or buyer demand was only one of several factors in determining the location and character of new apartment buildings. As various critics pointed out, the price and availability of land and finance continued to dominate these decisions.

Melbourne

Melbourne's post-war apartment boom was muted in comparison to Sydney's, although it shared many characteristics. One of these was a move away from rental apartments towards various forms of co-operative or company ownership, before the eventual introduction (in 1967) of individual strata title. A leading promoter of 'self-ownership flats' was Bernard Evans, an architect and businessman who became Melbourne's Lord Mayor during the 1950s. Evans campaigned for apartment buildings in the city: 'The time has now come when smart city apartments must be available if Melbourne is not to remain a provincial city.'[51]

Establishment links helped Evans to gain approval for substantial blocks on prominent near-city sites, notably Sheridan Close on St Kilda Road and Elizabeth Court on Queens Road.[52] In 1960 Evans designed an eighty-unit, five-floor block at 69 Queens Road, shortly afterwards redesigned by Robin Boyd as the John Batman Motor Inn.

Another establishment participant in apartment architecture was Yuncken Freeman Associates. Better known for the Myer Music Bowl and several city office towers, Yuncken Freeman also designed apartment blocks in South Yarra and Toorak for a variety of clients, including the housing and property company A. V. Jennings. The most notable was Fairlie, a nine-storey luxury block built opposite the Botanic Gardens in 1960. Fairlie is raised on concrete pilotis, which double as an entry portico, while concrete mullions support and delineate balconies and windows. In contrast to the nearby Domain Park, the concrete structure communicates delicacy and apparent lightness.

Fairlie was followed by several tall blocks built on Toorak's main thoroughfares, the result of a new apartment tolerance from a pro-development Prahran Council. The architect and writer Neil Clerehan argued that many Melbourne municipalities were 'in turmoil' over flat proposals. 'When so much variation in land value is caused by man-made regulations … certain things happen. At present councils are under enormous pressure to reclassify land to make it useful for flats and the size and cost of the projects involved will ensure that the new developers will not be content with the usual treatment.'[53] Robin Boyd commented sardonically:

For the rich and childless there are high-rise flats. Some of them rise high for perfectly valid reasons: they do so to overlook

↑ Although built in 1959, Edgewater still stands out from the mostly low-rise dwellings along the St Kilda water's edge. Mordecai Benshemesh's landmark was one of the few tall buildings permitted in Melbourne's major apartment suburb.

↖ Apartment living returned to the city of Melbourne during the late 1960s. Kurt Popper's 15 Collins Street was completed in 1969.

some magnificent view, as on the banks of Sydney Harbour. Some of them, however, climb high for less valid reason, as along Toorak Road ... In this case there is nothing special to look at ... The flats climb up on each other's shoulders only in order to fit as many as possible on to the land, because the land is very expensive. And the land is expensive only because the name Toorak still retains a certain snob value borrowed from the mansions of the rich ...[54]

A more typical critique of luxury flats was offered by the leader of the Country Party: 'The Government should cut down on the construction of luxury flats ... The money spent on these should be diverted to flats for ordinary housing needs ...'[55]

As in Sydney, the apartment-friendly heritage of émigré architects had a speedy impact. Among the most prominent was Ernest Fooks, who arrived in Melbourne from Vienna in 1939 as a refugee,

like Frederick Romberg, from Nazi anti-Semitism. Fooks was an articulate advocate of apartment living and, while working for the Housing Commission in 1946, he published a booklet titled X-ray the City!, a critique of Melbourne in terms of contemporary European thinking on city planning. Fooks argued that high population densities were necessary to generate the quality social and cultural infrastructure that were denied to low-density suburbs. Apartments were crucial to this goal: 'Better-class apartment areas usually show high population densities, although the housing conditions are by no means detrimental to the health and welfare of the population, whereas the same density in a region of single dwelling units would cause lot and area crowding in its worst forms.'[56]

After entering private practice in 1948, Fooks designed more than forty apartment blocks during the next three decades. Most were concentrated in the inner-eastern suburbs and were built for individual sale rather than rent.[57] However, these projects were primarily modest

Novelist David Malouf described 1950s Brisbane as a 'big country town that is still mostly weatherboard and one-storeyed'. A brief flurry of apartment-building during the 1930s did not fundamentally alter the city's 'sleepy, slatternly' character.[1]

In 1958 work began on Torbreck, the largest apartment block yet built in Australia for the private market. Following a Sydney and Melbourne tradition, Torbreck took its name from the 1870s house that previously occupied the site on Highgate Hill, overlooking the city of Brisbane and the South Bank district.

In other respects the new building was also a novelty, its concrete frame providing the visual and structural grid of a twenty-floor tower block and a seven-floor 'Garden block'. The tower block included a ground floor shopping area, restaurant and lounge, although the array of services provided was curtailed somewhat by municipal regulations. Thanks to its height and site, Torbreck was quickly dubbed 'the outstanding landmark of Brisbane'.[2]

Promoted as 'a new concept in modern living', Torbreck's 150 apartments were modest in size, aimed at single people and couples, although all had individual balconies and access to views and cooling breezes. Steel louvres provided sun protection as well as a colour pattern to the tower's eastern and western facades. The spectacular views from above Highgate

Hill were a focus of Torbreck's marketing pitch. A helicopter flew interested clients to the height of their yet-to-be-built apartment so that the prospective view could be savoured. The advertising pitch was highly successful, and most Torbreck units were sold before the building's completion. Torbreck was marketed under company title, with purchasers paying a one-third deposit and the balance in four instalments during construction.

Torbreck attracted thousands of sightseers and lent its name to lottery syndicates and other popular pastimes. More than any other building, it remains synonymous in Brisbane with the transformation of the northern capital into a modern city.

⬆ The character of Toorak and South Yarra changed during the 1960s as Prahran Council began permitting high-rise flats along the main roads of the district. Herbert Tisher's Orrong Towers on Orrong Road was built in 1961.

three-floor walk-up flats. It was presumably frustration with this restrictive genre that fuelled Fooks' criticism of local governments 'groping in the dark', making it impossible 'for private enterprise to develop whole estates, where high-rise Flat buildings are intermixed with Maisonettes … where the planning and siting of the buildings of different height and size, could create the sense of variety, contrast and relief which everyone is aiming at.'[58] Fooks argued that 'only high cost of land justifies a multi-storey development'; consequently they were built 'even where they are not required'.

Larger apartment projects were produced by other émigré architects, notably Kurt Popper, Mordecai Benshemesh and Herbert Tisher. Although scarcely noted in architectural histories, this group of Viennese refugees had a profound impact on Melbourne's cityscape. During the late 1960s, Popper designed the first post-war city apartment blocks, Park Tower in Spring Street and the nearby 15 Collins Street

apartments, which is a sophisticated composition of offset balconies above two floors of shops and office suites. More ambitious still was Popper's 1970 design for a 250-room combination hotel and apartments at 131–137 Lonsdale Street, notable for its splayed banks of balconies, although neighbouring buildings have unfortunately crowded these.[59]

Benshemesh's Edgewater Towers at St Kilda introduced the multistorey slab block to the private market. Although Robin Boyd claimed Domain Park's novelty, Edgewater, a thirteen-floor slab block of 100 apartments by the waterfront, appeared a year or two earlier than Domain Park.[60] Prominent location has ensured Edgewater landmark status, although its appearance has been compromised by the enclosure of numerous balconies. As well as walk-ups, Tisher designed at least one substantial apartment block, the seven-floor Orrong Towers at Toorak.[61]

Divergent tendencies

The high point of public and private acceptance of the Modernist urban vision was the New South Wales Government's decision to demolish The Rocks' 'chaotic jumble of ramshackle structures and ill-planned streets' and replace them with office towers and apartment buildings for 10,000 residents.[62] Harry Seidler developed Lend Lease's proposal for the redevelopment of The Rocks district, justified by Dick Dusseldorp as a chance 'to make the area Sydney's leading beauty spot and set an example for the redevelopment of the rest of the city'. Seidler argued that 'the £30 million Rocks project was an example of good redevelopment planning … achieved because the State Government was able to offer a large area of land in one parcel'.[63]

After advertising worldwide in 1961, the government received nine redevelopment proposals from four development consortia. The proposals were created by the cream of Australia's architectural talent, including as well as Seidler, Grounds, Romberg & Boyd, Stephenson & Turner, and Gruzman, McKay, Rickard & Gordon. The favoured proposal envisaged thirteen apartment towers of varying heights, with the tallest being grouped to the west of the site, close to the Harbour Bridge approaches.[64] Its architects boasted that this plan conformed to 'the modern concept of inner-city design and planning, being based on a system of segregation of pedestrians and vehicular traffic, with high towers rising out of a base or podium of service and parking space, the top of which is entirely given over to pedestrian plazas and open space'.[65]

The Rocks project coincided with the scrapping of Sydney's longstanding 150-foot building height. In the resulting skyscraper construction boom, apartments and retail complexes could not match the investment returns offered by office and hotel towers. Developers and financiers transformed the city in the space of a few years. Among the numerous city landmarks demolished was Strathkyle, one of Sydney's first apartment buildings, and Marton Hall, a 1940 bachelor flat block overlooking Wynyard Square.

The Rocks project was a victim of the same economic logic, plus the election of Robert Askin's conservative state government in 1965. Among Askin's closest supporters were some leading figures of the property and building industries, notably Sir Paul Strasser of Parkes Developments. Although rumours of corrupt relationships between Askin's government and property magnates were never verified, there is no doubt that Askin was comfortable for his supporters in the industry to make planning decisions with minimum government oversight.[66] The Askin era saw both the peak of the Sydney post-war boom and the strongest reaction to it. The Canberra architect Roger Pegrum described the economic logic of the time:

> The game of building 'home units' in Sydney or 'villa units' in Melbourne has become popular with developers, who recognise the potential profits. Politically the game has been manipulated by rate-hungry councils and revenue-hungry parliaments, and the cost of inner-urban land has risen steadily. The picture is familiar to all city-watchers. Soon few people in the inner suburbs can afford to stay in their detached house, even if they do

⬆ This 1963 Lend Lease model was typical of those proposed for the redevelopment of The Rocks. Although these apartment and office complexes were not built, development of The Rocks remained controversial; during the 1970s inciting conflict between conservationists and the New South Wales Government.

> not object to living in the constant shadow of a large non-human ant-heap. None of this explains why 'home-units' should be so bloody ugly ...[67]

Even before the watershed of the Green Bans was reached, some architects were looking for ways of integrating apartments into the existing townscape. The architect forerunner was Ken Woolley, whose The Penthouses at Darling Point in 1967 started a fashion for terraced townhouse developments in the tradition of Wyldefel Gardens: 'This was the first major building of the type in Australia, although the type is ideal for development of harbour foreshores: it preserves the form of the land, reduces the bulk of building near the harbour edge and enables people further up the hillside to see over the top.'[68]

Numerous similar townhouse precincts were built, primarily on harbourside locations.[69] This genre found great acceptance in Melbourne, given its conformity to the city's low-rise apartment culture. Designed by Daryl Jackson, City Edge is a large-scale attempt to combine the best features of apartment living and suburban houses. Comprising 180 units, City Edge was built during the early 1970s on a large South Melbourne site.[70] Notable smaller townhouse projects included Bernard Joyce's Kurneh in South Yarra, 'a unique form of urban living, whereby each town house has its own private garden environment'.[71]

Queensland gained strata title legislation in 1965 and, with a pro-development government and the example of Torbreck, the inner suburbs saw a renewed apartment boom. Notable results included Glenfalloch, a fifteen-floor slab block designed by Maurice Hurst, which brought the Domain Park look to the New Farm riverside.

⬃ The Penthouses at Darling Point inspired a trend towards low-rise townhouse developments. Its architect Ken Woolley designed similar townhouse developments at Cremorne and Wollstonecraft.

⬅ The sprawling City Edge townhouse development revived the Melbourne tradition of low-rise apartments grouped around courtyards and enclosed streets. Since the 1970s its South Melbourne location has become home to numerous apartment developments.

⬆ Like many leading Queensland architects, Maurice Hurst, designer of Glenfalloch, was best known for adapting Modernist cottages and holiday homes to the tropical environment. Glenfalloch's deeply recessed balconies resemble those of Torbreck, the inspiration for several 1960s Brisbane projects.

Australia's first public housing was built

in The Rocks, Sydney, after the 1900 outbreak of bubonic plague. These pioneering structures included workers' flats that are still in use. The first public apartments initiated a tradition of innovation that was a feature of public housing for much of the twentieth century.

As well as setting higher standards for workers' housing, public housing has frequently created new urban and architectural forms. The New South Wales Housing Commission boasted during the 1960s: 'The State Government's multi-million dollar slum clearance and redevelopment programme is bringing new life and vitality to run-down residential areas … Designed and equipped for modern living, the multi-storey blocks bring new dignity and pride to the areas while providing homes for working couples and families with children.'[1]

Such claims are likely to meet with disdain, given today's association between public housing and social decay. It is widely assumed that public housing—certainly in apartment format—is a failure, costly both financially and socially. In this version of events, the importation of social housing practice from Europe and the USA also imported the consequences of flawed architectural and social theories.

For much of the twentieth century the Australian housing authorities worked at the cutting edge of housing theory and practice. This was all the more notable for being practised at the cheap end of the market. In the end the failings of some housing and architectural theories diminished the reputation and significance of public housing. These failures also represented a change in the purpose of public housing, away from the provision of exemplary housing to a form of emergency social security.

The Rocks

Following the plague The Rocks precinct was resumed by the Sydney Harbour Trust, which had been created to rebuild the docks and dockside precinct. The official intention was to reconstruct the entire area for commercial uses, although the resumed area included 430 dwellings. However, this strategy was compromised as a 'large number of the residents within the Area are what is known as waterside workers, being employed in and around the wharves … It is recognised

 '… bringing new life and vitality to run-down residential areas.' For thirty years from 1945, the state housing commissions were crusaders as well as demolishers and builders. This 1960s promotions booklet outlined the New South Wales commission's plans for Waterloo in glowing terms.

that these men … have to live close to their work, and hence special consideration has had to be extended to them.'[2]

Varney Parkes, son of former premier Sir Henry Parkes and a successful architect, chaired an Improvement Advisory Board that researched and proposed housing options, 'including £180,000 for the construction of tenement houses'.[3] Remarkably, the proposed solutions were exposed to public scrutiny by their prospective tenants.[4] According to R. R. P. Hickson, the Harbour Trust's chairman, 'there is a very strong feeling in all the areas under the control of the Harbour Trust against flats', especially large tenements.[5] The initial plan for European-style tenement blocks was quickly abandoned in favour of a combination of renovated existing housing plus infill housing on the sites of demolished buildings. This solution anticipated strategies adopted more than half a century later in inner-city areas of Sydney and Melbourne.

Between 1906 and 1917 new housing was constructed in a variety of forms, including two-storey terrace houses in Windmill Street. The new terraces flouted the official preference for suburban cottages.

⬆ Completed in 1910, the Sydney Harbour Trust's terrace-like flats in Lower Fort and High Streets, the latter pictured here, are still publicly tenanted, like much of the housing in The Rocks and Millers Point.

Even more contentious was the construction of flats in High, Lower Fort and Cumberland Streets: 'The limited space available … necessitated the construction of these dwellings on the flat system, and in order to compensate for the absence of yard space, the Commissioners have provided, in a central position, a common playground … for the younger children of the residents here and in the immediate neighbourhood …'[6] The seventy-two High Street flats completed in 1910 have the appearance of terrace houses with generous verandahs, but each terrace contains four flats. According to Henry Deane Walsh, chief engineer of the Harbour Trust, the flats 'which consist of three bedrooms, living room, wash-house, bathroom … each having a separate hall door, and with reinforced concrete floors between the upper and lower flats, thus rendering them fire-proof, water-proof, and nearly sound-proof, have proved most successful in providing homes for those who by the nature of their occupation must live in the vicinity of the wharves'.[7]

Also completed in 1910 were flats in Lower Fort Street. Designed by Government Architect Walter Vernon, who was responsible for the

Art Gallery of New South Wales and the first stage of the State Library, these flats are more functional in appearance but similar in concept, with twenty-seven three-bedroom flats grouped into five three-storey terrace-like structures.[8] The new flats coexisted comfortably with the colonial housing of Fort Street while offering a sophisticated balance of public and private spaces. They created a successful model of workers' housing, which unfortunately was rarely revisited in succeeding decades.

The *Daily Telegraph* compared 'the handsome new tenements erected by the Government' with the 'slum houses demolished' in the same area.[9] Elsewhere, the Harbour Trust attracted a storm of criticism from housing reformers. J. D. Fitzgerald, for example, bemoaned the fact 'the Rocks tenants … prefer the terrace, which eventually must become a slum, and the houses that the Government have recently built will become slums, because the principle is wrong'.[10] The architect James Nangle agreed: 'One of the great reasons for the Resumption of the Rocks was the removal of the slums, but similar congested conditions of life would return with the tenement buildings. Flats were an evil, whether as residences of the wealthy or the poor.'[11]

To the contrary, a century of use has vindicated the judgement of Hickson and his Trust. It is testimony to their success that The Rocks and Millers Point continue as a public housing precinct, a considerable achievement of social, architectural and heritage dimensions.

Small triumphs

The rebuilding of the wharves and harbourside precincts was Sydney's major public work before the construction of the Harbour Bridge during the 1920s. It created an ambitious integration of transport, commercial and social infrastructure.[12]

At the time, urban idealism was focused on the separation and zoning of urban functions, in moving residential life from the city to the suburbs. In 1912 this idealism was encapsulated by the New South Wales Housing Act, which established a Housing Board with powers to create new public housing, communities and urban forms as a model for the broader building industry.

Although the new Housing Board completed the Millers Point public housing, its urban preference was quickly indicated by its establishment of the Daceyville model suburb on the southern outskirts of Sydney. Rather than workers' flats, the Housing Board attempted to build 'a model garden village to show how workmen's homes should be built and grouped in order to provide pleasant homes and healthy suburbs and to show how cheaply they can be provided'.[13] Yet even this form of suburban public housing eventually fell foul of campaigns by private developers and conservative politicians. Daceyville garden suburb was only partially completed.

The Housing Act also permitted local governments to build public housing. Only the Sydney City Council took advantage of this provision,

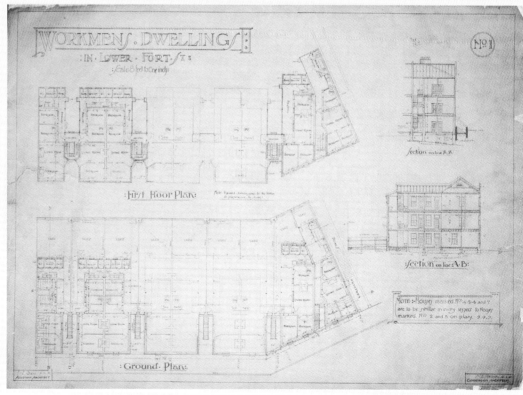

Walter Liberty Vernon was the first of many leading architects to attempt to design economical but pleasing public housing. Vernon's 'Workmen's dwellings' was more successful than the work of many of his successors.

quickly commencing the planning of two apartment buildings with 134 flats in the inner suburb of Chippendale. The outbreak of war in 1914 meant that only one of the planned two buildings was completed.

The City Council expected its flats to generate sufficient rental 'that the scheme should not be a burden on the city rates'.[14] However, the council made a substantial loss on the Strickland project primarily because of the cost of the land, despite its 'slum' status.[15] This experience was repeated with two further public apartment blocks built by the City Council during the 1920s: Ways Terrace, Pyrmont, and the Dowling Street Dwellings, Woolloomooloo.

As a dock area with a substantial working population and much poor-quality housing, Pyrmont Point resembled The Rocks. The council resumed and demolished housing in Ways Terrace, announcing a design competition for a replacement apartment block. The commission was won by Leslie Wilkinson, first professor of architecture at the University of Sydney, and his colleague Joseph Charles Fowell, who created a four-storey design of primarily three-bedroom flats. Most of these were planned over two storeys, with the bedrooms occupying the upper floor above the kitchen and living room.

⬆ '... best suited to the Australian ideal of block housing.' Completed in 1926, Ways Terrace at Pyrmont Point was typical of early public housing in matching the architectural and social scale of its setting.

The judging committee was chaired by Sir Charles Rosenthal, who had recently designed the exclusive Darnley Hall apartments at Elizabeth Bay. Rosenthal was also a decorated Great War officer, Nationalist Member of Parliament and champion of conservative causes, including the King and Empire Alliance. Any traditionalist thoughts Rosenthal may have harboured regarding workers' flats were allayed by Wilkinson's terrace-like design. The committee judged that 'the system of housing for working men proposed' by Wilkinson 'is to be commended as that nearly best suited to the Australian ideal of block housing, the general principle being that each flat or dwelling should be an independent unit or home with its own entrance from the street and where possible its own small garden'.[16]

In contrast, Florence Taylor had no hesitation in branding the design for Ways Terrace as 'an offence against the aesthetic senses of the city ratepayers ... The whole lacks symmetry, balance and repose, and

Samuel Lipson's 1934 proposal for perimeter-block public housing in the 'slum' suburb of Paddington. Although Lipson's plan was briefly adopted by the New South Wales Government, Paddington's terrace houses survived to become one of Sydney's most exclusive suburbs.

only requires the vari-coloured garments of its proposed tenants hanging from its balconies and openings to complete its ugliness.' Taylor's judgement was presumably shaped by her belief that Ways Terrace would 'help to create a new slum area'.[17]

Appointed in 1918, Wilkinson promoted a 'Mediterranean' style of architecture in Sydney, pointing to similarities of climate and waterside topography. Although Wilkinson is best known for his houses and university buildings, with Ways Terrace he created one of the best sited and most architecturally singular apartments in Australia. A Hollywood version of Spanish architecture became popular stylistic clothing for Sydney flats during the 1920s, but Wilkinson's Iberian statement evoked a more vernacular air, its forty flats appearing as a random cluster of terraces above the harbour. This simplicity resulted in part

from the loss of elements of Wilkinson's original design, notably small cantilevered balconies.

The quality of Ways Terrace was recognised seventy years later, when new public housing was built on neighbouring sites in Bowman Street. Integrating shops, terrace houses and apartments, the new complex copies many aspects of Ways Terrace's appearance and structure.

Ways Terrace was the leading achievement of what was initially intended by the City Council to be a much more ambitious program of slum demolition and apartment building.[18] The Lord Mayor believed that 'the shortage of houses was so great that it could not be met by private enterprise'.[19] However, budgetary constraints and the demise of Labor administrations at both City Council and State Government combined to terminate this brief experiment.

Paddington Municipal Council was the only local government to consider public housing during the 1930s, commissioning the architect Samuel Lipson to design 120 workers' flats for a triangular site on the corner of Oxford Street and Glenmore Road. The project was abandoned in the face of local opposition, including that of the local MP Norman Thomas, who said: 'If any such building were erected they would in the years to come prove far worse slums than those the council seeks to abolish today … The excessive flat building of the past few years will ultimately prove of great harm to this city …'[20]

A changing climate

Anti-flat opinion was crucial in keeping governments out of the public housing arena, but various schemes to encourage cottage ownership could not cope with the shortage of adequate housing evident in the wake of the 1930s depression. Campaigns for housing reform came from both ends of the political spectrum, including middle-class Christians concerned at the moral consequences of slum life and trade unions, communists and Labor supporters angry at evictions of the unemployed and their families.

In the face of these campaigns the conservative governments of Victoria and New South Wales were compelled to enter the public housing sphere for the first time. The first major public housing project in Melbourne, built at Fishermen's Bend from 1939, was composed of free-standing cottages rather than flats.

Although the Erskineville flats project in inner Sydney stirred a torrent of criticism—as detailed in chapter 1—it illustrated the potential of public apartments, and was an important forerunner of post-war public housing. Unlike The Rocks and City Council flats, these were not buildings designed to conform to existing streetscapes but an attempt to form a new environment. Morton Herman, architect of the Erskineville flats, was convinced of their exemplary character, describing them as 'the first real attempt in Australia to provide urban housing with all the pleasant attributes that planning and controlled nature can produce …'.[21] Herman designed 200 mainly two-bedroom flats in two-storey blocks of eight flats, occupying only 30 per cent of open ground with at least 20 metres space between each block. Thanks to Erskineville Council's opposition, only fifty-six dwellings in seven blocks were built on unused land; no existing houses were demolished.

Each flat has two bedrooms and a balcony that could be used as a sleep-out. The blocks are oriented north to south, restricting direct sunlight during the hot part of the day. Following similar London County Council schemes, the scheme included provision for gardens, playgrounds for children, 'perambulator sheds', day nurseries and laundries, separate from the flat buildings.

According to Morton Herman, the Erskineville flats were significant beyond the public sector. 'The Erskineville scheme is important not only as a slum clearance effort, but as showing the first Australian attempt at the scientific planning of flats. Flats in this country have a bad name, and one that is unfortunately justified to a large extent.'[22] *Building* agreed that 'in respect of light, air and open space, the Erskineville development is far better than in the case of many of the flats in the more wealthy suburbs and even excels that found in many individual cottages'.[23]

The Erskineville flats were one of three schemes planned by the New South Wales Government and its Housing Board 'for the removal of what are regarded as slum blots' and their replacement with flats. The others were intended for Newtown and Paddington, on the site first proposed in 1934.[24] These projects were halted by the outbreak

Apartment living   Mrs Philomene Watson

'I thought the flats were lovely. I went berserk for one. We were hand-picked. When you came in there was inlaid lino, a beautiful cream and green pattern, and linen closets. Everything was up-to-the-minute … the built-ins were the best thing and the cleanliness. We paid 19 shillings per week, gas was a penny in the slot and for tuppence you could have a good bath.'

When Philomene Watson got the news that she and her husband had been selected for one of the new 'home units' at Erskineville in 1938, the newly married couple was 'thrilled to pieces'. At the time the estate was highly controversial because it provided those who needed public housing with flats and not detached houses. Her son Peter remembers the stigma of living in public housing in Erskineville. When he bought a train ticket from the Catholic school he attended in Lewisham, he was regularly greeted with 'Child return to Erskineville … Child return to Dirtyville'.

In spite of the social stigma of living in a 'slum' area, Philomene, her husband, who was then a seasonal worker at the wool stores and latterly in the air force, always loved living here. With a full-time on-site caretaker and a fence and gate demarcating it from the street, the estate felt like an oasis: 'There were a lot of families, and we had lots of friends on the estate for the first few decades. People made use of the perambulator sheds and the shared washing lines, and the estate was like a community.'

Now a sprightly ninety-five-year-old, she continues to talk up her domain despite rising estate crime problems: 'I love the freedom and the fact that you can look out both windows and see space and greenery. I live next door to my church and for decades have been very active in the local community, running the tuckshop, and doing the gardening for my own patch and for many of my neighbours.'

⬆ '... the first real attempt in Australia to provide urban housing with all the pleasant attributes that planning and controlled nature can produce ...' Sam Hood photographed the new Erskineville flats in 1938.

of war, and the Erskineville controversy emphasised the complications created if local governments were involved in public housing. This lesson was not wasted on the McKell Labor government, which was elected in 1941.

The product of a Redfern childhood, William 'Bill' McKell made his political career in the inner city. This experience and his political acumen made housing scarcity and quality a central element of Labor's platform. McKell made common cause with middle-class slum reformers as well as more traditional slum reformers, arguing that 'private enterprise has failed—and is still failing—to provide houses for the people. It must also be recorded that all Governments before this one have failed, equally with private enterprise. In the previous nine years of UAP (Liberal) Government, the ONLY dwellings erected by the State were the grandiloquently publicised 56 flats at Erskineville!'[25]

McKell created the New South Wales Housing Commission as soon as he was elected, which then placed pressure on the Labor federal government to take some responsibility for housing. When the Commonwealth Housing Commission was formed in 1943 it adopted a more open-minded attitude to apartments than governments had previously exhibited. The architect Walter Bunning, executive officer of the newly created commission, used the slum image as justification for this change: 'This happens to be Sydney, but it could be part of Melbourne, Adelaide or Brisbane. It has narrow ugly streets, lanes, alleys and mean pocket-handkerchief allotments. In this whole square mile you will not find one park or playground. The children play in the lanes and alleys; they live a lane life and their parents sit on their doorsteps ... At the back they try to grow flowers—they grow sooty stunted flowers like their own withered lives ...'[26] Bunning argued that modern flats would overcome objections: 'a concentrated slum area ... can be replaced by the same number of units in an apartment block set in spacious surroundings ... sunlight and fresh air coming into every window; every flat having a view of the gardens that surround it ...'[27]

The Commonwealth–State Housing Agreement of 1945 provided federal funding for multi-unit dwellings as well as cottages. The policy

⬆ Premier McKell's home suburb of Redfern was one of the first parts of Sydney to be redeveloped by the Housing Commission. Built in Walker Street about 1955, these flats were among the first to provide car parking for tenants.

was justified on the grounds that opposition to apartments arose 'because of the poor standard of these dwellings in many Australian capitals' and that well-designed apartments held many 'economic and technical advantages' over single homes.[28] However, federal funds were initially available only for blocks of four storeys or less; taller blocks required specific approval from the federal government.

As Member for Redfern, William McKell bore no sentimentality for the streets and terrace houses of his youth. A similar attitude formed fellow Redfern boy J. M. 'Jack' Bourke, who headed the New South Wales Housing Commission from 1951 to 1981. Under Bourke's guidance the Housing Commission became the largest housing developer in New South Wales, building a fifth of the state's new housing during the 1950s and 1960s. Its main activity was the creation of suburban estates of cottages; flats accounted for less than a fifth of its activities, and the great majority of these were two- and three-storey walk-ups.

Nonetheless, the Housing Commission began a series of inner-Sydney slum clearance projects, producing apartments for workers

in areas including Redfern (Walker and Elizabeth Streets), Waterloo (Cooper and Raglan Streets), Balmain (Elliot and Glassop Streets) and Surry Hills (Devonshire Street). By 1954 the Housing Commission had built 2358 flats in Sydney.[29]

Greenway and Wandana

In 1948 the New South Wales Housing Commission sent P. J. Gordon of the Sydney architecture practice Morrow & Gordon to study public housing in Sweden and England. Gordon was impressed by Sweden's use of neighbourhood plans in which community centres, railway stations, laundries and kindergartens were integrated with home and working life.[30] He was also pleased by the landscaping and open space surrounding Stockholm's mainly low-rise apartment buildings.

Despite its suburban image, Canberra is home to some notable apartment buildings. Most were built during the 1960s and 1970s, when the city was struggling to cope with an unprecedented influx of population. Canberra languished during the first half of the twentieth century; in 1958 its population was only 39,000. However, the determination of the Menzies government to create a genuine national capital saw numerous government departments and their staffs transferred to the 'bush capital'. By 1988 Canberra was home to 279,000 people.[1]

Because Canberra's small building industry was incapable of meeting the demand for housing, most new flats and houses were commissioned by the newly created National Capital Development Commission. As a result, Canberra has the highest proportion of public housing of any Australian city, much of it built to accommodate public servants and their families. The structures were designed by some of

Australia's leading architects, including Sydney Ancher, a member of the generation of architects to encounter European Modernism during the 1930s peak of its influence and credibility. Despite being 'completely bowled over' by the work of Mies van der Rohe, Ancher found few opportunities in his Australian projects, which were largely confined to cottages and hotels, to explore these influences until 1959, when his Northbourne Housing design won a limited design competition.[2]

The Northbourne Housing group has been praised as 'Canberra's (and probably Australia's) first and only true application of … the Bauhaus principles used for public housing'.[3] Ancher created a variety of simple and expressive structures in a variety of formats (duplexes, three- and four-storey flat blocks, three-storey maisonettes and courtyard flats), using expressed concrete frames to permit a variety of window and wall designs. However, the outstanding feature

of the housing group is its comprehensive site design, intended as an urban entrance to Canberra on Northbourne Avenue, 'with a unifying expression of town scale and character to conceal existing building sprawl of average suburban development each side of the highway'.[4] In contrast to the nearby sprawl, Northbourne's diverse buildings are linked by pergolas and symmetrical landscaping, and car access is limited to the rear of the sites.

The National Capital Development Commission permitted cottages but not flats to be sold from the public housing portfolio. The Northbourne Housing group was therefore less sought-after by tenants than cottage properties and, poorly served by maintenance, has lost some of its lustre.[5] Now one of numerous apartment and other buildings lining Northbourne Avenue, the Northbourne Housing group remains a surprising star among Canberra's architectural showpieces.

↥ '... the Big House near the Bridge.' When completed in 1954, Greenway was the largest building north of Sydney Harbour, and it towered over Kirribilli. Only the bridge and its approaches matched Greenway's scale.

On returning to Sydney, Gordon began work on Australia's first large-scale public housing project. Situated by the northern approach to the Harbour Bridge, Greenway Flats occupied a site resumed some decades earlier for bridge construction. Comprising 309 one- and two-bedroom flats, housing 900 tenants, Greenway was Australia's largest residential development when completed in 1954. For a decade or so, it was one of Sydney's largest buildings.[31]

Apart from its integration with an established suburb, well served by public transport and other social infrastructure, Greenway did not imitate Gordon's description of the European pattern. Instead of three- and four-storey walk-up flats, Greenway took the form of four connected blocks, two of eleven floors, one of five floors and one of three. The two tall blocks consist of three narrow wings radiating from a central lift and services tower, permitting unbroken views for each flat, and easing access to the ground and other buildings.

In many respects, Greenway was a half-hearted application of contemporary housing theory. The large towers are steel framed and clad with face bricks, unrelieved by balconies on most sides, creating a ponderous appearance and dominating its steep site. Unimaginative interior design, lack of balconies and cross-ventilation for most flats meant that Greenway fell some way short of its architectural potential, as did the fact that its construction cost per flat was higher than that of a suburban bungalow.[32]

Harry Seidler was perhaps the most vehement of Greenway's critics: 'People here don't like flats, mainly because of the monstrosities that were built in the past. Take the Greenway Flats ... the site is one of the most beautiful in the world, yet look what they have done with it! No wonder people would rather travel to an unsewered weatherboard in Bankstown. I don't blame them.'[33]

Much of the substantial press comment was more positive, *Post* magazine observing that 'more than 900 people live in the Big House near the The Bridge ... Some complain, others are deliriously happy, but if anyone moves out, 30,000 others fight to get in'.[34] Indeed, the major controversy of Greenway's early years was accusations of a tenant ballot rorted in favour of Labor supporters and friends of Housing Minister Clive Evatt.[35]

⬆➡ Wandana flats, 1956. Western Australian Minister for Housing Herb Graham, one of the men looking out over Subiaco from Wandana, was responsible for the construction of this pioneering International Style public housing block, some years before similar blocks appeared in the eastern states.

A more predictable controversy was ignited by Perth's first public housing tower Wandana Flats, built near the city at Subiaco between 1954 and 1956. This 242-flat complex consisted of a ten-storey slab block and two three-storey walk-up blocks. With its cantilevered balconies and extensive landscaping Wandana was a closer approximation to international practice than Greenway, not surprisingly given its design by Harold Krantz, Perth's leading promoter of contemporary architecture.

The siting of Wandana Flats opposite Kings Park increased tenants' amenity as well as opposition to the project. The *West Australian* complained that the project 'conjures up visions of the slums of Tokyo, the tenements of London and Glasgow or at best the skyscraping "housing projects" which have proliferated upstream from the United Nations glass house on Manhattan Island'.[36] Despite such criticism,

⬆ 'Darby and Joan' flats at Moe, 1962. Designed for elderly couples, these were one of the standard walk-up types built by the Housing Commission of Victoria before its mid-1960s switch to high-rise construction.

⬎ During the 1960s, the Housing Commission of Victoria was unapologetic in its preference for high-rise public housing. Its publications were proud endorsements of tower block economics and architecture. The cover of the 1962 *Annual Report*, featuring the Emerald Hill Court estate at South Melbourne, was typical.

Wandana was the first of several Western Australian public housing complexes built during the 1950s and 1960s.

The 'windscreen survey'

In Victoria the slum clearance catalyst was Henry Bolte, premier from 1955 to 1973. Despite his leadership of the Liberal Party, Bolte was the son of a country publican; he exploited his background as a Melbourne 'outsider' to challenge established policies.

Although the Housing Commission of Victoria was formed in 1937, it had achieved little in the way of slum clearance by 1955, concentrating instead on the construction of new suburban estates of cottages and walk-up flats. Bolte used the Housing Commission's slow progress as a weapon against the Labor incumbents. On becoming Premier, he appointed a royal commission into the commission, using its findings to justify a greatly accelerated program of slum clearance. A new Housing Act gave the commission wide-ranging powers to declare Slum Reclamation Areas without having to condemn individual houses.

The ensuing slum clearances were largely based on a survey performed in 1960 by two commission officers,

Debney's Estate, Flemington, was one of the first tower blocks built in Melbourne using prefabricated concrete sections.

Grahame Shaw and and the newly appointed slum research officer J. H. Davey, which 'showed there were in the inner metropolitan area of Melbourne at least 1,000 acres of housing so sub-standard in nature that economic repair was out of the question'.[37] Derisively dubbed the 'windscreen survey' because it was conducted by driving around inner Melbourne, this document became the basis for demolitions and their public justification.

Although inner-city slum clearance did not begin in earnest until the late 1950s, the commission had already generated considerable expertise in flat construction. For a few years of the 1950s, the commission built most of the flats completed in Victoria, so slow was the private sector to meet demand for this form of accommodation. In 1955, 600 of the 800 apartment dwellings completed in Victoria were the work of the Housing Commission, including many of those initially used as the Olympic Village at Heidelberg.[38] These construction numbers exploded into the thousands during the 1960s, as flats became the commission's preferred means of rehousing.

The cost of inner-city land was a significant incentive to this policy. According to the commission: 'In the first place, many people say, "Why build flats … These flats you build will be the slums of the future" … Obviously the Commission cannot build and rent and sell individual

homes on such dear land, particularly as its charter is to house the low-income group. Economic considerations therefore force the Commission to increase the density of building, and this can only be done by building row-houses or flats.'[39]

In 1959 the commission began work on its first major slum clearance project, Emerald Hill Court at South Melbourne. The estate featured a sixteen-floor tower containing 120 one- and two-bedroom flats and walk-ups with eighty-eight three-bedroom 'family flats … thereby providing balanced housing for families, couples and elderly people living alone. The high-level development will permit more open space to be made available, which is important where families are housed.'[40]

The Emerald Hill Court tower was constructed largely of concrete sections cast on site. However, the commission's walk-up flats were already primarily built of prefabricated concrete sections produced at the commission's own casting factory at Holmesglen. Using a wartime munitions factory, the Concrete House factory began producing precast concrete houses, maisonettes and walk-ups during the 1950s. According to the commission, 'casting under a factory roof cut down on delays

⬆ 'As the cost of lifts could not be justified in low-level flats ... the Commission decided to delete walk-ups and build wholly in high-rise blocks.' A combination of twelve- and twenty-storey blocks, Hotham Estate at North Melbourne was one of Melbourne's largest.

on site'. By 1963 'full advantage of precasting is now being taken on 4-storey flats in that all structural components are now factory made'.[41]

These four-storey blocks were the main components of Debney's Estate at Flemington. A twenty-floor tower was added in 1964, an innovative structure comprising load-bearing walls of precast elements. Trialled in 1962 on an eight-storey block in Altona Street, Kensington, the precast system was then used at Debney's Estate and Reeves Street, Carlton. Most of the commission's 1960s towers used this system, which differed from the combination of concrete framing, cladding and infill used in most apartment buildings. The towers used a variant of the slab block formula, with balcony access to each flat and narrow floor plans that permitted ventilation and light from both sides.

The possession of in-house construction resources added to the commission's formidable bureaucratic momentum, and to its domination by engineering and building professionals, with surprisingly little political or public oversight. Slum clearance and rebuilding was planned and carried out by the same department, with the result that local communities and their concerns were overridden by the commission's need to keep its program moving. The economist Colin Clark claimed that the Housing Commission 'has a tiger by the tail, having invested heavily in a large-scale plant for making concrete panels ... and it has to be continually building high blocks of flats in order to keep its plant operating'.[42]

The extent of this program was breathtaking. In one year of the late 1960s, the commission completed seven multistorey towers at

Carlton, Collingwood, North Melbourne, Prahran and Williamstown, as well as commencing or continuing work on a further ten towers. These projects totalled 2943 high-rise dwellings, as well as hundreds of low-rise flats.[43] Horace Petty, Minister for Housing and Member for Toorak, justified the program for its capacity to repopulate the inner city: 'One of the features of Melbourne's inner suburban development in recent years has been the struggle to maintain an adequately and suitably housed population near the heart of the city.'[44]

The 'slum reclamation' program at least achieved this goal. For example, the Hotham Estate at North Melbourne replaced 159 houses with 374 flats. The population of the site increased from 439 to 1470. The commission boasted that 'Hotham Estate provides 7¾ acres, or 82 per cent of the site as open space comprising gardens, playgrounds for children of different ages, and off-street parking'.[45]

Robin Boyd described the multistorey apartments built by government housing authorities as 'an extraordinary official repudiation of the Australian dream', an 'assault on the conventional Australian housing pattern of a vast, sparse villadom interrupted only by one or two tight pockets of high density high-rise for migrants and misfits'.[46] The Victorian Housing Commission was unapologetic for providing an alternative to suburbia, 'where women complain of boredom, men complain of the road hazards, the long tedious travelling to work, the isolation from social, communal and education centres'.[47]

Waterloo

Like the Victorian Housing Commission, the New South Wales commission developed a set of standard designs for walk-up flats during the 1940s and 1950s. Most featured individual entrances for each flat. When these designs were criticised during the 1960s for their monotonous appearance, the commission employed architects for individual projects. Despite criticism, commission walk-ups were notable for their siting and amenity, which were superior to most of those built by the private sector. Unlike the suburban 'six-packs', commission walk-ups were seldom short of space for recreation, parking and light. Some municipal councils used them as a standard-setter for new flat building regulations.

After Greenway, the Sydney City Council was next into the apartment tower field. In 1958 the Lord Mayor of Sydney, Harry Jensen, returned from a study tour of public housing and 'strongly advocated a population of higher density for Sydney'. Jensen's interest in public housing sprang less from a concern for slum clearance than a desire to maintain the city's population and stop the drift of business to the suburbs, which he noted in North America.[48] Schemes completed in 1960 for the City Council Housing Projects at Camperdown (a ten-storey, four-wing building with 153 flats) and Glebe (a twelve-storey, three-wing block with 120 flats) were substantial evidence of Jensen's commitment to alternatives in urban housing.

⬆ Glebe in inner-city Sydney has been the site of several interpretations of public housing, including the 1960 twelve-storey block in this photograph and the 1970s renewal of existing terrace housing.

Although extensive, the high-rise building program of the New South Wales Housing Commission did not match the size of its Victorian counterpart. While tower blocks became a major type of public housing in Melbourne, less than 5 per cent of New South Wales public housing was built in high-rise form. However, apartment towers were adopted as the main form of inner-city public housing in the immediate south of Sydney city, the area identified by the Housing Commission as having 'the majority of Sydney's worst slums … Slum conditions inflict misery and degradation on the occupants of dwellings in the blighted areas and can, in time, destroy the business and commercial heart of a city.'[49]

In 1958 the Housing Commission of New South Wales began construction of John Northcott Place, in Surry Hills near Central Station. Comprising 429 one- and two-bedroom flats in a fifteen-floor complex, Northcott was the largest flat building in Australia when completed, although its Melbourne counterparts quickly challenged for that title. The Housing Commission justified flats on the grounds that 'bad conditions are not necessarily related to the height of the building or the number of families it houses. It is the space between the buildings that matters and consequently as buildings are made bigger, so the space between them should be made greater. In other words, there is no sound reason why a building should be high provided the space around it is sufficient … it may provide better views and give more light and fresh air …'[50]

After Northcott, the neighbouring suburbs of Redfern and Waterloo became the focus of slum clearance, with 442 houses being demolished in Redfern alone. The first tower constructed in Redfern was William McKell Place, composed of 'four ten-storey blocks of flats grouped together in a huge elongated "X" design', accommodating more than 800 people in 282 flats.[51] Three neighbouring sixteen-storey slab blocks named Poet's Corner—the towers are individually named after Australian poets—were completed in 1966. Designed by the leading Sydney firm of Peddle, Thorp & Walker, the Poet's Corner towers each comprised 192 one- and two-bedroom flats.

In Waterloo the commission demolished more than 600 houses to create a 30-acre development site for the Endeavour Project. Four

seventeen-storey blocks for families were completed by 1974, followed by Matavai and Turanga, two thirty-storey towers for pensioners. Designed by the private practice Stafford, Moor & Farrington, these towers featured precast concrete elements. The commission claimed that the towers 'will become a Sydney landmark'. In fact the concentration of towers in Redfern and Waterloo came to epitomise the Housing Commission's activities in the eyes of its critics.

This perception was reinforced in 1972 when the Housing Commission released plans to build more than 2000 new dwellings in Waterloo, including six more thirty-storey towers. These proposals were the focus of opposition from the newly formed South Sydney Action Group, an organisation initially dismissed by the commission on the grounds that 'the existing residents who are at present complaining may in any case not be there in ten years' time, their houses brought out by more affluent people or businesses, while piecemeal rebuilding would lead to visual chaos'.[52]

This dismissive attitude ended when the Builders' Labourers Federation banned work on the towers, ensuring widespread media coverage of the controversy. With the project delayed, in 1974 the commission commenced a detailed consultative process with residents and tenants. The majority supported construction of further public housing in Waterloo, although most preferred it in low-rise format.

Northcott Place was 'my biggest job, my biggest victory', according to its architect Samuel Lipson. This idealistic attempt to marry a public tower block to new urban infrastructure is today stigmatised as an island of social dysfunction.

A significant influence was the federal Labor government of Gough Whitlam, whose housing minister, Tom Uren, favoured urban renewal and rehabilitation programs. With the power to direct federal housing funds, Uren was a major player in the defeat of the New South Wales Askin government's plans to transform the inner suburb of Woolloomooloo into office and other commercial developments as well as building further high-rise public housing.[53]

After the election of the Wran Labor government in New South Wales, Housing Commission activity in both Waterloo and Woolloomooloo was redirected to the rehabilitation of existing housing and the creation of architecturally compatible infill housing. The last public housing tower constructed in Sydney was Sirius Apartments, completed 1979 in Cumberland Street, The Rocks, for residents displaced by the commercial redevelopment of the area. Tellingly, this solitary residential tower, the result of a tenant consultation process, replaced the several office and apartment towers planned for the area during the 1960s.

For decades Fitzroy was considered to contain the worst slums in Melbourne, featuring prominently on the 'slum reclamation' map created during the 1950s by the Housing Commission of Victoria.

Comprising four twenty-storey towers as well as walk-up blocks, Atherton Gardens contains 800 flats that house almost 3000 people. Built over four years from 1968, these were among the last public housing towers built in Melbourne. A similar development planned for Fitzroy was not built owing to community protest.

Unlike the Strickland and Northbourne public housing, Atherton Gardens was not designed for a particular site or suburb. It employed the Housing Commission's standard building system of prefabricated cast concrete components, used to create a series of identikit structures across the twenty-one high-rise housing estates built in Melbourne during the 1960s. Every aspect of these buildings conspired against identification with their tenants. Instead

of individual or tightly grouped entrances, each ten Atherton Gardens flats are entered by a common balcony, which creates problems of security and privacy.

Construction of Atherton Gardens began in the year the British Government terminated the various subsidies that encouraged high-rise public housing, amid wide agreement of the program's failure.[1] Only the bureaucratic and political momentum created by the Victorian Housing Commission saw high-rise housing estates continue to be built in Melbourne after this model had been discredited in England and the USA. The Housing Commission's program was even more remarkable given the long-standing Melbourne suspicion of tall residential buildings for the private market.

Since the 1970s Fitzroy has been transformed into one of Melbourne's hippest addresses, which underlines the changing reputation of inner-city living. In contrast to their affluent neighbours, 95 per cent of Atherton Gardens tenants receive public

income support as single parents, unemployed, disabled or aged. By the late 1990s, the estate's main economic activity was drug trafficking, which has caused numerous violent incidents and increased the social isolation and insecurity of the tenants.

Since 2002 considerable resources have been devoted to a 'renewal' program for Atherton Gardens. Some of the results are obvious, notably the vegetable gardens and other enhancements of the ground-level spaces. Other changes are less visible, such as improved security measures, including a concierge service. The buildings themselves are being redecorated to produce some individuality for flats and precincts.[2] Perhaps most remarkable is the creation of an estate website and local internet connection between tenants. A majority of Atherton Gardens tenants are of Asian (primarily Vietnamese) origin, and tenants have enthusiastically embraced the opportunity to communicate within the estate's many communities.[3]

⬆ Although its apartment construction was concentrated in the inner city, the Housing Commission of New South Wales also built flats in suburban areas, including Riverwood, Maroubra, Eastlakes and Dundas, illustrated here.

Housing residents who did not wish to move from the area, Sirius signalled a return to Australia's first public housing projects, preserving 'million-dollar views' and city life for public tenants. After two decades of intense pressure to privatise the historic harbour sides of The Rocks and Woolloomooloo, this was an emphatic victory for the public realm. The majority of the established houses of The Rocks and Millers Point district remain as public housing.

In Melbourne, the Housing Commission juggernaut stalled with surprising speed after residents' campaigning saw the Housing Commission forced to obtain individual planning approvals for its projects. By 1973, three years after completing the thirty-floor Park Towers at South Melbourne, Housing Commission construction was at its lowest point for twenty-eight years, the commission complaining that the 'time delays involved impeded site development'.[54]

Developments in Carlton and Fitzroy were delayed by court injunctions and community opposition. By 1976 the Victorian commission was also talking the new language of urban renewal and community consultation: 'The Commission ... is devising and using methods of making contact with existing communities so that, whilst moving quickly towards housing the families presently on the waiting lists, full account is taken of the people who already live in these towns ... recognizing that "housing" means development of a community.'[55]

Both in Melbourne and Sydney the housing commissions' rehabilitation programs met considerable success, both socially and architecturally, with many architects producing innovative interpretations of infill housing. The solutions trialled at The Rocks seventy years before were reborn.

The issues
The Victorian Government used the language of slum clearance throughout the 1960s, with its Minister for Housing boasting of 'the

⬆ The Waterloo public housing precinct was one of Sydney's largest construction projects of the 1960s. Four decades on, the demolition of these towers is a possibility, as the New South Wales Government promotes a privately funded redevelopment of the area.

accelerated rate of reclaiming decadent areas' through 'slum reclamation and development'.[56] Although the commission's programic determination became a synonym for bureaucratic myopia, for some years its activities met with surprisingly little opposition apart from affected residents and property owners. The councils of Melbourne, Prahran, Port Melbourne, Williamstown, South Melbourne and Richmond contributed financial and political support, placing the Housing Commission's interests ahead of those of their ratepayers.

During the 1960s and 1970s few social groups were as extensively studied and surveyed as the tenants of public flats. Many of these studies supported the commission's work. A 1966 survey by social workers of the Brotherhood of St Laurence, a long-standing proponent of slum clearance, focused on the Hotham Estate, North Melbourne. It concluded that 'for most, the flat was a vast improvement on their previous accommodation ... Though there were criticisms made about the flat interiors, on the whole most people found the flats themselves pleasant ... the most satisfied tenants are those in the high-rise block where life is made easier by lifts, convenient

laundries and a well-finished building ...'. Significantly, the study also found that 'for many the standard of facilities and life on a big estate were not pleasant at all and did not measure up to the comfort of the flat'.[57]

Although several of the academic and charitable studies of high-rise public towers found their residents to be happy with their lot, most were critical of the consequences for children.[58] The New South Wales Housing Commission initially refused apartment tenancies to families with children younger than seven, and attracted criticism for this policy. A Liberal MP claimed that the government was 'legislating against people having children and when and where they wanted to'. Others noted that such discrimination was unlawful if practised by private landlords, who were regularly prosecuted for it.[59] This policy was

Opened in 1964, William McKell Place brought high-rise public housing to Redfern. Max Dupain's photo captures the building and its milieu.
As the participants in its opening ceremony suggest, the eight-storey Purcell block was the first constructed specifically for aged tenants. Its apparent success led to the construction of the much larger Matavai and Turanga towers.

changed as families and single mothers formed an increasing proportion of the commission's tenants. In Melbourne, the Housing Commission claimed that high-rise flats were more suitable for families than walk-ups; the towers made lifts, drying areas, communal laundries and other facilities economically viable.[60]

Although the housing commissions made much of these shared facilities and open space, they were a failure of many high-rise estates. According to a landscape architect employed by the New South Wales commission: 'At ground level there is no incentive for anyone to maintain even the immediate environment outside their home because of a lack of direct internal/external access and because there is no way of securing external areas to form private, defensible territory. Residents cannot risk investing time or effort in gardening when they have no control over people wandering through the area.'[61]

Street-level neglect of housing estates was an element in the changing dynamic between public housing and its setting. During the 1960s public housing tenants in Melbourne and Sydney were of 'comparatively high social status' in their neighbourhoods owing to the vagueness of the means tests used to decide eligibility. Most had

jobs or received the aged pension.[62] Within a decade or two, many public housing estates had become pockets of urban poverty, with the majority of residents existing on social security.[63] Housing estates also came to be regarded as sources of crime and disorder, recreating the fears of the campaigners for slum clearance. Similar problems dogged many of the new suburban estates of cottages and townhouses.

Surrounded by rapidly gentrifying neighbourhoods, the new tower blocks quickly lost the distinction of providing better and cheaper housing than their neighbours. However, this market-driven form of 'slum clearance' also provided a new justification for public housing. The New South Wales Housing Commission argued that 'the need for public housing close to the centre of the City is becoming more and more apparent as redevelopment and/or renovation force lower income earners out of the inner City'.[64] Recent proposals for private

⬆ Max Dupain's 1965 construction photo of Gilmore and Kendall, two of the three sixteen-storey Poet's Corner blocks. Apart from generic problems—lack of individual access to flats, security and so on—many Waterloo towers suffer from poor orientation; their east–west aspect rendering the balconies vulnerable to extreme winds.

owners to build on inner-city housing estates are intended 'to dilute the social effects of clustering … public tenants on one site'. They have also been criticised for threatening the future of public housing.[65] Ironically, the recent decline in housing affordability has recreated a housing shortage for wage-earning families, increasing the need for public investment in affordable housing.

Northcott Place became emblematic of the failures of public housing towers and their changed relationship to former 'slum suburbs'.

⬆ Tom Zubrycki's documentary film *Waterloo* recorded resident campaigns against the New South Wales Housing Commission's 'slum clearance' program. The production of the film became an element of the campaigns, especially the filming of re-enactments. *Waterloo*'s 1981 premiere coincided with the final abandonment of the commission's plans for Waterloo.

➡ When completed in 1976 Matavai and Turanga were intended to set a new standard for public housing towers. The square tower design was believed to be more appropriate for pensioner tenants than the long walkways of slab blocks, while the common areas and landscaping were themed to reflect the South Sea journeys of James Cook.

Northcott was designed by Samuel Lipson and Peter Kaad, one of Sydney's leading Modernist practices. Born in Britain of Lithuanian parents, Lipson came to Australia in 1925 and quickly became a leading importer and interpreter of international practice. Northcott Place gave Lipson a long-awaited chance at a major 'social architecture' project. When interviewed some years later he described it as 'my biggest job, my biggest victory. It was the biggest job in Australia at the time.'[66]

Northcott was an uncompromised expression of the model of the skyscraper in

'Sirius'

Sirius Tower, located in The Rocks, was built after extensive consultation with residents, many of whom had been involved in the Green Bans against redevelopment plans. An important part of the resulting brief was 'a design … that was neither of orthodox square or rectangular design but which would blend in with the then existing skyline'.

⬆ As well as restoring more than a hundred terraces, the Housing Commission built almost 400 new infill dwellings in Woolloomooloo, including these in Brougham Street designed by Philip Cox.

the park—an attempt at standardising and ordering both the land and built environment and, in doing so, providing an economy and efficiency of living. Incorporating meeting rooms, shops and other social facilities in an attempt to create a partly self-contained community, the estate bears little relationship to the traditional street and is evidence of the potent influence of the ideas and theories of European Modernists in Australia.

The journalist Gavin Souter observed that some of the people who lived in the demolished Surry Hills streets 'were sorry to leave them':

They were given the choice of waiting for flats at Sir John Northcott Place or taking a Housing Commission home in one of the western suburbs. Only five families waited for flats; the rest of the little world in O'Sullivan and Pearl Streets was swept out to Villawood and Lalor Park. Billy Jarvis, born in O'Sullivan Street some forty years ago, is a case in point. He lives at Lalor Park now but every chance he gets he is back in the bar at the Forresters, on the corner of Riley and Foveaux.[67]

Northcott was initially viewed as a success, sufficiently worthy to be accorded a visit by the Queen in 1963; the Waterloo towers were similarly blessed a decade later. Interviews with long-term Northcott residents

confirm the early success and the dominance of wage-earners among the pioneering tenants.[68]

In recent decades Northcott has attracted the unwelcome but accurate nickname of 'Suicide Towers', averaging five suicides a year as well as several other violent incidents. The tower's situation in what is now one of Sydney's grooviest addresses has ensured that its problems are well publicised. The neighbouring Belvoir Street Theatre is one of several arts organisations to work with tenants to produce works of art, including performances, documentaries and exhibitions.[69] The results have included improved consultation between police, the New South Wales Department of Housing and tenants to improve Northcott's social amenities.

Northcott is a contemporary of Blues Point Tower, highlighting the

⬆ The 1980s saw leading architects working with the new policy of housing commissions to conform their projects more closely with the inner-suburban architectural and social context. Kay Street Housing in Carlton was designed by Maggie Edmond and Peter Corrigan, Melbourne's best-known practitioners of post-modern aesthetic recycling.

striking difference between the social and political success of private and public apartment towers. Architecture embodying social status and exclusivity quickly became, when built for public tenants, a symbol of exclusion and disadvantage. Melbourne's prefabricated towers proclaimed their public status with repetitive appearance, as did the rarity of private apartment towers. Sydney's public housing towers were more varied and, apart from the Redfern–Waterloo precinct, less

Dave Tacon's photo was taken in 2005 at Atherton Gardens housing estate, Fitzroy. Tacon's summary: 'Twelve-year-old Osman came to Australia from Somalia five years previously. Few members of his team, and the opposing team the Fitzroy Lions, were born in Australia; many of them arrived as refugees.'
Doris Condon, Labor mayor of South Melbourne, is pictured in 1970 presenting an award to the director and chief architect of the Housing Commission for Park Towers, the last and largest tower built by the commission. The support of the mainly Labor inner-city councils was crucial to the 'slum reclamation' program.

brutal to the inner-city environment. They were quickly outnumbered by towers built for the private market.

Public tower blocks still punctuate the skylines of inner Melbourne and Sydney. The rental income the towers produce has declined with the increase in tenants existing on social security. The resulting need to sell public housing assets means that the future of public housing is again in question.

The liveability of the estates varies considerably, depending on the social compatibility of tenants and the efforts made by housing departments, police, tenants and others to remediate problems and conflicts. Drug users are now common among public tenants, bringing a new

⬆ One of the last major public housing developments built, Newcastle East's 1989 completion preceded the redevelopment of its industrial surrounds as a leisure and entertainment precinct. Local architects Suters & Snell grouped apartments and balconies in apparently random stacks.

set of problems and conflicts. In 1972 the Victorian Housing Commission conceded that to 'outsiders and casual passers-by', commission towers appear 'huge and foreboding … Nothing can be further from the truth. Inside is a community, warm and bustling with human activities, imbued with the spirit of neighbourhood and togetherness.'[70] Reconciling these hopes with reality is a continuing effort.

To talk of suburban flats is to talk primarily of 'walk-ups', the two- and three-storey blocks of usually less than twelve flats that began spreading across the suburbs of Sydney and Melbourne before 1920. Although the attention of architecture journals and the press centred on high-rise flats, these were never the most numerous type of flat building.

Located in Windmill Street, Millers Point, the first purpose-built apartment building in Sydney was also its first walk-up block. Following a fire in his hotel, John Stevens built a four-storey 'boarding house' on the site in 1900 to house waterfront workers. Stacking four identical flats on each floor—all with stoves and enamel baths—around a common stairway and balconies, the Stevens Building set the mould for thousands of similar blocks.[1]

In Brisbane and Perth apartment living remained primarily a near-city experience until the 1960s. But in Sydney and Melbourne apartments reached the suburbs during the 1920s and 1930s, following the outward march of cottages along the railways and tramlines. By 1933 flats accounted for more than 10 per cent of the residences in the western Sydney suburbs of Ashfield, Petersham, Annandale and Burwood.[2]

The streets around railway stations and shopping strips were remade with squat blocks of texture brick, tinted glass windows marked the stairwells, plaster decorations trawled the vocabulary of exotic architecture and prominently displayed names mostly recalling the 'Old Country'—Stratford, Lyndhurst—or the new urbanity of the USA—Pasadena, Monterey. Between these concentrations of unorthodoxy stretched the even plains of cottages. In 1947 the average suburban flat contained four rooms (usually two bedrooms, living room and kitchen) and was occupied by three people.[3]

As the suburban frontier expanded again from the 1950s, the same process was repeated further into the periphery. Flats appeared in numbers in Sydney suburbs like Canterbury, Rockdale, Sutherland and Strathfield. Melbourne's flat-dwellers remained concentrated in the eastern suburbs as Camberwell and Caulfield followed the pre-war flat booms of South Yarra, Toorak, St Kilda and Hawthorn. Adelaide stands out as the only Australian city where suburbia has always been the primary location of apartments, notably Unley in the inner southern suburbs and the seaside resort of Glenelg.

Eastern suburbs

The strongest trend in Sydney was to harbour and beach-side suburbs, particularly those well served by tramlines. By 1933 Sydney's eastern municipalities of Waverley, Woollahra and Randwick hosted almost as many flats as the city and inner Sydney. Waverley, including Bondi, Bronte and Dover Heights, went from 9 per cent flats in 1921 to 32 per cent in 1933. At the end of the war, Waverley had more flats (8087) than any other Sydney municipality. These were more modest affairs than those of wealthy Woollahra, where the streetscapes of Double Bay, Rose Bay and Edgecliff were also dominated by flat buildings.

In 1939 the New South Wales Government's Housing Improvement Board joined aldermen and other critics in warning of 'the decline of the Eastern Suburbs. Sydney is exchanging old slums for new … in the Eastern Suburbs particularly, private houses are disappearing … There is a need for a comprehensive form of flat-planning …'[4] These fears were evidently not shared by eastern suburbs flat-dwellers, who paid higher rents for their domicile than neighbouring cottage-dwellers.[5] Given the existence of cheaper alternatives, it appears that for these people flat living was a choice rather than a last resort. The urbanist Max Kelly observed of Waverley flat life: 'Residents were not crammed into these types of buildings as they were to be when "flats" became "units"; nor were they forced to live a life divorced from the street below or the shops nearby … it seems that the accommodation supplied, and the services provided, represented a real contribution in qualitative terms to post-war housing shortages. And always, in Waverley, there was the beach at the end of the road.'[6]

In the rush to retrospectively brand Australia a nation of home-owners, the apartment tenants of these affluent suburbs have been forgotten. So have the landlords who profited so handsomely from them. Woollahra and Prahran, which includes South Yarra and Toorak, have long been two of Australia's wealthiest municipalities, yet their concentration of flats meant that until the 1960s they were mainly peopled by tenants, who were apparently no less prosperous or

⬆ Windmill Street turns out for the photographer. Stevens Buildings in Millers Point set the pattern for walk-up flats.

◤ Texture brick, tinted glass and tiles: 1930s walk-up flats at Petersham, Sydney.

'comfortable' for this status. In 1947, in Prahran as in Woollahra, flats rented for substantially more (47 s. 9 d.) than houses (29 s. 3 d.).[7]

In Melbourne the municipality of St Kilda stood out as apartment headquarters. In 1914 the Melbourne City Council introduced new building laws, setting out minimums for allotment and frontage sizes. These laws also required that all dwellings have a street frontage, effectively outlawing most types of flat. However, municipal councils could add their own amendments to permit flats.[8] St Kilda City Council was one of those that did, with the result that by 1947 the bayside suburb boasted 6075 flats, a quarter of the Melbourne total.

With easy access to the city, ample entertainment and shopping facilities, St Kilda resembled Sydney seaside suburbs like Bondi and Manly, which are popular with both residents and holidaymakers. But architecturally and socially St Kilda was unique in Melbourne.

Some of St Kilda's first apartment buildings were as distinctive as the suburb; others set the mould for flats throughout Melbourne. In the first category were conversions of rows of terrace houses into one flat block, such as Grosvenor Mansions in Williams Street and Marli Place on the Esplanade. Despite their visible staircases, both conversions were successful and lucrative.[9] Summerland Mansions is another St Kilda original, a mansion flat built above shops on the corner of Acland and Fitzroy Streets, the latter being the main shopping and entertainment thoroughfare. Completed in 1920, Summerland was aimed at tenants wealthy enough to hire servants, although it also offered a communal dining room.

Like most St Kilda flats, Summerland Mansions stood apart from those of nearby South Yarra and Toorak largely for their generous balconies and unabashed functionality. Grosvenor Mansions, Marli Place and Summerland Mansions did not pretend to be Tudor villas and suchlike. The Canterbury, probably St Kilda's first purpose-built apartment building when completed in 1914, was designed to make its apartment role clear. Although its balconies are now glazed, the Canterbury's exaggerated height and viewing tower still communicates its purpose. Other early St Kilda flats resembled the brick walk-ups of Sydney suburbia, although often with an extra stylistic flourish as with Howard Lawson's 1923 Biltmore flats in Eildon Road.[10]

Initially a wealthy locality like Kings Cross, St Kilda was favoured by the city elite. By the 1940s, to the jaundiced eyes of the novelist Hal Porter, 'St Kilda, once a fashionable and grandiose seaside suburb, a sort of Aussie Cannes with a better beach, has become tawdry, its one-guinea waves now cheap as a penny. Its mansions along the Esplanade … have become boarding houses, or have been subdivided into flats, flatettes and hives of bed-sitters smelling of gas-rings.'[11]

St Kilda's blue-collar urbanity attracted European immigrants old and new. Robin Boyd observed during the 1960s:

Many New Australians, especially those from central Europe, are used to high-density city living, and prefer it and seek it here … The more successful European migrant … created a demand for flat buildings near the cities … Thus cheap walk-up blocks of eavesless flats, made of yellow or orange bricks, according to region, were built in great quantity in areas which tolerated them such as St Kilda … In block after block they replaced all the old single houses and the trees and created

⬆ Mansion flats above shops are a feature of European cities. Architect Christopher Cowper's Summerland Mansions is perhaps Australia's best-known example of the genre. Built in two stages during 1920 and 1921, Summerland's reputation declined during the mid-century years—like St Kilda—but has recently regained its original status.

another separate zone of their own, isolated and insulated from the old Australian suburbia.[12]

St Kilda's flats formed the background to a bohemian identity comparable to that of Kings Cross. It has been home to artists and writers including Albert Tucker, Joy Hester, Hal Porter, Mirka Mora and George Johnston. St Kilda today is unavoidably more monied than even twenty years ago, when Nick Cave, Dave Graney, Deborah Conway, Stephen Cummings, Howard Arkley and others dominated its arts scene. Even contemporary St Kilda produces cultural moments, notably the television drama of singledom, *The Secret Life of Us*, located in an Esplanade apartment block.

Walk-ups and the building laws

In St Kilda as elsewhere walk-up flats predominated. *Architecture and Arts* pointed out in 1960 that 'this type of development represents at least 90% of Melbourne's flat building boom'.[13]

Walk-up flats represented the accommodation of the apartment format to Australian suburbia. The official denial of the functional differences between single and multi-unit dwellings had many consequences. It allowed apartment development to be accommodated to the existing street and subdivision patterns, but it also limited their architectural, urban and living potential. In a sense the 'Australian dream' took its revenge in this suburbanisation of apartments, simultaneously ensuring that their image was forever compromised.

By determining the growth of flats through regulations originally conceived for cottages, state governments and local councils initially ignored the flat as a minority of the housing spectrum. The first legislation that drew distinctions between different types of urban housing was New South Wales's Ordinance 71, introduced in 1921 under the Local Government Act. Although this legislation allowed local councils

to regulate housing density, building and subdivision, resume land and control new roads, it failed to make adequate controls for flat buildings beyond setting minimum distances from buildings and site borders.[14] Although these regulations made little specific allowance for flats, they did not discourage them. To the contrary, New South Wales building laws encouraged the walk-up format, and rent controls favoured flat construction generally.

Melbourne's building laws imposed limitations on height and site coverage, although individual councils added their own regulations.[15] Again, these more rigorous regulations encouraged low-rise walk-ups, although on more generous sites than was generally the case in Sydney.

By the 1940s councils in Sydney and Melbourne, after decades of complaining and campaigning, had powers to set building and urban standards for flats. An observer of suburban streetscapes would be surprised at this fact, given the obvious decline in the architectural and urban standard of post-1945 walk-ups. Especially, the power to zone flats into particular areas created streets of walk-ups, undermining their potential for views, light and quiet.

⬆ The addition of external staircases and landings to the existing houses forming Marli Court lends a surprising charm to this makeshift apartment building. Converted in 1911, Marli Place is still a feature of St Kilda's Esplanade.

Clearly, the generation of council rates and population took precedence in the minds of many aldermen. Developers and builders sought those municipalities with the least restrictive building codes. Sydney's Canterbury municipality, for example, has many more 1960s walk-ups than neighbouring Bankstown, which enforced stricter minimum standards. The social status of both municipalities was similarly modest; the Canterbury aldermen apparently believed that this justified the construction of rudimentary dwellings.[16] Eventually the New South Wales Government was forced by local campaigning to overrule Canterbury Council's approvals of 'irregular home unit development'.[17]

Architects have generally been leading proponents of apartment living, but they were leading critics of walk-ups. Morton Herman lamented in 1937: 'Sydney is fast becoming swamped by innumerable

The Canterbury was designed by H. W. & F. B. Tomkins, architects of the Myer Emporium and other notable Melbourne buildings. Each of its floors contain a single flat, apart from the two-flat top floor added five years later in 1919.

box-like blocks which march, cheek by jowl, down uninteresting streets in increasingly dull suburbs. In the design of the flats the light area is the dominant motif, and the amenities, aspect and gracious planning are passed over with contempt. The resulting dwellings can only be regarded as mere shelters, and the addition to the cultural and civic benefit is nil.'[18]

Forty years later, Harry Seidler was scathing at the walk-up flats replacing houses throughout the suburbs: 'The total effect of this demolition of individual houses for replacement on the same site by now quite standard three-storey flats is truly horrifying. The results are barrack-type buildings, their long dimensions filling the depth of the narrow allotment. What used to be yards at the back and on the sides … are denuded of vegetation and paved for cars. On floors above, the living rooms of adjacent blocks face each other across the five-metre wide canyon …'[19] Architect Norman Edwards concurred: 'The red texture brick home unit block has done even more to desecrate Sydney's fine natural environment than the proverbial red brick and tile bungalow … The result, functionally and visually, is disastrous.'[20]

As Seidler pointed out, the assignment of the ground level to parking space further reduced the amenity of many 1960s and 1970s walk-ups. Architect and writer Howard Tanner was similarly critical: 'Throughout our cities where once sat the small brick bungalow, complete with appendages such as "Hill's hoist", hydrangeas, frangipani trees and buffalo lawn, now exist three storey buildings constructed from similar bricks and red tile roofs. The streetscape for the pedestrian is one for cars.'[21]

However, many well-sited and well-designed walk-up flat buildings were also built, particularly in more desirable suburbs. Some have even been recognised for their architecture, including the Chilterns, built at Rose Bay in 1953. According to *Building*, ' "The Chilterns" is certainly unusual! … The architect Mr D. Forsyth Evans says the design is an adaptation of a principle introduced by the famous French architect, Le Corbusier … This building is the only one of its kind in Australia, if not in the world.'[22] Douglas Forsyth Evans, who also designed the nearby Caprice harbourside restaurant, designed this three-storey walk-up block around a row of Le Corbusier-style concrete pilotis. Evans' engineer Peter Miller recalled: 'I must have seen Corb's Paris building so I said, "Why don't we do this and put the thing up on some stilts and put the cars underneath? …" '[23]

Walk-ups and the building industry

Like the laws, the building industry was geared towards the construction of small blocks in a suburban context. Most of the flat development industry retained a similar structure to the cottage building industry, which was dominated by builder–entrepreneurs who generally completed only a small number of houses each year. This remained the case despite the advent of large 'project' building companies like A. V. Jennings, which was unable to secure more than a small percentage of the cottage building market.[24] Not surprisingly, many builders worked in both sections of the building industry.

A 1960s study by the Commonwealth Department of Housing found that in the construction of slightly more than half of new apartment buildings the developer and builder was the same person. These developer–builders usually built one walk-up block at a time, which was financed with high-interest loans from finance or insurance companies. The study concluded that the 'picture that emerges is of an industry organised on a relatively small scale. Professional builders are

⬆ Born in the Greek island of Kastelorizo, Mick Kanis ran a café in Richmond. Local status is evident in this 1940s snapshot of Mick Kanis with his Pontiac and flat in Punt Road, Richmond.

quite significant but there has also been a lot of activity in the industry from individual investors.'[25]

The building industry was easy to enter—there were no licensing or educational requirements—and rewarded conservatism in design and construction rather than the financial risks of amalgamating cottage sites and seeking council approval for tall blocks.[26] Small-scale builder–developers preferred 'two and three-storey blocks of flats which offered little risk'.[27]

But while the builder–developers churned out suburban 'six-packs', the broader industry was changing with the entry of large property companies into the apartment market. Like Reid Murray, the company that built Torbreck in Brisbane shortly before going bust, the property companies were highly geared and dependent on rapid cash flow to remain profitable. This was in turn dependent on the speculative boom in land prices and ample credit from banks and finance companies.

During the 1960s and 1970s the city flat markets reached a new level of speculative intensity. The advent of strata title introduced

many individual home unit owners to the industry, as investors as well as residents. Among the companies to take advantage of this new market and source of finance was Home Units of Australia, a Sydney company that built hundreds of suburban walk-ups a year during the 1960s, mainly in Ashfield, Burwood, Strathfield and Brighton-Le-Sands, before collapsing in 1974 with debts approaching $180 million. By this time the company's principals were safely ensconced in Monaco, far from their many creditors.[28]

Although immigration and affluence continued to provide a solid demand for new flats, speculation and profiteering gave the apartment industry an unsavoury image during the 1960s and 1970s. This image was underlined not only by the many builders and property companies that failed but also by the poor quality of the products.

For most of the twentieth century, apartment buildings had to conform to building regulations formulated for suburban cottages. The resulting compromises produced many unsatisfactory buildings—including a significant proportion of suburban walk-up flats—which undermined the reality and image of apartment living.

Some more successful attempts to marry suburban streetscapes and apartments were built in Melbourne's inner-eastern suburbs during the 1920s and 1930s. Although the affluent suburbs of Toorak and South Yarra were among the first to host concentrations of flats, building laws restricted them to two-

or three-storey height. As the architect Robert Hamilton observed, 'our municipal councils have adopted a policy of viewing flats with disfavour and this is having a marked bearing on the development of our housing accommodation'. In Toorak the result was: 'A more spacious layout in regard to general planning and garden surroundings of flat buildings … such buildings present an appearance of large houses and do not have the somewhat objectionable character of the tenement class … each flat has a separate entrance and the occupier retains the psychology of home ownership. Numerous flats of this description in Toorak contain entrance hall, lounge, din-

ing room, two bedrooms, maid's room and one or two bathrooms.'[1]

Hamilton's Denby Dale was typical in that 'the design of the scheme has been derived from Old England, and this character of the past, combined with the amenities of the present, has been admirably sustained'.[2] Consisting of three blocks of four flats, Denby Dale's apartment function was further disguised by individual designs for entry doors, lights and other external fittings.

Robert Hamilton was Melbourne's master of Tudor Revival, often disparagingly described as 'stockbroker Tudor' for its popularity with the wealthy. An alderman for the

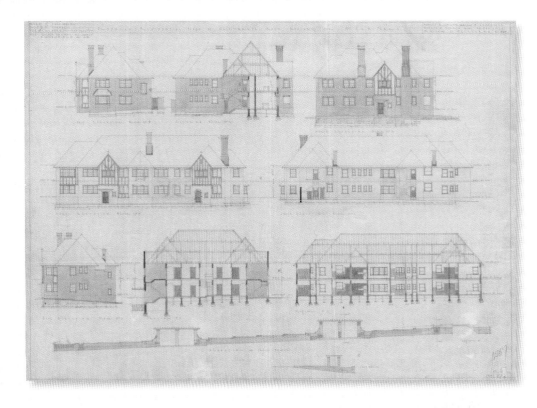

City of Prahran during the 1930s, Hamilton also designed numerous houses and shops in Tudor style. The concentration of his shop designs on Toorak Road led to the shopping centre gaining the title of 'Toorak Village', an appellation since repeated at numerous ambitious town centres.[3] Although Hamilton believed that the City of Melbourne was 'unwise' to obstruct the construction of city flats, he was a creative defender of Melbourne's suburban character.

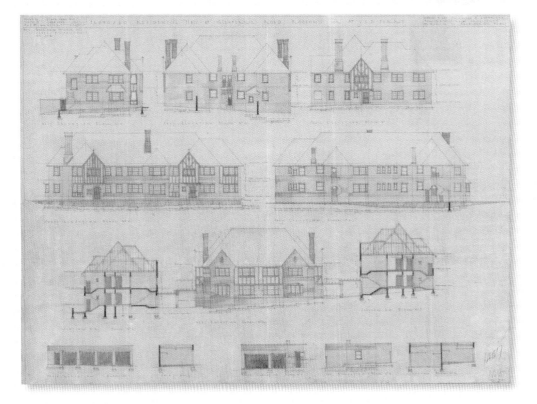

↑ Walk-up flats in Brighton-Le-Sands, Sydney.
→ Although walk-up flats are perhaps the most criticised building type, many transcend the limitations of the genre. Among these is the Chilterns, built at Rose Bay in the early 1950s. Other walk-ups are being retro-fitted with balconies and other improvements to their original design.

Henry Pollack, a refugee who arrived in Sydney from Poland via Russia, Japan, China and Hong Kong, recalled that 'in 1964 when I graduated and commenced architectural practice, the standard of apartment design was dismal … The few well-planned and attractive buildings dated back to the 1930s. Apartments provided rudimentary living space ("2 brms, cons and lnge"), cooking and sanitary facilities. They were built on a tight budget and both planning and external appearance was basic.'[29] When Pollack set up business as an architect–developer, he found that 'I had to compete with low-cost builders who ran one job at a time and walked around the jobs collecting

discarded cut bricks and putting them back in the walls … In the 1960s hardly anyone built home units of good quality.'[30]

Pollack's preference for quality buildings pushed him towards the more affluent end of the suburban market. Erwin Graf, founder of Stockland Trust, took a similar attitude, avoiding walk-up projects because 'I didn't want to create future slums'.[31] There were many other émigré developers willing to cater to the immigrant market for walk-ups. It was a truism of the industry that 'migrants are helping to foster the demand for flats and home units … They are taking up many of the new flats especially those in the western suburbs [of Sydney]. Unlike Australians, they are mostly accustomed to apartment blocks … The way Australians have for years clung to their suburban cottages standing in its own plot of land is unique.'[32]

Paul Strasser's Parkes Developments specifically targeted the immigrant market. A flamboyant Hungarian famous for establishing Double Bay's Cosmopolitan restaurant and hotel, social centrepiece

⬆ Delcana at Spit Road, Mosman, was built in 1959 by Dick Dusseldorp's construction company Civil & Civic. With generous balconies and views towards Sydney Heads and Manly, Delcana is one of many walk-ups that takes advantage of Sydney's topography.

of eastern suburbs immigrant society, Strasser in the early 1960s purchased the former Rosebery racecourse at Eastlakes south of Sydney. Parkes filled most of the large site with rows of walk-up flats, taking advantage of its siting near two large immigrant hostels. During the late 1960s the company even ran its own immigrant sponsorship scheme, meeting its immigrants at Sydney airport, assisting them to find employment and, in numerous cases, to purchase a Parkes flat at Eastlakes.[33]

According to Jack Mundey of the Builders' Labourers Federation, Parkes 'had originally gained permission to develop the racecourse on the basis that it would put up a kind of garden city with large eight-storey buildings separated by green areas ... Instead, a series of three-storey buildings, close to each other and utilising every available centimetre, had gone up.'[34] In 1971 the BLF joined Eastlakes residents to block a plan to build more flats on the last two hectares of vacant land.[35] The controversy was one of the first indications of a new popular appreciation of the urban environment, and specifically the need for apartments to be appropriately sited. This and other controversies finally persuaded councils to end the walk-up era.

Some notable exceptions to the walk-up malaise were constructed in Perth during the 1950s and 1960s. In Perth Harold Krantz formed a partnership with Viennese émigré Robert Schläflik (who changed his name to Sheldon). Krantz and Sheldon employed thirty-nine nationalities of immigrant architects and draftsmen. Rather than allow speculators and developers to dominate decisions, Krantz and Sheldon invited investors to finance each of their numerous suburban apartment projects. Harold Krantz believed that this approach gave him design freedom as well as the financial resources for amalgamated sites and cheaper materials: 'So I collared the flat market and we were building, at one stage, at least a thousand flats a year. So I could go to Bunnings and I could say I want 1000 feet of skirting ...'[36] Perth's suburbs are dotted with the resulting towers, slab blocks and walk-ups, all constructed on generous sites, including local landmarks such as Hillside Gardens and Mount Eliza (also known as 'the thermos flask' for its distinctive circular plan).

Next to the Greek Orthodox Church and opposite the new Kogarah Town Centre Library and Cultural Centre on Belgrave Street live Carmen and Leon Donovan, with Leon's niece, the talented Aboriginal singer, Emma Donovan, who is in her early twenties.

Apartment living Carmen and Leon Donovan

'It's a friendly block with a mix of owner-occupiers and renters. It is very diverse culturally, which is what we like. There are Brazilians, Tongans, Chinese, Anglos, Peruvians, Greeks living here; it's like the United Nations in one block.'

The trio lives in a two-bedroom, two-bathroom apartment in a street of new blocks, with local shops and businesses below. Both from big families, they grew up in houses, Leon as part of his extended family from the Gumbaingirr peoples on the New South Wales mid-north coast, and Carmen with her Chilean parents in south-west Sydney.

'We're the Kogarah crew; we live together and we travel together. We wanted to take Emma under our wings, and living together just feels right. For now we can't imagine living anywhere else. The apartment has it all; it's spacious and self-contained and, although it's part of the new town centre, it's very quiet.'

They happened upon this development and Kogarah itself when visiting family in nearby St George Hospital, and they bought into the new development with the initial help of Carmen's family, who were determined that the newly

married couple should own a place of their own rather than rent.

'I wanted to live in an apartment because Leon used to travel extensively for work and I wanted the security of a home with cameras at the entrance. We liked the quiet, the space and light of the apartment; the proximity to the train station, the police station below and the local Thai and Chinese restaurants when we don't feel like cooking.'

Proximity to cosmopolitan Brighton-Le-Sands and the nearby Westfield mall were also big draw cards.

In 2005 the photojournalist Dean Sewell photographed flats and their residents at Hillsdale, southern Sydney. Occupied primarily by families, the flats create a busy street life as well as unusual uses; for example the male members of a Pakistani family eat in the garage of their flat.

↥ Eastlakes is perhaps Australia's most concentrated walk-up precinct, almost devoid of public spaces or other types of building.

Meriton

Unlike Parkes Developments, the conservatively managed firms of Mirvac, Stockland, Lend Lease and Meriton were among the few major apartment builders to survive the 1974 property crash. Meriton stood apart in retaining a focus on plebeian suburbs. Its founder Harry Triguboff was born in China of Russian Jewish parents. After settling in Australia he drove taxis before entering the property business. In 1967 he built his first apartment block in Meriton Street, Gladesville. ' "Nobody built 18-unit apartment blocks," explains Triguboff, who sold the entire block to one man …'[37] The success of this project confirmed Triguboff's strategy of building large blocks on suburban sites, often disused industrial land rather than established streetscapes. Meriton quickly moved away from the walk-up format, bringing apartment towers to Sydney's suburbs. Meriton buildings are especially prominent near railway stations, major roads and retail centres.

Having constructed more than 50,000 apartments, primarily in Sydney and on the Gold Coast, Meriton Apartments is now Australia's largest residential building company. Triguboff is one of Australia's richest men. Yet in many respects Meriton still functions like a 1960s builder–developer, remaining a private company with Triguboff being closely involved in all decision-making. The company seeks and buys its sites and employs the architects, engineers, construction managers and workers. It arranges finance for vendors, most of whom are investors and landlords. Meriton has long resisted unionisation of its building workforce.

In recent years the bland, repetitive character of Meriton buildings has attracted criticism, adding a new, unflattering term to urban slang—to 'Meritonise'. Some suburban councils have been less welcoming, demanding higher building standards; others remain accomodating. 'You can't have the same standard in every goddamn area in Sydney,' Triguboff responds. 'If you want to build units, you must give them a very simple standard. In America they build shit everywhere. Here everything has to be a mausoleum.'[38] Meriton now avoids

several of its former favourite suburbs in favour of city and near-city locations. The price of this shift is design competitions and high-profile architects including Harry Seidler, Graham Jahn and Bob Nation, but the rewards in rent and purchase are also greater.

Yet the suburban legacy of Meriton and its competitors survives, and during the 1990s it belatedly attracted the concern of governments and architects. The architecture writer Ian Perlman wrote: 'These developments have been going on for some years. But the numbness, the blind tolerance, may now be over. Making big blocks at the low end of the market is a game that leaves nobody smelling terribly sweet. Councils are accused of allowing the urban fabric to fray. Developers are pilloried for basing their business on, well, business. For architects, who are well aware of unrealized potentials, there is frustration at the limitation imposed on their own services.'[39] Graham Jahn, then president of the Royal Australian Institute of Architects, noted in 1999 that recent flat developments had moved beyond the 'popular notion of apartment living … government housing for people who couldn't afford the dream'. However, despite the

⬆ The Oaks, Roscoe Street, Bondi, was the second block of flats designed and built by Henry Pollack. Pollack's ambition to raise the standard of suburban flats was somewhat thwarted by the local council, which ordered a large oak tree between the two wings chopped down during construction.

trappings of quality housing, many of the standards of size, storage, acoustic privacy and floor-to-ceiling heights 'still reflect government housing'.[40]

While the Victorian Government responded by placing a three-storey height limit on most suburban areas, the former New South Wales Premier Bob Carr convened a Premier's Forum on Residential Flat Design, bringing together more than 200 architects, planners, developers and heritage and local government professionals. The result was a design pattern book for apartments and a new Design Code and Design Review Panels for apartment developments. Perhaps the major outcome was legislation to restrict apartment design to accredited architects and designers.

⬆ During the 1960s Krantz and Sheldon concluded that load-bearing walls allowed cheaper construction than the normal combination of concrete columns and floor slabs. Built for the Bond Corporation in 1968, Windsor Towers at South Perth is one of several Perth towers built to this unusual prescription.

⬆ Completed in 1965, Mount Eliza apartments was the first circular plan apartment tower in Australia; it was also innovative in having only one or two flats on each of its sixteen floors. Krantz and Sheldon's design was imitated extensively in the eastern states.

Carr had been alerted to the problem by the view from his government car as he was chauffeured to the city via the newly 'Meritonised' town centres of Maroubra Junction and Kensington. His concern was primarily aesthetic rather than the more functional concerns of leading architects. Although the profession welcomed the new rules because they 'delivered architects a monopoly in designing multi-unit residential buildings over two storeys', leading members were concerned by their prescriptive nature. Harry Seidler ridiculed the pattern book as 'an absurd, naïve and regressive design guide for apartment buildings' with 'enforced mediocrity [being] the ubiquitous result as illustrated in our Government's pattern book'.[41] Glenn Murcutt declared that any discussion of aesthetics needs to be eliminated from legislation and planning codes, while Alex Popov suggested that the very concept of a pattern book 'suggests that good architecture is just a matter of following rules and can simply be assembled by following prescriptive

Where it all began for Harry Triguboff: Meriton Street, Gladesville. Elizabeth Court is at centre.

guidelines'. It encourages formalism, which, he points out, resulted in the 'failure that was postmodernism'.[42]

These comments missed the pattern book's purpose, which is to improve the general standard of suburban apartments rather than those designed for the upper end of the market. The debate also neglected the issues raised by urban planners and demographers: that suburban 'six-pack' flats built in some areas during the 1960s and 1970s have already become pockets of urban disadvantage, the only form of rental housing available to those on the fringes of the labour market. Further low-cost development is likely to make this problem more general: 'Cramming more cheap flats into already socially stressed town centres, the outcome of the past 30 years of urban consolidation, is asking

In all Australian state capitals, beachside suburbs were among the first to host large numbers of flats: 'To meet the taste of holiday-makers large blocks of residential flats have been erected at Manly, Bondi, Coogee and other surf centres, and the high rents the owners get for suites during summer invasion are compensation for winter slackness … These investors are divisible into two classes—those who let the whole of their building, and those who occupy part of the building themselves. The latter are the more common …'[1]

In 1920 Coogee was home to perhaps Sydney's largest beachside apartment block, Beach Court in Arden Street, designed by Douglas Esplin and Stuart Mould, who were shortly to create The Astor in Macquarie Street.[2] This was Coogee's resort heyday, with an aquarium, amusement pier and seabaths attracting hordes of visitors and day-trippers. However, Manly's access to harbour and surf bathing was similarly appealing, and in 1929 a new standard in seaside apartments was set with the completion of Borambil at the southern end of Manly Beach.

Comprising thirty-four two-bedroom flats, Borambil was built for the grazier William Matchett of Borambil Park near Condoblin. It was one of several beachside flats built for graziers with the dual purpose of rental returns and ownership of a holiday apartment. The building was owned by the Matchett family until 1962. Peddle, Thorp & Walker won a limited contest to design the eight-storey building, situated 'within a few yards of the surf beach but at the same time being completely isolated from the weekend holiday throng'.[3] With basement parking and a 'Florentine' exterior, Borambil brought Macleay Street opulence to the seaside while adding holiday features that included 'separate entrances, with shower and change rooms for lady and gentleman surfers … on the lower ground floor'.[4]

Although Borambil included servants' accommodation in the central tower, its

marketing made much of the kitchens, 'a masterpiece of domestic architecture … The numerous new appointments, so essential to kitchen efficiency, will be the envy of every housewife.'[5] The architect and journalist Florence Taylor, formerly an opponent of flats for their diminution of women's domestic role, was sufficiently impressed by Borambil to concede that 'flats as a means of housing will always be popular in certain areas from now on owing to their humanitarian consideration for the women, for the age of women's emancipation from the household drudge …'.[6]

Borambil has outlived many fads and fashions of seaside life.

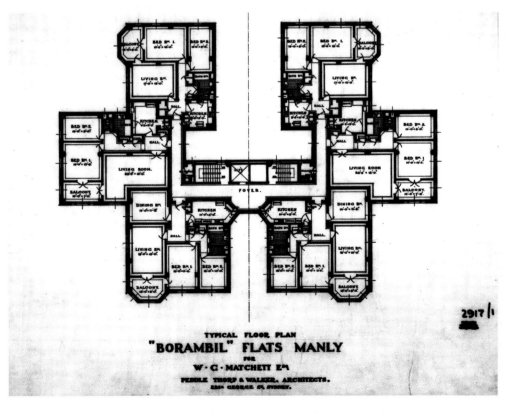

TYPICAL FLOOR PLAN
"BORAMBIL" FLATS MANLY
FOR
W·G·MATCHETT E⁵ᵈ
PEDDLE THORP & WALKER, ARCHITECTS.
&&& GEORGE ST, SYDNEY.

↑ As well as remaking the skyline of several suburban centres, Meriton has transformed their streetscapes. In Rockdale, shopping centres, parking stations and apartment towers create an ambiguous mixture of public and private spaces.

for trouble.'[43] According to urban demographer and commentator Bill Randolph, strata title ownership is entrenching architectural and social poverty: 'It is unclear that this framework is robust enough to deliver an acceptable product that many consumers will want to live in for a long period. These issues are poorly understood by those planning Sydney's higher-density future. Then there is the problem of what you do with a block of flats when it reaches the end of its structural life.'[44]

Towers by the water

Before Meriton, Sydney apartment towers were largely confined to the inner city and harbourside and beachside suburbs, areas with established apartment traditions, hilly topography and water views, and a population sufficiently affluent for a partial investment in large apartment blocks.

On Darling Point, Potts Point, Macleay Point and Blues Point, in Kirribilli, Neutral Bay, Cremorne, and Mosman, the construction of home-unit blocks has radically altered the appearance of the slopes and foreshores of the main harbour ... the most important midwives at the rebirth of Mosman were the high-density developers who bought two or three old properties, demolished them, amalgamated their titles, and threw up blocks of twenty or thirty units, all with harbour views. Home units craned their necks from every ridge ...[45]

The 1960s format of the suburban apartment tower was exemplified by Colebrook, a seventeen-storey, 108-apartment block built above Double Bay shopping centre for a target market of 'the business man and the housewife'. A square tower built around a central services core, Colebrook was designed by Peddle, Thorp & Walker, Sydney's oldest architectural practice, and occupied 'the site of the old Colebrook Mansion, many of whose fine trees have been preserved to provide a charming natural setting for the building'.[46]

Although the tower format has spread to the suburbs, a class division persists between low-rise and high-rise apartments, except in the

← ↑ 'Home units craned their necks from every ridge.' Completed in 1961 at Double Bay, Colebrook was one of the first towers built in Sydney's waterside suburbs.

Apartment living Abdul Alizada, Homa Shojaie, Omid and Navid Alizada

Abdul Alizada fled his home city of Hazarajat in the central rugged, mountainous country of central Afghanistan and arrived illegally by air in Australia in 1999. After twenty-eight days in Villawood detention centre in Sydney's south-west, he lived in a series of different apartments in western Sydney close to the Auburn area, which now is home to more than 4000 Afghanis. Abdul, his wife Homa Shojaie, who joined him in 2003, and their two young children now live in an orange-brick 1970s rented walk-up in nearby Berala. The interior is colourful and immaculately presented; children's toys, flower arrangements and comfortable furniture make the most of a roomy apartment. Their neighbours in the block are all immigrant families: Chinese, Turkish, Arab.

A teacher in his home country, Abdul now works as a tiler on houses and commercial properties. They live in an apartment by necessity: 'Of course we would love to live in our own house with a garden and space for the children to play, but at the moment, with such a small family and little money, this is not a reality.'

House or no house, he is thrilled to be in Australia and is forever elated that, unlike in Afghanistan, where his own Hazara people have been a persecuted minority for centuries, he no longer needs to hide from the police and the military. Abdul explains that only Afghani families with many children live in houses in Australia; most of their friends live in nearby apartments. A leading personality in the Hazar community, Abdul has concentrated his efforts on fundraising with others to purchase space for a community centre to assist other Hazar immigrants with their many social problems, which stem from a lack of English, few skills, difficulty finding work and unfamiliarity with a new country's systems and rules. The community is closeknit, and the family's social network revolves around the community.

Having never lived in apartments in their home country but rather in large houses with facilities shared by several families, they have had to adapt to apartment living. Their current home has advantages and disadvantages, say Abdul and Homa: 'The car park is poorly planned, which makes parking the car very difficult, but we like that the kitchen is partly closed to the living room, therefore preventing cooking smells wafting through.'

Abdul and Homa are saving for their own apartment close to Olympic Park, where their children can grow up close to parks and gardens. They hope to save a deposit on a two-bedroom apartment within the next year. One day they hope to leave apartment living behind and buy a house so that their two energetic boys can stretch their legs.

forces with Stuart Mould to design The Astor at Macquarie Street. Thanks to its height and scale, 'sightseers would catch the ferry across to marvel at its height and admire its grandeur'.[48] Built on a deep narrow block, the seven-storey building features nineteen flats, caretaker's quarters and a flat roof. The interior spaces are relatively generous, having a typical floor plan of three rooms, kitchen, bathroom and balcony. Costing £17,000 for land and construction, the apartments renting for up to £2 per week, Montreaux was seen as 'a sound and splendid return on capital outlaid'.[49]

Manly's urban character changed dramatically during the 1920s, as flats replaced boarding houses and cottages on several of its main streets, notably Ashburner Street, which runs between the harbour and ocean beaches. Connected to the city by ferry and tram, Manly doubled as a commuter suburb and holiday resort, as did many of the first concentrations of apartments. As well as Bondi, Bronte and Coogee in Sydney, these included St Kilda, Brighton and Elwood in Melbourne and Redcliffe, the first Brisbane suburb to attract substantial numbers of apartments. Similar clusters developed in Adelaide's Glenelg and Perth's Cottlesloe. According to the *Australian Home Builder*, 'Flats at the seaside favour the "community living" which is beloved by holiday-makers, not only in Sydney, but wherever holidays are enjoyed … Even in Melbourne cases are known where a three-roomed flat will yield as much rent as a seven-roomed villa.'[50]

Melbourne would have to wait until the 1960s for a seaside building of similar size to Manly's Borambil, although St Kilda boasted no shortage of distinctive structures, including Geoffrey Mewton's Euro-influenced Bellaire in Cordery Street and the Belvedere, crowning the Esplanade above the beach.

Not all seaside suburbs draw holidaymakers, but most feature plenty of red-brick walk-ups. In places this combination has brought the worst features of suburban flatland to the seaside. In her Sydney travelogue, Ruth Park considered the southern beach suburb of Maroubra a strong contender 'in the Ugliest Suburb contest … it is the endless blocks of home units that really curdle the blood, jungles of identical buildings, all the same design, same brick, same height, same nothingness around their feet, in which crouch rows of identical scared little cottages. It is petrifying, even worse than Bondi and Coogee.'[51] The journalist John Clare remembers 1940s Maroubra more fondly: 'The red and liver-coloured

⬆ Influenced by the pioneering tall buildings of Chicago, the Montreaux at Manly shares architects with The Astor at Macquarie Street. Although Manly was soon dotted with flats, the Montreaux still lacks the high neighbours appropriate to its deep floor plan.

case of public housing. In Melbourne, Brisbane and Sydney, the 'households in high-rise flats are relatively better off compared to those in low rise flats', largely because towers continue to cluster in city or waterside locales.[47]

This phenomenon has existed since the infancy of flats in Australia. Built at Manly in 1917, Montreaux was designed by Douglas Esplin six years before he joined

bricks of bungalows and flats seemed an extension of the heath, which underlined the brightest skies with Aboriginal solemnity.' Whatever their aesthetic failings, seaside flats at least ensured a social diversity. 'Opposite our Duncan Street place, brick blocks of flats began to rise in what had been a scrub-filled hollow. These were for refugees. One boy of about my own age used to walk up and down, singing "I'm John from Budapest".'[52]

'Surfers'

Although the east coast capitals led the way in apartment development, they were about to be usurped by a racy newcomer. The 30 kilometres between Coolangatta and Surfers Paradise had been named the Gold Coast for only a year when Kinkabool was completed in 1959. The first Gold Coast apartment tower, Kinkabool was designed

⬆ Like his Woy Woy flats at nearby Elwood, Geoffrey Mewton's Bellaire was built in 1936. The unrendered red brickwork of this three-storey bachelor flat block aligned it with Sydney's first modern flats as well as with later generations of walk-ups.

by Brisbane architects Lund Hutton & Newell, and set the pattern for numerous beachside towers with basement car parking, shops at ground level and two penthouses on the top floor. In between were ten floors containing thirty-four flats.[53]

The Gold Coast is the only Australian city with no history of building height restrictions. It quickly became Australia's leading apartment city, with flats forming a third of its dwellings by 1966. The first major Gold Coast apartment developer was a Queenslander, Ron McMaster, who built forty apartment towers during the 1970s and 1980s. Increasingly

⬆ One of St Kilda's best-known flat buildings, the Belvedere was built in 1929 to the design of William H. Merritt, architect of several suburban flats. The Californian Spanish of the Belvedere (recently renamed the Esplanade) extends to the interior detailing of its thirteen flats and still stands out among the exotic stylings of St Kilda flats.

the scale of Gold Coast projects and a development-friendly City Council attracted entrepreneurs from all over Australia.

One of these was the hotelier Eddie Kornhauser. A sometime associate of the Sydney nightclub czar Abe Saffron, Kornhauser's suspect reputation dogged him when he attempted to expand his hotel empire in Melbourne. Plans to redevelop his Chevron Hotel into an international hotel complex were stymied by Melbourne City Council, despite Kornhauser's commissioning of Harry Seidler as architect. An outraged Kornhauser transferred his operations to the Gold Coast, where in 1975 he built the twin thirty-one-floor towers of the Paradise Centre at Surfers Paradise. However, Kornhauser's association with the corrupt politician Russ Hinze harmed his business prospects. Kornhauser was charged and cleared of paying bribes to Hinze. George Herscu, another Melbourne property developer with Gold Coast interests, was jailed on similar charges.[54]

The first decades of Gold Coast development were aimed at Australian holidaymakers as well as retirees from the southern states. Helen Garner's story of a Melbourne woman visiting her retired parents captures the flavour of Surfers during the early 1980s:

'What do you do all day, up here?' I say on the way home.

'Oh … play bowls. Follow the real estate. I ring up the firms that advertise these flash units and I ask 'em questions. I let 'em lower and lower their price … It's bloody crook up here,' he says, 'Jerry-built. Sad. "Every conceivable luxury"! They can't get rid of it. They're desperate. Come on. We'll go up and have a look.'

⬆ Pioneer of Gold Coast apartment towers, Kinkabool still offers holiday accommodation. Its jaunty 1950s colour scheme has not survived, but Kinkabool's ground-breaking status is widely recognised and has been assigned heritage protection.

⬆ ⬆ In 1957 Robin Boyd dismissed the Gold Coast as 'a fibro-cement paradise under a rainbow of plastic paint'. Boyd had the first generation of Gold Coast flats in mind, including the Alston and Halmar flats at Labrador. ⬆ By 1970 Surfers Paradise was established as a leading holiday destination, creating numerous rooftop and poolside scenes like this one. However, Queensland's abolition of death duties was about to change the character of the Gold Coast, which attracted ageing residents from the southern states.

The lift in Biarritz is lined with mushroom-coloured carpet. We brace our backs against its wall and it rushes us upwards. The salesman in the display unit has a moustache, several gold bracelets, a beige suit, and a clipboard against his chest … Just inside the living room stand five Ionic pillars in a half-moon curve. Beyond them, through the glass, are views of a river and some mountains …

'From the other side you can see the sea,' says my father.[55]

Other Gold Coast fiction is more racy, focusing on the area's combination of wealth, ostentation and shady property dealings. Perhaps the best known is the 1981 feature film *Goodbye Paradise*, starring Ray Barrett.

During the 1980s the Gold Coast was transformed by the sudden interest of Japanese investors, tourists and retirees. The Gold Coast was the first offshore resort to attract significant investment from Japan, with major multinational companies including Matsushita, Mitsui and Toyomenka diversifying into its resorts and apartments. The developer Jim Raptis had already established a trend towards exotic architectural themes with the Copacobana and St Tropez at Surfers Paradise. The Japanese projects took theming, size and luxury a step further. Notable was the forty-three-storey pink, purple and blue Grand Mariner at Paradise Waters, designed by the Canadian Hulbert Group. Responsible for resorts and apartments in Miami and Vancouver, Hulbert established a Gold Coast office in 1985 and designed most of the Sanctuary Cove resort. Grand Mariner was created at the request of Mitsui and Orient

Finance for 'a building that doesn't melt into the rest of the skyline, people should always know it's there'.[56] A similar strategy was followed with Belle Maison, a French chateau-themed tower at Broadbeach, designed for a Japanese retail company with specialities in women's clothing, accessories and toiletries. The France–Gold Coast–shopping alliance proved a marketing triumph.

In the same decade a Queensland royal commission into corruption weakened the association between the Gold Coast, crooked property deals and unplanned development. By the 1990s, when Japanese investment began to cool, the Gold Coast had been transformed into an internationally recognised holiday destination. As of 2004 the Gold Coast boasted 216 apartment buildings of twelve storeys or more, with another twenty-five being under construction.[57] By then Surfers Paradise was the sixth largest city in Australia. With 500,000 people and Australia's fastest population growth rate (3.5 per cent per year), the city can afford to ignore the prejudices of southern metropolises.

Some developers now claim that Gold Coast apartments are decidedly superior to those of the capital cities. One to make this claim is Harry Triguboff, whose Meriton Apartments has constructed several Gold Coast towers since the early 1980s, including the Florida, Xanadu and Solaire. 'Mr Triguboff ... agreed that his Gold Coast towers have improved greatly in quality and design since his first Main Beach venture. He said that the Gold Coast market of today demands bigger apartments than Meriton builds in Sydney ...'[58]

Perhaps the most prominent of contemporary developers is the Sunland Group of Soheil and Sahba Abedian. This father and son combination is best known for Q1, for a few years the world's tallest residential tower. This eighty-storey, 522-apartment, 322-metre tall 'vertical suburb' has created an international reputation for the apartment architecture of the Gold Coast, which is now regarded as competitive with those of Asia and the Americas. Through the creation of themed and highly identifiable towers, the Gold Coast has successfully differentiated itself from the apartment architecture of Australia.

Meanwhile, apartment development stretches along the Pacific coast north and south of Brisbane, and parts of the New South Wales North Coast and North Queensland are similarly affected. The transformation of sleepy holiday towns into high-rise resorts is not universally popular especially when, as in the northern New South Wales town of Tweed Heads, local politicians formed associations with property developers.[59] Like the transplantation of brick-veneer suburbia to the seaside, the relationship between the beach and apartment living creates continuing controversies.

↲ Completed in 1976, Focus was the forerunner of a new generation of Gold Coast apartment towers. Designed by Sydney architects Clark Gazzard, Focus' circular floor plan and thirty levels brought new height and architectural sophistication to Surfers Paradise.

↥ '... a building that doesn't melt into the rest of the skyline': Grand Mariner at Paradise Waters, created for the influx of investors and visitors from Japan.

The Gold Coast hosts several theme parks, a concept also influential with its architecture since the 1980s. The Moroccan, like the Phoenician, the Mediterranean, St Tropez and so on, is notable for its themed architecture and interiors.

When completed in 2005, Q1 overtook Dubai's 21st Century Tower as the world's tallest residential building, although its status is already threatened by new projects in Dubai and elsewhere. Despite the challenge of Eureka Tower, Melbourne, Q1 remains the tallest structure in Australia.

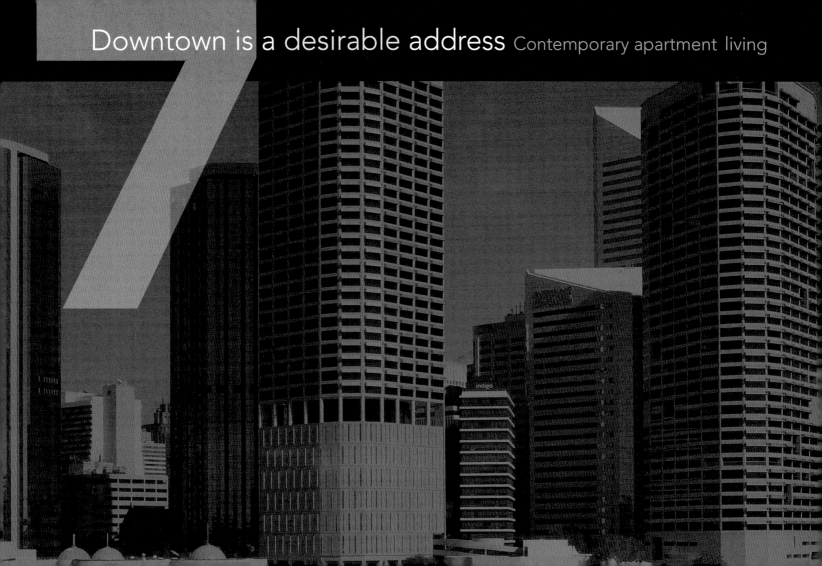

7

Downtown is a desirable address Contemporary apartment living

Overlooking Sydney's Hyde Park from Liverpool Street, the thirty-storey Connaught opened in 1984. With a total of 239 units, the Connaught quickly attracted attention for its celebrity residents, including at various times the notorious hit man Christopher Dale Flannery, television personality Jana Wendt, flamboyant lawyer Chris Murphy, Sydney Airport chief Max Moore-Wilton and singers Michael Hutchence and Barry Crocker.[1]

A decade or so earlier the Park Regis had become the first major apartment building constructed in Sydney's CBD since the 1930s. The Park Regis was designed and built during the late 1960s by Stocks and Holdings (later Stockland Trust), a property and building company founded on the Lend Lease model by Hungarian immigrant Erwin Graf. But whereas Lend Lease's experience with the failed Rocks project rendered the company pessimistic of city apartment projects, Graf's forty-four-storey Park Regis, claimed to be the tallest apartment tower outside the USA, was a success, if less lucrative to its developer than the new office towers surrounding it.[2]

The market for city apartments was slowly building. Another city tower, the York at Wynyard Park, created a buying frenzy for Mirvac when placed on the market in 1980: 'Some buyers lined up at night, one parked outside in a caravan. By 9am, the opening time, a crowd of impatient and excited people was waiting at the door ... The prices were escalating daily and the building was sold out before the official opening.'[3]

Designed by Robertson & Marks, experienced architects of city commercial buildings, the Connaught set a new standard in size and luxury for city apartments. Its construction contradicted early 1980s predictions of a low-rise future. The 1970s backlash against tall apartment developments and a new appreciation of urban and architectural heritage saw many local governments plan for a low-rise future with an emphasis on townhouse and other medium-density projects.[4] By the end of the 1980s, however, multistorey apartment buildings were back on the housing agenda, helped somewhat by an oversupply of office space.

In 1991 just 7000 people were living in the City of Sydney, but this number had increased to 32,000 by 2003, and growth to 40,000 by

The Connaught's construction required the demolition of the well-loved Paris Theatre; one form of city life replaced another. Home to many of Sydney's 'great and good', the Connaught exemplifies the complications of maintaining a vibrant urban culture.

Forerunner of Sydney's contemporary apartment boom, the Park Regis remains one of the city's most striking towers. Later extended on its southern side, the Park Regis now offers hotel and backpacker accommodation as well as apartments.

⬆ When completed in 1997, the fifty-three floors of Century Tower formed the tallest residential building in Sydney, dominating the southern skyline of the CBD. Its prominence has since been diminished by the apartment boom around Chinatown.

↗ Developed by Meriton, designed by Bob Nation, World Tower soars above Sydney's towers. Its World Square site, once occupied by Anthony Hordern's grand department store, lay deserted for decades as developers, unions and governments argued over its future.

2006 was projected.[5] Since 1995, 97 per cent of central Melbourne housing developments have been in medium- or high-density form, and a further 13,500 dwellings are projected to be constructed in the City of Melbourne before 2010.[6]

The city apartment has become respectable as well as trendy. As significant as the raw numbers is the renewed association of city apartment living with affluence. The signature elements of the contemporary upmarket high-rise include a twenty-four-hour concierge, gymnasium, heated pool, tennis court, marble and granite finishes, secure parking for two cars per apartment, and an 'oversized' balcony to make the most of the views.[7] In many ways the contemporary acceptability of city apartment living has repeated that of the early city flats, such as The Astor, The Albany, Melbourne Mansions, Lawson Flats and Ruthven Mansions. City living has regained its glamorous image but among a wider social milieu than during the 1920s and 1930s.

This prominent 'lifestyle' trend has attracted the interest of journalists and the media. Typical was Deidre Macken in *Good Weekend* magazine: 'The CBD used to be home to pigeons, not people. But now downtown is a desirable address.'[8] Or Guy Allenby on housing the upwardly mobile: 'Not so long ago living in a city apartment didn't

⬆ Partly owing to their proximity to the revered Sydney Opera House, East Circular Quay's 'toaster' apartments were the subject of protest rallies while under construction. The success of the apartments' colonnade and other public spaces has ameliorated the precinct's reputation.

figure on anybody's wish list. Inner-city terrace yes, medium-density pied-à-terre on the city's fringe maybe, but a tower block in the dead heart of Australia's biggest city?'[9]

The journalistic focus highlights the rapid change to our cities' architectural and social fabric. A resident of four city apartments since 1987 observed:

> When we first moved in to the city, the weekends were dead because there was no one here. Come 5pm and people got into their cars and they went home. If you didn't have milk before the shops closed in the afternoon then that was it, you wouldn't have any milk until the next morning … It was almost like a village. You could go out to a show and then go back to someone's apartment for a coffee … The people are still here but you don't see each other because you get lost in the crowd.[10]

High-rise residential now makes the city centres resemble mini versions of Hong Kong: 'A few years ago, this synthetic landscape wasn't there; it is now a fair bet that more of the films and novels of our reflective popular culture will be set in such flats.'[11] The embrace of CBD apartment life has been swift.

City apartment development has been fuelled by a relatively affluent middle-class group prepared to move to the city, who work a 'particular set of jobs that are demanding between 80 and 100 hours per week … and the best place to do it is just down the road from where you're living in the big end of town'.[12] The new city colonists conform mostly to three demographic categories: empty-nesters (couples whose children have left home); DINKS (double income, no kids); and 'millennium families' who 'see a city lifestyle as a better and more sophisticated way for their kids to grow up'.[13]

Consistent with the direction of change in age distribution and labour force status, the income distribution of people living in high-rise housing also changed relative to that of the Australian population. In 1981 high-rise residents were slightly overrepresented in middle- to

The appointment of Italian star architect Renzo Piano as designer of Macquarie Apartments was widely viewed as an attempt to justify the demolition of its site predecessor, the State Office Block, a standard-setting 1960s office tower. Piano's appointment has proved to be more than public relations; his ability to create buildings unique to their place has produced an engaging and individual structure.

higher-income brackets. By 2001 they were strongly overrepresented. For example, 11 per cent of high-rise residents aged 15 years and over received a gross weekly income of $1500 or more in 2001, compared with just 4 per cent of all Australians in this age group. High income was more common among high-rise residents born in Australia than among those born overseas.

Immigrants form the other significant demographic in the city residential renaissance. In 2001, 50 per cent of high-rise residents were born overseas, usually in Asia or Europe, which is twice the overseas-born share of the total population. This results partly from an increase in the number of foreign citizens residing in Australia on temporary student visas. In 2001 a fifth of overseas-born high-rise residents were full-time students, up from 4 per cent in 1981. In blocks with four or more storeys, Asia supplied the largest group of immigrant residents.[14] High-rise apartment buildings with access to Asian supermarkets, specialty food stores and restaurants are marketed to Asian investors and

renters. A high percentage of those buying into the area adjacent to Sydney's Chinatown are investors from Singapore, Hong Kong, Indonesia and Malaysia.[15]

The southern part of Sydney's CBD, centred on Chinatown, is the densest precinct of Australian city living, being home to more than 10,000 people, 4000 of them new residents. This population is complemented by a daily influx of 35,000 workers each day. A handful of large blocks have attracted the bulk of residents, and the seventy-five-storey World Tower has swallowed up many of the new arrivals. It is one of a profusion of new Chinatown towers that include Century Tower (fifty-three storeys), Meriton Tower (forty-eight storeys), Latitude (fifty-one storeys), Aspect (forty-one storeys) and Cassia Gardens (twenty-six storeys). Some of these towers mix residential with office space and at ground level include shops to service the increase in residents and workers to the area. The newsagent at World Square sums up the transition: 'This area will be unrecognizable in 10 years

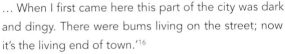

The Cove, completed in 2004, was a stylish return to Sydney city projects for Harry Seidler. Notable for respectful integration with its historic streetscape, the Cove retains its architect's signature aesthetic. 'They are running naked, crawling naked, topless and beautiful on a mysterious, rock landscape.' The prospectus for Republic 2, now a collector's item.

Towers, The Connaught, Grand Central, Waterford Tower, Paramount, The Peak. These are the suburbs of the CBD.'[17]

… When I first came here this part of the city was dark and dingy. There were bums living on the street; now it's the living end of town.'[16]

The lifestyle city

Apartment complexes have become the centrepiece of urban renewal, of the contemporary revisioning of the commercial, retailing, industrial city. In an attempt to create a sense of neighbourhood and identity in the city's residential renaissance, apartments are promoted as 'vertical villages', named and marketed as image-making commodities: 'They live not in addresses, but in names. Horizon, Republic Tower, The Domain, Observatory Tower, Quay West, Quay Grand, Melbourne Terrace, The Georgia, Highgate, Victoria Tower, Miramar, Parkland

Despite the language of neighbourhood, lifestyle is generally more narrowly defined. A 1998 apartment prospectus broke new ground, changing property advertising in Sydney: 'They are running naked, crawling naked, topless and beautiful on a mysterious, rock landscape. There are longing, intense gazes. And plenty of pubic hair. These images weren't for a cologne or Gucci. They were for a new block of apartments in East Sydney called Republic 2', designed by leading apartment designers Burley Katon Halliday. Heavy on picturesque nudes, the extensive brochure featured just two pages of architectural details.[18]

Mikkal Armstrong of Dakota Creative is one of the behind-the-scenes players in contemporary apartment advertising, having been the mind behind the names and image of the Grid, the Horizon and Republic 2. Of his brochure for the latter he says that he 'didn't want to have a brochure of "people drinking cappuccinos and kitchen finishes"', but preferred to 'establish the developer as somebody who is doing quality product and to use the black and white photography to speak directly to people about artistic integrity and quality'.[19]

While families flying kites and couples reading newspapers and drinking cappuccinos remain the norm in advertising suburban apartment developments, this image is apparently passé among inner-city advertising gurus. According to Anthony Denman, principal at the Double Bay advertising agency ADS: '… in the early 1990s the cappuccino-style brochure was the way of luring people to the city, which didn't have a history of a residential lifestyle. "It was basic stuff. It was like, getting your target market, 30 to 49, girl and boy, down at Darling Harbour, in situ having brunch." '[20]

Developers and architects

Architects have a long association with apartments, evident for example in the prominent role of architects such as Katsalidis, Seidler, Engelen Moore and Stanisic in the contemporary apartment boom. However, architects often struggle to find influential roles in an industry dominated by development companies.

The private sector is responsible for almost all of the apartment buildings of the last twenty-five years. Using the design and construct formula 'with a formularized adoption of tilt-slab construction techniques' such companies as Meriton, Mirvac, Australand, Central Equity and Multiplex control the design agendas closely.[21] Project managers delegate the design process as well as the construction, marketing and other elements of the major residential projects. During Sydney's controversial East Circular Quay development, project manager Bovis McLachlan became the 'intermediaries, and architects who work with them find it difficult to communicate directly with their clients'.[22] Peddle, Thorp & Walker's Andrew Andersons, principal architect of part of East Circular Quay, was required to sign a confidentiality agreement gagging him from speaking publicly about the project, itself the work of a bewildering collection of interests:[23]

> Lord Mayor Frank Sartor has consulted Hassell's Ken Maher and Denton Corker Marshall's Richard Johnson for ideas to tweak the purple-glazed facades of the internationally criticised apartment block … Even its architects don't seem happy with the way that this design-and-construct project has turned out. It is now said to have been 'planned and documented' by Dino Burattini & Associates before going to Peddle Thorp & Walker, who designed 'the outside 500mm' and negotiated the consent with close design input from the City of Sydney council.[24]

◄ The major element of Melbourne's urban redesign, Docklands is also one of the most controversial. Attempts to create an urban and cultural context for its apartments and parks—including the Docklands stadium and film studio project—have met with varying success.

▲ Docklands extends east to the several apartment buildings that form Yarra's Edge, designed and built primarily by developer Mirvac. Yarra's Edge includes the ninety-two-floor, 556-apartment Eureka Tower completed in 2006. The culmination of a lengthy attempt by the Grollo developer family to create a landmark building for Melbourne, the Eureka project survived changes of location and site.

⬆ Once a bustling working-class suburb, Pyrmont is now a concentration of upmarket apartments and vestigial social infrastructure. The suburb's industrial past survives in little but apartment names, including the Quarry and the Distillery. Designed by Melbourne architects Denton Corker Marshall, these towers are the centrepiece of Lend Lease's residential development of the former CSR refinery site.

The subject of public protests, satirically dubbed 'the Toaster' for its bland design, East Circular Quay evidences the unsatisfactory potential of architect–developer–government alliances.

Andrew Andersons: One Christmas holidays, I was on the receiving end of a very mysterious phone call. Somebody rang me up and wouldn't say who it was and asked me to ring a number and suddenly, at the other end of the line, was the Prime Minister … And as I recall we … all got down on our knees and looked at what the impact of lowering the height might be from different angles looking across the sea.
Paul Keating: I mean, it would horrify people to see what it would've been. I mean, they go on now in Sydney, about it, but God how they would go on, if it had been the way it was going to be.[25]

Property companies are today among political parties' most generous donors; the price appears to be privileged access to decisions over prominent sites. Meanwhile, architects are chosen as part of the builder–developer package and are employed by the developer or builder. 'Governments feel safe with this method—signing a contract with a developer who offers the best deal for public land, they sign away financial risk and design decisions for a set amount and delivery date.'[26] Hence the most prominent buildings, such as East Circular Quay, attract the well-known, well-connected architects who are well versed in getting plans through council. Only star international and national architects, such as Norman Foster, Renzo Piano and Nonda Katsilidis, have a greater chance to control their designs.

These high-profile names also create a more sympathetic consideration of proposals at odds with building and urban ordinances.[27] During the 1990s Victoria's Planning Minister 'called upon developers to disregard height limits if they could achieve higher standards … height limits were portrayed as limits to creativity, a story readily accepted by many architects … To oppose the height is to oppose the architecture.'[28]

Meriton has joined other developers in using architecture as a selling point, both politically and publicly. In the late 1990s Meriton started to draw on consultant architects, culminating in the World Tower site where a limited design competition attracted entries from Australia's leading apartment architects including Nation Fender Katsalidis, Peddle Thorp & Walker and Harry Seidler & Associates. Designed by Bob Nation, Meriton's World Tower became Sydney's first NFK building, and the nearby Meriton Tower proved to be one of Harry Seidler's last commissions.

Meriton joined other developers in promoting 'architecture as lifestyle accessory', part of the broader trend that has seen city apartments arriving in the social pages, discounts being given to celebrities to encourage 'names' to buy into developments, starring roles on television in programs like The Block, and talk in architectural, urban and social circles of which interior designer, developer and architect is doing which buildings:[29]

There was a baby-doll nightdress draped over the bed. So gay! And a Jacob Delafon conical basin in the bathroom. That's sooo Scott Weston. Yeah, he's the interior designer of the display unit; he did the Medusa Hotel. No, he's not the architect. Alex Tzannes is the architect. What do you mean, was Burley Katon Halliday busy? Alex is fabulous! He did Bistro Moncur. Anywaaaay, the Icon apartments have been mentioned in the 'Cool list'. The one done by the Sunday Telegraph's social writer, Melissa Hoyer. Who lives there? Well, no-one yet. But Ming Gan[30] is working on it. He's selling the units. He lives in Horizon. He should know …[31]

The leading example of high-end apartment living by an overseas architect is the sixteen-storey Macquarie Apartments by Italy's

The new apartment precinct of Wolli Creek will be home to 6500 residents in towers developed by Meriton, Australand and Multiplex. Representative of the exponential rise of 'apartment villages' across Sydney's former industrial sites, Wolli Creek is of mixed architectural pedigree, unlike its colonial neighbour, Tempe House, dwarfed in the foreground.

Typical of the medium-rise apartment and townhouse developments spreading along the Parramatta River are Balmain Shores and the neighbouring Balmain Cove, developed by Australand on the former site of the Balmain Power Station. On the water, working boats are replaced by marinas of pleasure craft.

The castellated walls, stores and brewing towers of Victoria Brewery, built from 1895, formed an unusually handsome industrial complex. Its apartment conversion included several existing buildings, as well as a spectacular marketing suite by French design guru Philippe Starck.

Renzo Piano. A return to Macquarie Street by luxury apartments, the building is notable for its glass-louvred facade, which responds to climactic changes and challenges the prejudice that facades of apartment buildings have to be uniform and repetitive. Macquarie is also distinctive for its borrowing of local building materials such as terracotta, used at the base and in mullions to screen the apartments for privacy.

Harry Seidler moved from designing high-rise apartment buildings in the inner city to the city area with North and the Cove, both of which are on restricted city sites. The Cove, comprising a podium and tower, is located on a tight 15-metre-wide site, sandwiched between two heritage-listed buildings. At pedestrian level, the height of the tower is not obvious as the street facade is of similar height to those of its neighbours. Seidler's facade is uncompromisingly modern with a highly distinctive rectangular composition of toughened glass, masonry and off-form concrete. It contains a dramatically spaced foyer at the base of the residential tower. The immediately identifiable Seidler wave-like balconies provide 'permanent open space' for the dwellers because, at this level of the apartment price range, as Seidler said, 'Nobody wants to look on to each other.'[32]

Built in a former industrial suburb, Mondrian encapsulates many contemporary trends in apartment design, notably a move away from stand-alone towers towards slab blocks built around courtyards. It also leads the way in incorporating eco-design, especially design for cross-ventilation, implemented with such success that no air-conditioning units have been fitted since Mondrian's completion in 2003.

Mondrian's architect Frank Stanisic designed Sydney's first contemporary court-yard development in 1990, using the site of the former Crown Street Hospital in Surry Hills. Stanisic has since designed several similar projects in inner-suburban sites: 'The communal courtyard is a very fundamental element of most European architecture … In Sydney for a long time all the focus was on towers, but the latest shift has been to brownfield or urban renewal sites where there are large blocks of land and no harbour views. There's no point in having a twenty-storey tower in an area where there's nothing to look at.'[1]

Mondrian is composed of 137 apart-ments in four narrow buildings up to seven floors in height. All apartments have balconies or courtyards, and the develop-ment surrounds a series of courtyards and a communal swimming pool. The buildings are similar to several eco-conscious designs created since 2000, notably Tina Engelen and Ian Moore's Altair, which attracted international praise.[2]

The trend toward courtyard apartments represents a renewal of post-1945

Modernism, a more urban-friendly version of the uncompromising work of Seidler, Boyd and others. Although the work of these Modernists is reflected in the grid-like exterior of Mondrian and similar projects, the aesthetic is driven by function rather than retro.

Stanisic was rewarded with the 2003 Wilkinson Award for residential buildings, conferred by the Royal Australian Institute of Architects' New South Wales chapter. As well as Mondrian's functional quality, the jury was impressed by its appearance: 'Mondrian is delivered in a stunning and refined "new modern" architectural script that is a welcome antidote to much of the regressive nostalgia permeating our cities and suburbs.'[3]

Success for an apartment design in such awards is a notable event in itself. Until the 1990s awards for residential architecture were the preserve of free-standing houses. However, cynicism lingers about the fact that such exemplary apartment architecture was restricted to the design-conscious inner-city: 'the high-end, not models for the masses'.[4] Stanisic shared these concerns, arguing that suburban councils continue to approve 'real shockers', notably when sites change owners, developers—and archi-tects.[5]

Others are optimistic that Mondrian will inspire a characteristically Australian apart-ment type that responds both to its urban and to its environmental setting.

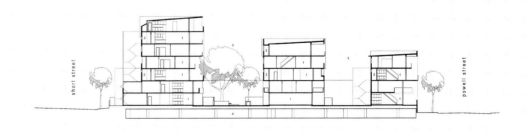

North South Section

1   Apartments

2   Gallery

3   Courtyard

4   Carpark

⬆ Barley and wheat silos are a feature of Richmond and Collingwood, landmarks in a primarily low-rise townscape. The future of these disused behemoths has incited debate among architects and conservationists. Nonda Katsalidis' Silo Apartments offered one solution.

⬆ Said to have the highest average apartment price in Australia when completed in 2001, The Melburnian on St Kilda Road is a statement of the continuing relationship between wealth and apartment living. Designed by Bates Smart, Australia's oldest architectural practice, The Melburnian comprises 230 apartments in three buildings.

➡ Harry Seidler's Riparian Plaza combines twenty-five floors of office space below ten floors comprising fifty penthouse apartments. The lower levels are occupied by a car park, as well as retail foyers. Located by the Brisbane River, Riparian's mixed use concept may become a common response to shortages of city real estate.

A new geography

Although high-rise buildings attract media attention, only a small proportion of Australians live in buildings with four or more storeys. Most of these are in Sydney. In 2001 apartments in Sydney's city and harbourside suburbs housed 42 per cent of the country's high-rise dwellers; another 18 per cent lived in Sydney seaside suburbs. Fourteen per cent of high-rise residents resided in Melbourne, followed by 11 per cent in Brisbane and other parts of Queensland.[34] Sydney's highrise waterside phenomenon was mirrored on the Gold Coast, on the Brisbane River and in Melbourne at Southbank and Port Phillip and in Geelong on Corio Bay shorelines.

The growth of higher-density development in the city and inner-ring areas was established during the 1980s, before urban consolidation policies had been formalised. While the last quarter of a century has seen intensification of flat construction in existing areas, a new geography of apartment living has emerged in Sydney and Melbourne in the middle-ring suburbs, 'a diffusion of higher density housing into suburban areas hitherto not characterized by this form of housing'.[35] Because of their suburban character, these areas have been the focus of controversy about government urban consolidation policies.

Developers, state and local governments promote the language of neighbourhood, in part to persuade a questioning public that higher density does not mean anonymity but can mean a more concentrated, better connected community. This approach has extended to the development of entire apartment precincts, usually involving the literal replacement of industry and trade with lifestyle—Docklands, Southbank (Melbourne), South Bank (Brisbane), Walsh Bay, East Darling Harbour and Pyrmont Point are among the most prominent examples. The most comprehensive use of apartments to revision a city's image and infrastructure is undoubtedly Melbourne's Docklands project. In many

⬆ Colloquially known as the 'stealth bomber' for its shadowy colours, Observatory Tower gives no hint of its former life as an office tower. The completion in 1996 of Observatory Tower, which contains 200 of Sydney's most expensive apartments, brought wealthy residents to the public housing precinct of Millers Point.

↗ ➔ Ercole Palazetti was engaged by developer Australand to design the Dorchester as a building appropriate to the historic fabric of Macleay Street. Although disdained by the architectural cognoscenti, the retro-luxury of Palazetti's 'neo-classical' apartments has found numerous patrons and buyers. The Dorchester prospectus encapsulates Palazetti's style.

respects the development of the derelict Victoria Dock precinct reflected the 1980s makeover of Sydney's Darling Harbour docks. However, both the residential and urban impact of Docklands is greater, as is its ambition to create a waterside, leisure-focused identity for Melbourne.

Occupying 200 hectares, Docklands is currently the largest construction project in Australia and when completed will almost double the size of Melbourne's CBD. The precinct is already home to more than 3000 people and workplace for more than 5000. These numbers are expected to reach 20,000 residents and 25,000 workers at the completion of the project. Although developers have persuaded the Docklands Authority to permit taller apartment towers, the 'Authority takes comfort that "there is a consensus that Melbourne has more top quality architects, urban designers and landscape architects than any other Australian city" '. Or, as claimed by architect Peter Corrigan, 'Melbourne has the ideas ... Sydney has the money.'[36] Yet given the involvement in Dock-lands of a *Who's Who* of major developers, a certain cynicism is in order. As Kim Dovey observes: 'The planning and urban design process was essentially ... subcontracted to developers.'[37]

Many of Sydney's 'brownfields' sites are located in the south-east around Waterloo and Zetland and along the Parramatta River. As Graham Jahn explained: 'the rats, oil slicks and drifting detritus trapped in Sydney Harbour backwashes west of the Bridge were cleaned up ... As the water got cleaner, industry got less visible, the land got more valuable and so it was rezoned for consolidation.'[38] From Glebe, Balmain, Abbotsford and Cabarita out to Breakfast Point, paint and soap factories, coal mines, saw mills and ammunition factories have been transformed into prime real estate. The change in land use has occurred because industry no longer needs the river as an access point. At Breakfast Point alone, 1850 apartments are being built, and 1600 at Rhodes Waterside and 2500 at Homebush Bay.[39]

Some industrial sites have seen the conversion of warehouses, wharves and other buildings to residential use. One of the largest is the redevelopment of the former Victoria Brewery in East Melbourne. The new title of Tribeca East was not the only image-making element of this project; the involvement of celebrated French designer Philippe Starck provided marketing clout as well as expertise. The large-scale and inner-city locations of many breweries have also seen them provide sites for apartment redevelopments in Adelaide (Brewery Apartments, Kent Town), Perth (Old Swan Brewery), Brisbane (Carlton Brewery, Fortitude Valley) and Sydney (Waverley Brewery, Moore Park and Kent Brewery, Broadway).

Meanwhile, Nonda Katsalidis' 1996 Silo Apartments established a trend in apartment architecture with a sculptural conversion of the reinforced concrete wheat silo of Daly's Malthouse at Richmond. More recently six former flour mill silos in Sydney's Newtown have been reworked by the architects Tonkin Zulaikha Greer. The project was both an architectural and an engineering challenge as it involved 'cutting into the 180mm-thick reinforced concrete walls of the 1936 cylindrical structure, and then attaching services and new wings'.[40] Other silo conversions have been completed at Dulwich Hill (Sydney), Bunbury (Western Australia), and Hobart, where the Battery Point silos are now the city's tallest apartment building.

Silos attract relatively few conservationist voices compared to

Apartment living John A. Pickles

For more than twenty-five years, John Pickles has been resident and chairman of the owners' corporation of one of Sydney's most prestigious apartment buildings, the twenty-one-storey President Towers in exclusive Darling Point. The round floor plan, reminiscent of Australia Square, has 360-degree views of Sydney Harbour, is surrounded by lush gardens and, most unusually for this part of town, has four street frontages. With the block having only one apartment per floor, its postcard views of Sydney Harbour

marry well with its opulence and seclusion. Pickles notes that the building used to be on the rich and famous itinerary for sightseers as a number of famous and influential people have occupied the block at various times.

A descendant of the Van Heusen shirt-making dynasty and an English immigrant from 1964, John and his family bought into the block in the late 1970s, setting a new price record for strata plan apartments. They decided that they needed to move with the three children to avoid 'rattling in a large house when the children left home'.

'In 1978 I counted the number of traffic lights between Warrawee, a leafy suburb on the upper North Shore of Sydney, and Marrickville, where I ran my business. That realisation propelled us to move here where we could adopt an eight-day week with the time that

we saved commuting. Researching the climate closely, I decided that we had two choices, either to live on the point itself or on the ridge to avoid the extreme summer hot and winter cold that applies to properties on the east and west side of the point.'

As chairman of the body corporate, Pickles prides himself on the way the building is run as a commercial proposition with a huge emphasis being placed on maintenance and security. Levies are larger than the average annual rent of most blocks, ensuring that the building is impeccably maintained and has for example the tidiest garages of arguably any apartment building in Australia.

'I have been called Adolf for the way I've run this block for more than twenty-five years, but no one complains when they realise that the value of

their apartment continues to rise exponentially, compounding at more than 9 per cent per annum. I am like the captain of a ship, with clear oversight for the technical crew—the executive—and all passengers—the residents. There is not one surface of the common areas, including the roof, garages, pool and fitness room, which has not received some attention in the last ten years. We even have the only bore water system of any apartment building in Darling Point.'

Although Pickles also spends a significant amount of time in Surfers Paradise at his alternative home, another multi-million-dollar apartment building, he still manages to expend at least 250 hours per year voluntarily chairing the owners' corporation, saying he will remain 'as long as my party wants me'.

office conversions, including some notable former government buildings. Melbourne's Railways Administration Office and the former Queensland Government Offices are now hotel and apartment complexes.

A new demography

Between 1991 and 2001 Australia's total of high-density dwellings increased by 37 per cent, compared with an 18 per cent increase in separate houses.[42] The contemporary apartment boom signals the urban reality that the 'traditional' family is no longer the dominant social unit of Australian society. Since the 1980s one- and two-person households have become the most common household type, undercutting the long-standing ideological association between the social mainstream and suburban cottages, and boosting the popularity of apartment living.

The growth in high-density living is prompted by changes in the age structure of the population, household and family composition and size, as well as demand for lower-priced accommodation and housing

⬆ Standing out from the established apartment precincts of Kings Cross and Darlinghurst, the Horizon has attracted more criticism that any of Harry Seidler's apartment projects since Blues Point Tower. As with the latter building, Horizon residents are not numbered among the critics.

wharves, which are more romantic structures in most people's eyes. The residential conversion of timber wharves at Sydney's Woolloomooloo and Walsh Bays provoked long-running heritage debates. Less controversial has been the conversion of city office towers to apartment use. Sydney's first office tower precinct, at the Observatory Hill end of Kent Street, is now largely residential following conversions of the Esso Building, Caltex House and the IBM Building during the 1990s.[41] Designed in 1964 by Stephenson & Turner, the IBM tower was reborn by Crone Associates as Observatory Tower, 199 prestigious residential apartments, the city pads of Paul Keating and David Williamson among others. Brisbane and Melbourne have also hosted several

close to employment centres.[43] The key demographic fact influencing the rise of apartment numbers is the decreasing percentage of the population fitting the subdivision profile, namely the nuclear family of Mum, Dad and kids. The proportion of couple families with children has declined to 47 per cent (2,321,165 families) of all families in 2001, down from 49.6 per cent in 1996 and 50.2 per cent (1,569,868 families) in 1971. For this group, the suburbs continue to offer the preferred lifestyle, but for the remainder, be it singles, unmarried couples, married couples with no children or divorcees, apartments are often the preferred residence.

Shrinking family sizes have created a disjuncture with the vastly increased size of many new suburban houses. The 'McMansion' phenomenon has invigorated debate about the ecological sustainability of new suburbs. With state governments adopting 'urban consolidation as their economic and planning mantra', apartments have become the favoured building type of government planning bureaucracies.[44]

The Elan apartments at Kings Cross is well known for the widely satirised public artwork on its forecourt. Thanks to this photo by Roslyn Sharp, the Elan is also associated with Wally Murray, evicted from his dwelling at the head of William Street by construction of the Elan. Murray returned from his rural exile to symbolically reclaim his former home.

One of the main arguments for the pursuit of urban consolidation is that it 'improves the range of housing choice open to households in terms of dwelling type, tenure and location'. Obviously this is pressing given the rise in diversity of household types since the 1970s and 1980s with shifts in demography, culture and lifestyle.[45] The 'compact city discourse' has remained central to government policy since the 1980s, but its implementation has been uneven.[46] It is also far from certain that the more prominent apartment developments will increase local social diversity. Kim Dovey's critique of Docklands is applicable to most upmarket precincts: 'the docks are set to become the residential preserve of a rather narrow social group of empty-nesters and younger managerial classes. The issue of social mix in the Docklands vanished, even from the rhetoric …'[47]

Although the better-off suburbs fight flats primarily on aesthetic and amenity grounds, several social scientists and planners have questioned the social consequences of urban consolidation, specifically the construction of many more flats in the western suburbs of Sydney and Melbourne where design and construction is already of a poor quality thanks to the last flat boom. This story is not about the architect-designed towers of the inner city but about the blocks built in the middle-ring suburbs of Sydney, which have been described by Bill Randolph as 'the slums of the future'.[48]

Randolph sees the new 'McMansion' suburbs as encouraging 'the "ghettoisation" of new housing choice … The newest suburbs are certainly socially exclusive—few renters, no affordable housing, no flats, and few old people or single people.' On the contrary, flats are clustered around existing town centres and transport routes, and are usually the domain of those without children and those who rent.[49] Higher-density housing is considerably more likely to be rented at 60 per cent, with separate houses registering just 18 per cent rental occupation. Most city houses are owned outright (47 per cent) with a third being purchased. In high-density housing the reverse was true; only a quarter of higher density dwellings being owned outright (24 per cent) and 13 per cent being purchased.[50]

Randolph fears for the future of the 'gleaming new blocks' built adjacent to transport nodes in the suburbs, arguing that 'a highly mobile population of youthful tenants may not be a secure base on which to rebuild declining town centres, although it should stimulate the latte trade'. The issue of maintenance of blocks is crucial. The ageing red and cream walk-up blocks in middle and outer-ring suburbs, in 'secondary or unfashionable locations' today, might give us some idea of what might become of hastily built apartments in the current boom.[51]

Apartments—the new great Australian dream?

In the ten-year period between 1991 and 2001, Sydney's higher-density housing increased more than three times the rate of separate houses; 36 per cent of the city's private housing stock being classified as higher density in 2001. This sharp growth was mirrored in Melbourne, Brisbane and Canberra.[52] Flats are now viewed as an inevitability and a necessity of the capital cities; debates are concerned less with questioning the consequences of apartments and more with their location, quantity, type and quality.

Even Canberra, Australia's suburban showcase, has adopted policies to 'create a more compact city'.[53] Northbourne Avenue and surrounding areas of Braddon and Dickson are now home to a range of new developments as part of a major infill housing program, the result

BE WHERE THE ACTION IS

Kingston Foreshore will offer a style of living completely new to Canberra. Imagine a pre-breakfast stroll or jog along the lake shore, waterside cafes and restaurants offering a tempting variety of cuisines, a cosmopolitan buzz from early morning until late in the evening—and it's all on your doorstep! Right from the start, Kingston Foreshore's own special ambience and its proximity to the shops and cafes of Kingston and Manuka will create a unique community lifestyle.

But there's more to this community than the rhythm of the city. At its soul is a feeling for Canberra's heritage. Historic buildings, including the Powerhouse, will provide facilities for cultural, arts, leisure and community activities. And peaceful landscaped parks will offer opportunities to chat with friends or simply relax and watch the world go by.

⬆ 'Kingston Foreshores: The Place to Be.' With an outdoor emphasis, Canberra advertises the apartment lifestyle.

of considerable neighbourhood planning and consultation with local residents. Townhouses and apartments formed a quarter of Canberra's dwellings in 2001, and this surprisingly high proportion is likely to increase as former industrial 'brownfields' sites are transformed into residential spaces of 'vibrant, cosmopolitan lifestyle and community'. An eight-year staged project, the mixed-use residential and commercial 37-hectare Kingston Foreshores development, is representative of this. It is the first major apartment development to take advantage of water views over Lake Burley Griffin and is marketed as 'already Canberra's most talked about address'. Brochures for the development proffer 'Kingston Foreshore: The Place to Be: Be entertained, be active, be well located, be inspired, be involved, be where the action is, be at the centre of things, be right at home, be yourself.'[54]

Improved apartment design has become a focus of bureaucrats and government architects. Former New South Wales Government Architect Chris Johnson ironically uses the life of house and garden in Australia as the referent: 'Apartments have now swung from a cheap alternative to being almost a preferred lifestyle. They need to exhibit some of the characteristics we associate with a freestanding house.'[55] These characteristics include more outdoor space, generous ceiling heights, a feeling of openness and a sense of individuality and space. The desire for apartments by a middle-class market is driving a 'phenomenal revolution in design', according to architect and former president of the RAIA Graham Jahn. He argues that contemporary apartment-dwellers seek the desired qualities of a house in apartments: increased outdoor space, larger living areas—'everything they enjoyed about living in a house re-created in an apartment'.[56] According to Mirvac's Henry Pollack, each generation wants 'more space, better finishes, more inventive design. Today my innovations are taken for granted. I might have been a trailblazer. Now the track is well established, wide and crowded.'[57]

Jahn asserts that we are in the second stage of city apartment living with the recognition that if you have a million dollars you might actually choose to live in an apartment. But he argues that we need to move to stage three, 'where apartment living would be a viable and attractive alternative for all the people living in semi-detached cottages, with the appropriate infrastructure and local amenities such as schools, shops and a high-quality public transport system'.[58] However, Jahn's ambitions continue to be sacrificed on the altar of capital gains and marketing. Leading apartment architect Camilla Block says: 'Architectural names now carry weight and the whole apartment lifestyle is being marketed as an urbane and sophisticated option. The downside, though, is that the market is still developer-driven.' The result is 'a greedy market. Designing and building for the quickest and biggest return, that's not the environment you get great architecture in and that's what we're working in.'[59]

Periods of rapid urban growth have usually featured a dramatic rise in the number of apartment buildings constructed. Conflicts between individual architectural statements and their relationship with the streetscape, adjoining building and even waterfront locations have made many apartments targets of criticism.[60] Harry Seidler's 1999 Horizon tower was widely judged to be both physically and socially inappropriate to its East Sydney location as it overlooked a street frequented by prostitutes and their clients.[61] Yet Horizon's A-list residents were among many gentrifiying the demographic and cultural milieu of the Kings Cross district.[62] That Kings Cross is today just another upmarket apartment district tells its own story.

'Jack and Jill go down the lift to fetch a babycino'

Owing to the declining affordability of housing and the desire to be close to the city, more families are living in flats, swapping the house with a backyard for an apartment. Although there has always been a quota of families in flats, the 'story of Australian childhood is being quietly rewritten'. Megan Mason explains that, instead of the nursery rhyme about Jack and Jill, she and her two-year-old daughter sing 'Jack and Jill go down the lift to fetch a babycino'.[63]

Do families choose apartments or are they forced into them because of the crisis of affordability, finding themselves priced out of over-priced suburban real estate markets? The answer appears to be yes to both questions, although there is growing evidence that many couples with one or two children are willing to forgo limited space and lack of back garden for a short commute and the retention of some form of their pre-baby cultural and urban life. This type of family is represented by Melissa Belanta and Luke Morey and their three-year-old daughter Eva Rosa. They argue that 'there was no question of swapping their Kurraba Point apartment for something 45 minutes up the Wakehurst Parkway'. Although this was partly a financial decision, it was also a lifestyle decision in that they wanted to continue to live centrally.[64]

For decades flats were criticised as being unsuitable for children; today such criticism is muted, which is perhaps the surest sign of the new acceptability of apartment living in Australia. At a private level, however, judgements are still made. Suzanne Greeves, husband Oliver and four-year-old daughter Annie moved to Sydney from New York in 2004 and lived in a Kirribilli apartment. Although apartment living is viewed as mainstream in North American and English capitals, this couple found their domestic arrangements encountered criticism: '… often other parents will just be shocked, and we come away feeling like we're depriving Annie somehow. I find myself always apologising for it or saying it's transitional.'[65]

The apartment debate has altered, but remains familiar.

Apartment living John Sharpe, Claire Armstrong and Rosie Sharpe

'We love living in an apartment, even in a family, because it's spacious, it's warm, it is north-facing with a huge deck, it's private, quiet, secure, low on maintenance and, most importantly, it's got light. We're told that every child must have a backyard. I had a backyard throughout my childhood, but I played in the street. If you know

anyone living in New York or other big metropolises, they all bring up children quite happily and successfully in apartments. It suits our lifestyle. We go out a lot, often all together as a family, and this will continue even after the second child. As soon as we go out we're in it, among urban life, not staring at the high fences and bunkered houses with blank facades that you often find in more suburban locations.'

John, like many others in their fifties, had bought an apartment off the plan for an investment, with no real intention of ever living in it. He had lived his whole life in houses and had not really considered apartment living as an alternative. When his

partner died in 2002, he decided, as an interim measure, to try living in an apartment, on Macleay Street in Sydney's groovy Potts Point, and was hooked. So too Claire had rented in a series of shared apartments in Sydney's eastern suburbs before meeting John.

Together they moved into his investment property, a penthouse on the sixth floor of Paddington Green in Sydney's eastern suburbs, before their first child was born. The apartment, designed by Devine Erby Mazlin, had more space than an average house with its three bedrooms and more than 250 square metres of internal and external space. The couple was captured by the space, light,

seclusion, harbour views and clever mix of historic site, such as the smokestack from the former Royal Hospital for Women, and the contemporary design. Theirs, like many in the upmarket range of contemporary apartments, has a selection of different architects to reduce the homogeneity of individual blocks.

Its proximity to everything means that they have all the benefits of inner-city living as well as having children's entertainments at their disposal. They can walk to places of interest, such as galleries, restaurants, cinemas and Kings Cross. It is also close to work, a ten-minute bus ride into the city, which means they rarely use their cars.

Notes

Introduction

1 Bill Randolph, quoted in Mary O'Malley, 'Storm clouds ahead: The cities of our future', *Uniken*, Issue 28, October 2005, p. 8.

2 Patrick Troy, 'Introduction: House and home', *A History of European Housing in Australia*, Cambridge University Press, Melbourne, 2000, p. 2.

3 Robin Boyd, *Australia's Home* (1952), 2nd edn, Penguin, Melbourne, 1978, p. viii.

4 Miles Lewis, *Suburban Backlash: The Battle for the World's Most Liveable City*, Bloomings, Melbourne, 1999, p. 77.

5 Peter Brew, 'Modern flats', in Simon Anderson and Meghan Nordeck, *Krantz & Sheldon Architectural Projects*, University of Western Australia, Perth, 1996, p. 5.

6 Helen Bennett, *Borrowed Mythologies: Recycling Brisbane's Inner City Heritage*, Queensland Heritage Council, Brisbane, 2005.

7 Australia has a rich tradition of survey studies, including Richard Apperly and Peter Lind, *444 Sydney Buildings*, Angus & Robertson, Sydney, 1971; Robert Irving et al., *Identifying Australian Architecture*, Angus & Robertson, Sydney, 1989; Graham Jahn, *Sydney Architecture*, Watermark Press, Sydney, 1997; Philip Goad, *Melbourne Architecture*, Watermark Press, Sydney, 1999; and Davina Jackson and Chris Johnson, *Australian Architecture Now*, Thames & Hudson, London, 2000.

8 Apartment design is a feature of several architect studies, including Kenneth Frampton, *Harry Seidler: Four Decades of Architecture*, Thames & Hudson, London, 1992; Conrad Hamann, *Cities of Hope: Australian Architecture and Design by Edmond and Corrigan*, Oxford University Press, Melbourne, 1993; and Trevor Howells, *Allen Jack + Cottier, 1952–2002*, Focus Publishing, Edgecliff, NSW, 2003.

9 Elizabeth Hawes, *New York, New York: How the Apartment House Transformed the Life of the City*, Knopf, New York, 1993, pp. 19–23.

10 Stephen Gardiner, *The Evolution of the House*, Constable, London, 1975, p. 93.

11 Seamus O'Hanlon, *Together Apart: Boarding House, Hostel and Flat Life in Pre-war Melbourne*, Australian Scholarly Publishing, Melbourne, 2002, p. 101.

12 Andrew Alpern, *Luxury Apartment Houses of Manhattan: An Illustrated History*, Dover Publications, New York, 1992, p. 11, quoted in ibid.

13 E. A. Partridge, *Short Etymological Dictionary of Modern English*, Greenwich House Crown Publishers, New York, 1983, pp. 473, 219.

14 Hawes, *New York, New York*, pp. 19–25.

15 *Decoration and Glass*, January 1938, p. 10.

1 Slums of the future?: A century of controversy

1 *Sydney Morning Herald*, 26 September 1925.

2 ibid.

3 *Sydney Morning Herald*, 13 June 1968, p. 7.

4 *Sydney Morning Herald*, 9 June 2006, p. 3.

5 Bill Randolph, 'Higher density communities: Current trends and future implications', *Strata and Community Title in Australia for the 21st Century Conference*, 31 August–3 September 2005, Gold Coast, p. 6.

6 *Building*, May 1911, pp. 76–7.

7 *Royal Commission for the Improvement of the City of Sydney and Its Suburbs*, NSWPP, 1909, vol. 5, question 3070, evidence of the Rev. George Campbell.

8 'Sydney, the Cinderella of cities', *Lone Hand*, vol. 1, no. 1, May 1907, p. 56.

9 Frank Walker, 'The passing of the "The Rocks" ', *Australian Field*, 25 January 1902, p. 26.

10 Deyan Sudjic, *Home: The Twentieth-century House*, Laurence King, London, 1999, p. 12.

11 *A Tenement Story: The History of 97 Orchard Street and the Lower East Side Tenement Museum*, New York City, Lower East Side Tenement

12 Sudjic, *Home*, p. 12.

13 *Royal Commission for the Improvement of the City of Sydney and Its Suburbs*, p. lv.

14 J. D. Fitzgerald, 'The improvement of Sydney', *Sydney Mail*, 10 June 1908, p. 1513.

15 *Royal Commission for the Improvement of the City of Sydney and Its Suburbs*, question 2707.

16 ibid., p. lv.

17 ibid., p. xxviii.

18 *Sydney Morning Herald*, 10 April 1914, p. 7.

19 J. J. C. Bradfield, 'The trend of modern railway development in thickly populated cities: With special reference to the requirements of the city of Sydney', Lecture to Sydney University Union, 27 July 1917, p. 40.

20 J. J. C. Bradfield, 'Sydney—Health and the traffic problem', written commentary to showing of slides 34, 35 and 36, Lectures and Addresses, 1915–17, No. 2, National Library of Australia, 4712/3/2, pp. 14–15.

21 J. J. C. Bradfield, 'Population and transportation problems of the city of Sydney', Town Planning Association of New South Wales, Royal Society's Hall, Elizabeth Street, Sydney, 6 November 1916, p. 19, Bradfield Papers, Lectures and Addresses 1915–17, No. 27, National Library of Australia, 4712/3/2.

22 *Building*, May 1925, p. 55.

23 *First (Progress) Report: Slum Reclamation*, Government Printer, Melbourne, 1937, p. 5.

24 Speech of Mr Prendergast, *Parliamentary Debates: Legislative Assembly*, Victoria, 13 August 1936, p. 924.

25 *Sydney Morning Herald*, 25 August 1937, p. 15.

26 *Sydney Morning Herald*, 24 August 1937, p. 11.

27 Petition,1938, New South Wales Department of Housing Library.

28 *Sydney Morning Herald*, 4 October 1937, p. 11.

29 *Sydney Morning Herald*, 25 August 1937, p. 15.

30 *Sydney Morning Herald*, 27 August 1937, p. 11.

31 John Henderson, 'One family one house', *Australian Home Builder*, April 1924, p. 33.

32 'The home—or the flat', *Building*, May 1915, pp. 125–6.

33 *Daily Telegraph*, 13 August 1921.

34 'How not to house', Editorial, *Evening News*, Sydney, 29 October 1919, n.p., clipping in scrapbook, Bradfield 50, 'Town planning and housing', Materials from the Professional Library of J. J. C. Bradfield relating to engineering, railways, bridges, etc., Sydney University Rare Books Library.

35 *Art and Architecture*, August 1905, p. 120.

36 *Sydney Morning Herald*, women's supplement, 26 September 1935, p. 10.

37 Kylie Tennant, *Time Enough Later*, Macmillan, London, 1945, p. 163.

38 George Johnston, *My Brother Jack*, William Collins, Melbourne, 1964, pp. 28–9.

39 Quoted in Geoffrey Dutton, *Kenneth Slessor: A Biography*, Viking, Melbourne, 1991, p. 41.

40 Stonnington Thematic Environmental History, Section 8.6, City of Stonnington, www.stonnington.vic.gov.au.

41 Hal Porter, *The Paper Chase*, Angus & Robertson, Sydney, 1966, p. 30.

42 *Hornsby Advocate*, 7 June 1929.

43 *Sydney Morning Herald*, 22 August 1939, p. 12.

44 New South Wales Parliamentary Debates, 21 November 1928, pp. 1952–3.

45 *Building*, September 1937, p. 87. See also *Sydney Morning Herald*, 1 October 1937, p. 20; 7 October, p. 10.

46 *Sydney Morning Herald*, 28 July 1936, p. 10.

47 Donald Dunbar, 'Virtual dreams—Living realities', *Fifth Australian Urban History Planning Conference Proceedings*, University of South Australia, Adelaide, 2000, p. 139.

48 Nora Cooper, 'The modern flat in Sydney', *Australian Home Beautiful*, February 1934, p. 20.

49 Jenny Gregory and Robyn Taylor, ' "The slums of tommorrow"? Architects, builders and the construction of flats in interwar Perth', in Frank Broeze (ed.),

Private Enterprise, Government and Society: Studies in Western Australian History, Centre for Western Australian History, Perth, 1992, pp. 82–6.

50 Harold Krantz, 'Flats: The sociological and economic aspect', *Building*, February 1942, p. 11.
51 *Sydney Morning Herald*, 24 July 1956, p. 11.
52 Harry Seidler, *Houses, Interiors and Projects*, Horwitz, Sydney, 1954, p. xii.
53 *Building*, January 1951, p. 30.
54 Denis Winston, 'What makes a city "great"?', *Journal of the Town Planning Institute*, vol. 61, no. 3, February 1955, p. 65.
55 Denis Winston, 'The problem', *Architecture in Australia*, June 1962, p. 56.
56 *Sydney Morning Herald*, 6 May 1958, p. 3.
57 Alan Gilbert, 'The roots of anti-suburbanism in Australia', in S. L. Goldberg and F. B. Smith (eds), *Australian Cultural History*, Cambridge University Press, Melbourne, 1989.
58 *Sunday Telegraph*, 23 February 1964.
59 J. H. Shaw, 'Planner's support of C.C.C. code on foreshores', *Sydney Morning Herald*, 17 November 1959, p. 27.
60 *Sunday Mirror*, 24 May 1964.
61 *Sun-Herald*, 24 March 1968.
62 *Nation*, 30 May 1964, p. 21.
63 Rob Hillier, *Let's Buy a Terrace House*, Ure Smith, Sydney, 1968, p. 7.
64 Vincent Smith, 'The battle of Victoria Street', *Architecture in Australia*, June 1976, pp. 36–45.
65 Jack Mundey, *Green Bans and Beyond*, Angus & Robertson, Sydney, 1981, p. 111.
66 Meredith Burgmann and Verity Burgmann, *Green Bans, Red Union: Environmental Activism and the New South Wales Builders' Labourers' Federation*, UNSW Press, Sydney, 1998.
67 *Sydney Morning Herald*, 21 June 1982.
68 Ruth Park, *Poor Man's Orange* (1949), Penguin, Melbourne, 1977, p. 38.
69 *The High Rise: A Paper Profiling Ministry of Housing and Construction High Rise Accommodation*, Ministry of Housing, Melbourne, 1990.
70 Quoted in George Tibbits, ' "The enemy within our gates": Slum clearance and high-rise flats', in Renate Howe (ed.), *New Houses for Old: Fifty Years of Public Housing in Victoria*, Ministry for Housing, Melbourne, 1988, p. 143.
71 Kay Hargreaves, *This House Not for Sale: Conflicts Between the Housing Commission and the Residents of Slum Reclamation Areas*, Centre for Urban Research and Action, Melbourne, 1976, p. 4.
72 John Larkin, 'Fears and dreams of high-rise kids', *Age*, 24 December 1971, p. 7.
73 Quoted in Lauren Costello, 'From prisons to penthouses: The changing images of high-rise living in Melbourne', *Housing Studies*, January 2005, p. 55.
74 Randolph, 'Higher density communities: Current trends and future implications', p. 8.
75 Michael Duffy, 'Sydney isn't full, so let's stop the rot', *Sydney Morning Herald*, 17 September 2005, p. 37.
76 'Fitzroy gets set for new development battle', *Age*, 1 June 2002.
77 'Another big night for the Espy', *Age*, 20 February 2003; Richard Peterson, 'Esplanade Hotel', *A Place of Sensuous Resort: Buildings of St Kilda and Their People*, St Kilda Historical Society, Melbourne, 2005, www.skhs.org.au/SKHSbuildings.
78 'Three-storey height limit for suburbs', *Age*, 29 October 2002.
79 T. Dick, 'Our days in the sun may be numbered', *Sydney Morning Herald*, 22 June 2004, p. 1.
80 Quoted in K. McKenzie, 'Battle of Ku-ring-gai', Domain, *Sydney Morning Herald*, 16–17 November 2002, p. 4a.

Case study: Blues Point Tower
1 Anne Susskind, 'Harry's dream', *Sydney Morning Herald*, 31 July 1995.
2 *Sydney Morning Herald*, 9 February 1960.
3 David Dale, 'Eyeful tower', *Sydney Morning Herald*, 18 May 1991, p. 46.

Case study: Melbourne Terrace
1 Craig McGregor, 'Stretch of the imagination', *Good Weekend*, 3 June 1995, pp. 24–5.

2 Commodious and comfortable flats: The first apartments
1 *Report of the Commission of Inquiry into the Question of the Housing of Workmen in Europe and America*, Government Printer, Sydney, 1913, pp. 98–9.
2 *Sydney Morning Herald*, 26 October 1923, p. 8.
3 Jan Roberts (ed.), *The Astor*, Ruskin Rowe Press, Sydney, 2003.
4 Streeton produced *Sydney Harbour from The Astor* in 1922. Will Ashton's *Macquarie Street from The Astor* was painted about 1925.
5 *Sands' Directory*: Cromer Club, W. Marshall, caretaker, 1900, p. 110; Cromer, Mrs Alfred Wilshire, manageress, in *Sands' Directory*, 1905, p. 116; Cromer, residential chambers, Mrs Alfred Wilshire, 1915, p. 128.
6 *Art and Architecture*, February 1905, p. 214.
7 *Art and Architecture*, August 1905, pp. 120–1.
8 *Building*, January 1910, p. 39.
9 *Evening News*, 23 July 1921.
10 *Building*, January 1915, p. 70.
11 Michael Gross, *740 Park: The Story of the World's Richest Apartment Building*, Broadway Books, New York, 2005, pp. 19–25.
12 Fitzgerald, 'The improvement of Sydney', p. 1513.
13 *Art and Architecture*, August 1905, pp. 120–1.
14 Letter of Charles Turner to David Syme, 2 March 1905, Syme Papers, State Library of Victoria, MS9751, Box 1190/4.
15 *The Leader*, 15 December 1906, p. 14.
16 Boyd, *Australia's Home*, p. 110.
17 *Sydney Morning Herald*, 27 February 1919, p. 6.
18 'A new and handsome two-flat home', *Australian Home Beautiful*, October 1927, p. 19.
19 *Building*, September 1937, p. 87.
20 Fitzgerald, 'The improvement of Sydney', p. 1513.
21 Ruth Thompson, 'Sydney's flats: A social and political history', PhD thesis, School of History, Philosophy and Politics, Macquarie University, 1986, p. 22.
22 *Sydney Morning Herald*, 16 March 1912.
23 *Real Property Annual*, 1913, p. 23, quoted in T. Sawyer, 'Residential flats in Melbourne: The development of a building type to 1950', research report, 5th year Architecture, University of Melbourne, 1982, p. 10.
24 *Sydney Morning Herald*, 26 October 1923, p. 8.
25 Thompson, 'Sydney's flats: A social and political history', pp. 100–3.
26 *Evening News*, 23 July 1921.
27 *Building*, February 1915, p. 92.
28 Bradfield, 'Population and transportation problems of the city of Sydney', p. 34.
29 Dymphna Cusack, *Jungfrau* (1936), Penguin, Melbourne, 1989, pp. 6–7.
30 The percentage of increases in tenements and flats in capital cities were: Hobart 959%; Sydney 611%; Melbourne 541%; Adelaide 289%; Brisbane 156%; Perth 83%. Source: Commonwealth Census, 1921; *Sydney Morning Herald*, 3 November 1923, p. 17.
31 Thompson, 'Sydney's flats: A social and political history', p. 55.
32 ibid., p. 20.
33 M. A. Harris, *Where to Live: ABC Guide to Sydney and Suburbs*, Marchant & Co., Sydney, 1917, p. 6.
34 Rockcliff Mansions, Neutral Bay, prospectus belonging to Messrs Raine & Horne, Stanton Library Local History Collection; *Building*, January 1930, p. 115.
35 These plans were part of a full account of his Sydney Harbour Bridge and City Railway Scheme, submitted for Bradfield's thesis, 'The city and suburban electric railways and the Sydney Harbour Bridge', Doctor of Science in Engineering, University of Sydney.
36 ibid., p. 31, and repeated verbatim in *Architecture*, 15 October 1921, pp. 101–2.

37 Bradfield, 'The town planning aspect', in ibid., p. 265.

38 *Building*, December 1912, p. 64.

39 *Building*, March 1919, p. 90.

40 Basil Burdett, 'Melbourne takes to flats', *The Home*, April 1936, p. 30.

41 'Lawson Flats', Register of Heritage Places—Assessment documentation, Perth, Heritage Council of Western Australia, 2001.

42 James Weirick, 'Spirituality and symbolism in the work of the Griffins', in Anne Watson (ed.), *Beyond Architecture: Marion Mahony and Walter Burley Griffin*, Powerhouse Publishing, Sydney, 1998, p. 68.

Case study: Strickland Flats

1 *Sydney Morning Herald*, 27 March 1914, p. 10.

2 ibid.

3 *Building*, August 1916, pp. 46–8.

4 John Sulman, *Town Planning in Australia*, Government Printing Office, Sydney, 1921, pp. 199–200.

5 Gina Ghioni, *Waterloo: A Case Study of Public Housing and Redevelopment in Sydney*, School of Architecture, University of Sydney, 1990, pp. 16–18.

Case study: Kingsclere

1 *Building*, December 1912, p. 64.

2 *Building*, January 1915, p. 68.

3 Jennifer Hill, *The Development of the Architecture in the Kings Cross Elizabeth Bay Area*, Architectural Projects for the New South Wales Heritage Office, Sydney, 2004.

3 The pulsing heart of city life: Inner-city apartments 1920–50

1 *Evening News*, 6 April 1921.

2 *Building*, November 1923, p. 44.

3 Harris, *Where to Live*, p. 93.

4 *Sydney Morning Herald*, 16 March 1927, p. 11.

5 Richard Cardew, 'Flats in Sydney: The thirty per cent solution?', in Jill Roe (ed.), *Twentieth-century Sydney*, Hale & Iremonger, Sydney, 1980, pp. 73, 77.

6 *Sydney Morning Herald*, 10 November 1937, p. 16.

7 'The locality and surroundings of to-day', Stanton & Son Ltd, Sydney, n.d.

8 Potts Point, Tusculum House and Grounds Estate, Subdivision Plan, 1922, Mitchell Library.

9 *Sydney Morning Herald*, 16 March 1927, p. 11.

10 Kenneth Slessor, 'A portrait of Sydney', *Bread and Wine: Selected Prose*, Angus & Robertson, Sydney, 1970, p. 4.

11 Peter Kirkpatrick, *The Sea Coast of Bohemia: Literary Life in Sydney's Roaring Twenties*, University of Queensland Press, St Lucia, Qld, 1992, p. 50.

12 Thompson, 'Sydney's flats: A social and political history', p. 39.

13 *New South Wales Parliamentary Debates*, 9 May 1940, p. 8415.

14 *Decoration and Glass*, October 1938, pp. 32–3.

15 Marion George, 'The flat-dweller: Tortured by noise', *Sydney Morning Herald*, 27 February 1929, p. 16.

16 'A small flat in the new manner', *The Home*, May 1934, p. 47.

17 Peter McNeil, 'Decorating the home: Australian interior decoration between the wars', *Art & Australia*, Summer 1995, pp. 222–31.

18 *The Home*, January 1929, p. 36; May 1934, p. 21.

19 *The Home*, November 1926, p. 38.

20 Lionel Frost, 'The urban history literature of Australia and New Zealand', *Journal of Urban History*, vol. 22, no. 1, November 1995, p. 143.

21 *Australian Home Builder*, July 1924, quoted in O'Hanlon, *Together Apart*, p. 123.

22 'Rising residential land values', *Australian Home Builder*, March 1924, p. 55.

23 'A new and handsome two-flat home', *Australian Home Beautiful*, October 1927, p. 18.

24 Burdett, 'Melbourne takes to flats', pp. 30, 32.

25 Dunbar, 'Virtual dreams—Living realities', p. 143.

26 *Building*, August 1938, p. 25.

27 Nora Cooper, 'Home life in the modern flat', *Australian Home Beautiful*, October 1933, pp. 8, 12.

28 Donald Dunbar, 'Australian flats: A comparison of Melbourne and Sydney flat developments in the interwar period', PhD thesis, University of Melbourne, 1998, vol. 1, p. 101.

29 *Building*, July 1930, p. 123.

30 W. Watson Sharp, 'Records the young architect's lecture on flat design', *Decoration and Glass*, August 1937, p. 14.

31 *Building*, July 1943, p. 8.

32 Quoted in Geoffrey Serle, *Robin Boyd: A Life*, Melbourne University Press, Melbourne, 1995, p. 55.

33 *Building*, October 1941, pp. 19, 21; November 1942, p. 8.

34 *Building*, February 1941, p. 36.

35 *Architecture*, September 1917, p. 55.

36 'A new factor in construction', *Building*, January 1910, p. 39.

37 *Sydney Morning Herald*, 28 July 1936, p. 10. See also the views of Leslie Wilkinson, Sydney University's professor of architecture, *Sydney Morning Herald*, 28 February 1936, p. 10.

38 Peter Kaad, 'We can have air, coolness and warmth …', *Art in Australia*, August 1940, p. 89.

39 Morton Herman, 'Urban housing', *Architecture*, October 1937, p. 226.

40 Philip Goad, 'Best Overend—Pioneer modernist in Melbourne', *Fabrications*, June 1994, pp. 106–10.

41 Best Overend, 'A minimum flat with maximum comfort', *Australian Home Beautiful*, September 1933, p. 29.

42 'Modern flats in Toorak', *Art in Australia*, March 1941, p. 78.

43 Robin Boyd, *Victorian Modern: One Hundred and Eleven Years of Modern Architecture in Melbourne*, Architectural Students' Society of the Royal Victorian Institute of Architects, 1947.

44 Harriet Edquist, *Frederick Romberg: The Architecture of Migration*, RMIT, Melbourne, 2000.

45 'Victorian scene', *Architecture*, January–March, 1951, p. 51.

46 *Building*, January 1949, p. 19.

47 Leslie Rees, 'Sydney after nine years', *The Home*, July 1936, p. 24.

48 *Decoration and Glass*, December 1936, p. 11.

49 *Sydney Morning Herald*, Women's Supplement, 26 September 1935, p. 10.

50 *Building*, February 1935, p. 105.

51 *Decoration and Glass*, July 1936, p. 10.

52 ibid., p. 9.

53 Nora Cooper, 'Wyldefels', *Australian Home Beautiful*, December 1936, pp. 10, 11.

54 Sydney Ure Smith, 'The aesthetic beauty of Sydney', *Architecture*, August 1938, p. 181.

55 *Sydney Morning Herald*, 4 June 1935, p. 3.

56 'Emil Sodersten', *Art in Australia*, November 1934, p. 92.

57 Donald Leslie Johnson, *Australian Architecture 1901–1951: Sources of Modernism*, Sydney University Press, 1980, p. 145.

58 *Building*, October 1934, p. 17.

59 *Building*, March 1936, p. 102.

60 'Cliffside Flats', Queensland Heritage Register, Environment Protection Agency, Brisbane, 2005; Robert Riddel, 'Avalon: A brief history', in Ricardo Felipe (ed.), *Avalon: Art and Life of an Apartment Building*, Museum of Brisbane, Brisbane, 2005.

61 'Julius Street Flats', Queensland Heritage Register, Environment Protection Agency, Brisbane, 2005.

62 *Building*, October 1934, p. 28.

63 Krantz, 'Flats: The sociological and economic aspect', p. 11.

64 Gregory and Taylor, ' "The slums of tommorrow"? Architects, builders and the construction of flats in interwar Perth', pp. 86–9. See also David Bromfield (ed.), *Aspects of Perth Modernism 1929–1942*, Centre for Fine Arts, UWA, Perth, 1986, pp. 29–30.

65 *Daily News*, 12 January 1938, p. 9.

Case study: Cairo

1 'The modern flat', *Australian Home Beautiful*, February 1934, p. 20.
2 Boyd, *Australia's Home*, p. 290.
3 Tulla Keating, 'Luxury-economy bachelor flats', *Australian Home Beautiful*, April 1937, p. 17.
4 Christopher Wilk (ed.), *Modernism: Designing a New World*, V&A Publications, London, 2006, pp. 184–7.

Case study: Marlborough Hall

1 'The Soderstens', *Decoration and Glass*, August 1936, p. 54.
2 *Decoration and Glass*, April 1938, p. 32.
3 'Luxury flats for moderate incomes', prospectus, Seven Elizabeth Street, Limited, Sydney, 1937.
4 'A young man with ideas', *People*, 10 May 1950, p. 27.

4 A new style of living: Inner-city apartments 1950–80

1 Ian McKay et al., *Living and Partly Living in Australia*, Nelson, Melbourne, 1971, p. 58.
2 *Architecture in Australia*, March 1964, p. 150.
3 McKay et al., *Living and Partly Living in Australia*, p. 58.
4 Prospectus, Domain Park Residential Suites, Lend Lease Development Pty Ltd, Melbourne, c. 1960.
5 *Age*, 18 August 1971, p. 9.
6 Frank Clarke, *Corporate Collapse: Accounting, Regulatory and Ethical Failure*, Cambridge University Press, Melbourne, 2003, pp. 55–65.
7 Dick Dusseldorp (1961) quoted in Lindie Clark, *Finding a Common Interest: The Story of Dick Dusseldorp and Lend Lease*, Cambridge University Press, Melbourne, 2002, pp. 174–5.
8 Dick Morath quoted in ibid., p. 176.
9 ibid., p. 181. Victoria's *Transfer of Land (Stratum Estates) Act 1960* introduced a form of strata title but was largely unworkable as it lacked provisions for the management of common property. The *Strata Titles Act 1967* introduced bodies corporate on the New South Wales model.
10 *Daily Telegraph*, 22 October 1958. The group of nine architects included Harry Seidler, Lyle Dunlop, Richard Fitzhardinge, Harry Howard, Ivan Seifert, Andrew Young, Philip Jackson, Douglas Gordon and Michael Boyle.
11 See Harry Seidler archives, 'McMahon's Point Planning', 1958, Mitchell Library, Locn no. MLMSS 7078/7.
12 *Sydney Morning Herald*, 12 January 1957, p. 9.
13 Harry Seidler and others, *Urban Redevelopment Concerns You!*, McMahons Point and Lavender Bay Progress Association, Sydney, 1957.
14 *Daily Telegraph*, 22 October 1958.
15 *Sun-Herald*, 26 October 1958.
16 ibid.
17 *Sydney Morning Herald*, 26 April 1957.
18 *Daily Telegraph*, 20 January 1962.
19 *Sunday Telegraph*, 23 February 1964.
20 *Sydney Morning Herald*, 12 May 1961.
21 'Rapid progress in communal housing plans abroad', newspaper clipping in Seidler archives, no publication given, Harry Seidler & Associates.
22 Prospectus, Ithaca Gardens Apartments.
23 *Building*, June 1951, p. 55.
24 *Nation*, 30 May 1964, pp. 21–2.
25 Harry Seidler, 'Blues Point Tower—A self-contained vertical community', *Architecture and Arts*, November 1958, p. 21.
26 *Building: Lighting: Engineering*, January 1961, p. 28.
27 *Architecture and Arts*, October 1957, p. 13.
28 *Architecture and Arts*, September 1960, p. 19.
29 *Cross-section*, February 1959.
30 *Building: Lighting: Engineering*, January 1961, p. 28.
31 *Sydney Morning Herald*, 7 July 1959, p. 17.
32 *Sydney Morning Herald*, 8 July 1958, p. 6; *Sydney Morning Herald*, 18 May 1959, p. 13.
33 *Building: Lighting: Engineering*, January 1960, p. 61.
34 *Sydney Morning Herald*, 18 May 1959, p. 13.
34 *Architecture and Arts*, February 1960, p. 32.
36 Rebecca Hawcroft, 'The untold story: Migrants and modernism', *Architecture Bulletin*, vol. 2, 2005, p. 6; 'A young man with ideas', *People*, 10 May 1950, pp. 25–7.
37 *New South Wales Official Yearbook*, 1976, p. 84.
38 A. R. Hall, 'Housing trends and economic growth', *Architecture in Australia*, June 1962, p. 61.
39 *Commonwealth of Australia Yearbook*, 1965, p. 352; *Commonwealth of Australia Yearbook*, 1968, p. 212.
40 *New South Wales Official Yearbook*, 1969, pp. 56, 425.
41 *Sydney Morning Herald*, 12 September 1959, p. 2.
42 April Hersey, 'Home units', *Australian House and Garden*, June 1966, p. 33.
43 Cardew, 'Flats in Sydney: The thirty per cent solution', pp. 80–1.
44 A. R. Hall, 'Housing trends and economic growth', *Architecture in Australia*, June 1962, p. 60.
45 *Commonwealth of Australia Yearbook*, 1965, p. 353; *Commonwealth of Australia Yearbook*, 1973, p. 194.
46 R. V. Cardew, *Flats: A Study of Occupants and Locations*, Ian Buchan Fell Reseach Project on Housing, University of Sydney, Sydney, 1970, p. 115.
47 Thompson, 'Sydney's flats: A social and political history', pp. 144–6.
48 *Sun-Herald*, 3 March 1968. See also 'Inside a high rise jungle', *Sydney Morning Herald*, 3 October 1970, p. 19.
49 For example, 'New "swinger" apartments at North Ryde', *Sydney Morning Herald*, 12 November 1970, p. 16.
50 Robert Drewe, 'Eighty per cent humidity', in *The Bodysurfers*, Picador, Sydney, 1987, p. 144.
51 *Age*, 17 April 1959, p. 18.
52 *Building*, October 1953, p. 58; May 1954, p. 61.
53 *Age*, 26 September 1959, p. 10.
54 Robin Boyd, 'The neighbourhood', in MacKay et al., *Living and Partly Living in Australia*, p. 36.
55 *Age*, 23 June 1960, p. 3.
56 Ernest Fooks, *X-ray the City! The Density Diagram: Basis for Urban Planning*, Ruskin Press, Melbourne, 1946, p. 69.
57 Harriet Edquist, *Ernest Fooks: Architect*, RMIT, Melbourne, 2001, p. 16.
58 Ernest Fooks, 'Two decades of flat developments in Australia', *Architecture and Arts*, October 1960, p. 31.
59 Harriet Edquist, *Kurt Popper: From Vienna to Melbourne Architect 1935–1975*, RMIT, Melbourne, 2002, pp. 18–19.
60 Peterson, 'Edgewater Towers', in *A Place of Sensuous Resort*.
61 *Architecture and Arts*, August 1961, p. 62.
62 *Building*, February 1959, p. 27.
63 *Sunday Mirror*, 24 May 1964.
64 *Building: Lighting: Engineering*, March 1963, pp. 15–22.
65 *Architecture Australia*, June 1963, p. 54.
66 David Hickie, *The Prince and the Premier*, Angus & Robertson, Sydney, 1985, pp. 75–84.
67 *Architecture in Australia*, October 1975, p. 93.
68 *Architecture in Australia*, August 1969, p. 617.
69 *Architecture in Australia*, August 1969, pp. 625–32, February 1970, pp. 123–5, Richard Apperly and Peter Lind, *444 Sydney Buildings*, Angus & Robertson, Sydney, 1971, p. 54.
70 Jennifer Taylor, *Australian Architecture Since 1960*, Law Book Company, Sydney, 1986, pp. 148–9.
71 *Architecture in Austalia*, June 1967, p. 420.

Case study: Wylde Street Cooperative Apartments

1 *Art in Australia*, August 1938, p. 62.
2 *Building*, September 1951, p. 20.
3 Interview with John Davis by S McHugh, 24 February 2003, Caroline Simpson Research Library Collection, Historic Houses Trust of New South Wales.

Case study: Torbreck

1   David Malouf, *Johnno: A Novel*, University of Queensland Press, St Lucia, Qld, 1975, p. 51.
2   *Architecture and Arts*, November 1961, p. 30.

5 Homes for working couples: Public apartments

1   Housing Commission of New South Wales, *Changing Face of a City*, Government Printer, Sydney, c. 1965.
2   *Annual Report of the Housing Board*, 1914, Government Printer, Sydney, p. 4.
3   ibid., p. 3.
4   Ghioni, *Waterloo*, pp. 7, 8.
5   *Royal Commission for the Improvement of the City of Sydney and Its Suburbs*, question 2436.
6   *Annual Report of Sydney Harbour Trust 1912*, Government Printer, Sydney, 1912, p. 3.
7   *Annual Report of Sydney Harbour Trust 1911*, Government Printer, Sydney, 1911, p. 24.
8   Max Kelly, *Anchored in a Small Cove: A History and Archaeology of the Rocks*, Sydney Cove Authority, Sydney, pp. 93–7.
9   *Daily Telegraph*, 2 February 1912, p. 1.
10 *Report of the Royal Commission for the Improvement of the City of Sydney and Its Suburbs*, question 2709.
11 *Building*, May 1911, p. 77.
12 Peter John Cantrill and Philip Thalis, 'The urban project in Sydney', *Architecture Bulletin*, July 1991, pp. 14–15.
13 *Annual Report of the Housing Board*, 1914, Government Printer, Sydney, p. 2.
14 *Sydney Morning Herald*, 3 December 1925, p. 11.
15 Dunbar, 'Australian flats: A comparison of Melbourne and Sydney flat developments in the interwar period', vol. 1, p. 161.
16 *Municipal Council of Sydney Competition for Workmen's Dwellings Way's Terrace Site Pyrmont Report*, 8 October 1923, City of Sydney Archives Record TC 2152/23, Part 2.
17 *Building*, November 1923, pp. 44, 47.
18 Shirley Fitzgerald, *Sydney 1842–1992*, Hale & Iremonger, Sydney, 1992, pp. 228–31.
19 A. Davey, 'James Peddle: Craftsman architect 1862–1930', vol. 2, thesis for Bachelor of Architecture, 1981, University of New South Wales, p. 99.
20 *Sydney Morning Herald*, 17 February 1934, p. 14. See also *Building*, February 1934, pp. 31, 32.
21 Morton Herman, 'The Erskineville Rehousing Scheme', *Art in Australia*, February 1939, p. 68.
22 ibid., p. 69.
23 *Building*, December 1938, p. 29.
24 *Sydney Morning Herald*, 4 May 1937, p. 16.
25 William McKell, *Five Critical Years: Story of the McKell Labor Government May 1941–May 1946*, ALP, Sydney, 1946, pp. 101–2.
26 Walter Bunning, *Homes in the Sun: The Past, Present and Future of Australian Housing*, W. J. Nesbit, Sydney, 1945, pp. 7–8.
27 ibid., p. 76.
28 'Multi-unit dwellings under the Commonwealth and State Housing Agreement', *Australian Housing*, June 1949, pp. 93–4.
29 Cardew, 'Flats in Sydney: The thirty per cent solution?', p. 79; Cardew, *Flats: A Study of Occupants and Locations*, p. 3.
30 P. J. Gordon, 'Housing in Sweden', *Building and Engineering*, June 1948, p. 38.
31 'Australia's largest flat development', *Building and Engineering*, March 1954, pp. 19–22.
32 *Annual Report*, Housing Commission of New South Wales, 1954, Sydney, p. 18.
33 Newspaper clipping from Seidler archives 1956, no publication given.
34 'Greenway is the new way', *Australasian Post*, 8 April 1954, p. 14.

35 Thompson, 'Sydney's flats: A social and political history', pp. 88–90.
36 'Wandana Apartment Block', Heritage Council of Western Australia, Register of Heritage Places—Assessment documentation, Perth, 2001.
37 Housing Commission Victoria, *The Enemy Within Our Gates*, Government Printer, Melbourne, 1966, p. 1.
38 Housing Commission Victoria, *Annual Report 1962–63*, Government Printer, Melbourne, 1963.
39 Housing Commission Victoria, *The Enemy Within Our Gates*, p. 5.
40 Housing Commission Victoria, *Annual Report 1959–60*, Melbourne, Government Printer, 1960, p. 11.
41 Housing Commission Victoria, *Annual Report 1962–63*, p. 9.
42 Colin Clark, 'The child on the balcony', *Sydney Morning Herald*, 3 December 1970, p. 2.
43 Housing Commission Victoria, *Annual Report 1967–68*, Government Printer, Melbourne, 1968.
44 *Age*, 12 September 1959, p. 3.
45 Housing Commission Victoria, *The Enemy Within Our Gates*, p. 4.
46 Boyd, 'The neighbourhood', in McKay et al., *Living and Partly Living in Australia*, pp. 38–9.
47 Housing Commission Victoria, *Housing is People: The Policy and Operations of the Housing Commission*, Housing Commission, Melbourne, 1972.
48 'Higher density city housing', *Building: Lighting: Engineering*, 24 October 1958, pp. 44–5.
49 Housing Commission of New South Wales, *Changing Face of a City*.
50 Housing Commission of New South Wales, 'Flats and shops', 1950, p. 1.
51 'Huge new flat project for Redfern', *Building: Lighting: Engineering*, April 1961, p. 28.
52 *Annual Report of the Housing Commission of New South Wales 1974*, Sydney, 1974, p. 5.
53 Ghioni, *Waterloo*, pp. 51–6; 'Minister hits at high-rise family units', *Sydney Morning Herald*, 7 August 1973, p. 11.
54 Housing Commission Victoria, *Annual Report 1973–74*, Government Printer, Melbourne, 1974, p. 1.
55 Housing Commission Victoria, *Annual Report 1976–77*, Government Printer, Melbourne, 1977, p. 3.
56 L. H. S. Thompson, 'Housing Commission of Victoria', *Architecture in Australia*, June 1962, p. 71.
57 Anne Stevenson et al., *High Living: A Study of Family Life in Flats*, Melbourne University Publishing, Melbourne, 1967, p. 81.
58 For example, A. J. Sutton and D. T. Richmond, *Walk Up or High Rise? Residents' Views on Public Housing*, Macquarie University, Sydney, 1977; *Waterloo Development Proposals: Analysis of Options and Environmental Impact Statement*, Housing Commission of New South Wales, Sydney, 1976, pp. 11–28ff.
59 *Sun-Herald*, 3 August 1958, p. 5.
60 M. A. Jones, *Housing and Poverty in Australia*, Melbourne University Press, Melbourne, 1972, p. 180.
61 Mora Main quoted in Ghioni, *Waterloo*, Appendix C2, p. 3.
62 Jones, *Housing and Poverty in Australia*, p. 179.
63 Julian Thomas, 'Wiring Atherton Gardens', *Griffith Review*, Autumn 2004, pp. 208–14.
64 Housing Commission of New South Wales, *Housing Commission Projects in the Sydney Region*, Sydney, c. 1970.
65 *Sydney Morning Herald*, 2 December 2004, p. 10.
66 Robert Staas, 'Samuel Lipson', *Architecture Bulletin*, May 1994, p. 19.
67 Gavin Souter and George Molnar, *Sydney Observed*, Angus & Robertson, Sydney, 1968, pp. 78–9.
68 Phillip Mar, 'Home in the tower block: Modernism, public housing and social memory', *Social Inequality Today*, Macquarie University, 2003.
69 *Sydney Morning Herald*, 23 November 2004, p. 12.
70 Housing Commission Victoria, *Housing is People*.

Case study: Northbourne Housing

1 Peter Ward, 'Leave a period piece in peace', *Weekend Australian Review*, 16 August 1997, p. 16.
2 ibid.
3 'Northbourne Housing Group', www.canberrahouse.com.au.
4 'Community housing', *Architecture in Australia*, March 1965, p. 135.
5 Personal communication with Professor Richard Clough, the first landscape architect for the National Capital Development Commission.

Case study: Atherton Gardens

1 Patrick Wright, *A Journey Through Ruins: The Last Days of London*, Radius, London, 1991, chapter 7.
2 Office of Housing, Neighbourhood Renewal Unit, www.neighbourhoodrenewal.vic.gov.au.
3 Thomas, 'Wiring Atherton Gardens'.

6 A series of three-storey buildings: Suburban and seaside apartments

1 Max Kelly wrote, 'It is a monumental structure, yet intimate, a skylight enclosing its public spaces', *Anchored in a Small Cove*, p. 97.
2 Cardew, *Flats: A Study of Occupants and Locations*, Appendix 1.
3 Census of the Commonwealth of Australia, 1947.
4 *Sydney Morning Herald*, 13 October 1939, p. 11.
5 In 1947 the average weekly rent of an unfurnished Waverley flat was 24 s. 7 d.; for a cottage the average was 32 s. 2 d. In Woollahra the gap was larger; flat rents averaged 51 s. 5 d. compared to 39 s. for houses. Census of the Commonwealth of Australia, 1947.
6 Max Kelly, 'Pleasure and profit: The eastern suburbs comes of age 1919–1929', in Jill Roe (ed.), *Twentieth Century Sydney*, Hale & Iremonger, Sydney, 1980, p. 14.
7 Census of the Commonwealth of Australia, 1947.
8 Dunbar, 'Australian flats: A comparison of Melbourne and Sydney flat developments in the interwar period', vol. 1, pp. 166–7.
9 Sawyer, 'Residential flats in Melbourne: The development of a building type to 1950', p. 53.
10 Peterson, 'Wimmera', in *A Place of Sensuous Resort*.
11 Hal Porter, *The Paper Chase*, Angus & Robertson, Sydney, 1966, p. 132.
12 McKay et al., *Living and Partly Living in Australia*, p. 37.
13 *Architecture and Arts*, October 1960, p. 36.
14 Thompson, 'Sydney's flats: A social and political history', p. 46.
15 Cardew, *Flats: A Study of Occupants and Locations*, p. 27.
16 Thompson, 'Sydney's flats: A social and political history', pp. 159–60; Cardew, 'Flats in Sydney', pp. 86–7.
17 *Sydney Morning Herald*, 22 August 1969, p. 10.
18 *Sydney Morning Herald*, 24 August 1937, p. 8.
19 Robin Boyd, 'Afterword 1979', *The Australian Ugliness*, 2nd rev. edn, Penguin, 1980, p. 255.
20 *Sydney Morning Herald*, 22 August 1967, p. 15.
21 Howard Tanner, *Australian Housing in the Seventies*, Ure Smith, Sydney, 1976, pp. 9–10.
22 *Building*, July 1953, p. 23.
23 Lecture at Rose Seidler House, 30 November 2003.
24 Don Garden, *Builders to the Nation: The AV Jennings Story*, Melbourne University Press, Melbourne, 1992, p. 213.
25 Commonwealth Department of Housing, *Flats: A Survey of Multi-unit Construction in Australia*, Government Printing Office, Canberra, 1967, p. 25.
26 *Sun-Herald*, 22 September 1968, p. 9.
27 *Sydney Morning Herald*, 20 July 1965, p. 16.
28 M. T. Daly, *Sydney Boom Sydney Bust: The City and Its Property Market 1850–1981*, Allen & Unwin, Sydney, 1982, pp. 105–6.
29 Henry Pollack, *The Accidental Developer: The Fascinating Rise to the Top of Mirvac Founder Henry Pollack*, ABC Books, Sydney, 2005, p. 319.
30 ibid., p. 226.
31 *Australian Financial Review*, 12 October 2000.
32 *Sydney Morning Herald*, 20 July 1965, p. 16.
33 Thompson, 'Sydney's flats: A social and political history', pp. 168–9.
34 Mundey, *Green Bans and Beyond*, p. 85.
35 Burgmann and Burgmann, *Green Bans, Red Union*, pp. 178–80.
36 Harold and David Krantz, 'A better job for less', in Simon Anderson and Meghan Nordeck, *Krantz & Sheldon Architectural Projects*, University of Western Australia, Perth, 1996, p. 2.
37 *Sunday Telegraph*, 16 April 2000, p. 112.
38 Lisa Allen, 'Give units a simple standard', *Australian Financial Review*, 4 May 2005.
39 Ian Perlman, 'Housing the upwardly mobile', *Sydney Morning Herald*, 7 March 2000.
40 Quoted in Guy Allenby, 'High society', Spectrum, *Sydney Morning Herald*, 12 June 1999, p. 4s.
41 H. Grennan, 'Mob rules', Domain, *Sydney Morning Herald*, 29 May 2003, pp. 6–7.
42 Quoted in Grennan, 2003, p. 7.
43 Bill Randolph, 'Plan for people, not just population', *Sydney Morning Herald*, 29 November 2005.
44 ibid.
45 Souter and Molnar, *Sydney Observed*, p. 128.
46 *Architecture and Arts*, September 1961, pp. 40, 65.
47 Randolph, 'Higher density communities: Current trends and future implications', p. 9.
48 Domain, *Sydney Morning Herald*, 23–24 August 2003, p. 4a.
49 Harris, *Where to Live*, pp. 10–11.
50 'Sydney seaside flats', *Australian Home Builder*, February 1924, p. 33.
51 Ruth Park, *The Companion Guide to Sydney*, Collins, London, 1973, p. 425.
52 John Clare, *Low Rent: A Memoir*, Text, Melbourne, 1997, pp. 37, 45.
53 Catalogue notes, Gold Coast City Council Local Studies Library.
54 'Creator of his own coastal paradise', *Australian*, 17 February 2006.
55 Helen Garner, 'Postcards from Surfers', in *Postcards from Surfers*, McPhee Gribble, Melbourne, 1985, pp. 9–10.
56 Joe Hajdu, *Samurai in the Surf: The Arrival of the Japanese on the Gold Coast*, Pandanus Press, Canberra, 2005, pp. 120–3.
57 'Gold Coast high-rise: Is tall beautiful?', 18 May 2004, www.abc.net.au/built/stories/s1110697.htm.
58 *Abode*, February 2006.
59 For example, 'Developer buys into local poll campaign', *Sydney Morning Herald*, 16 September 1989, p. 11.

Case study: Denby Dale

1 Robert B. Hamilton, 'Modern flat development in Melbourne', *Journal of the Royal Victorian Institute of Architects*, May 1938, p. 46.
2 *Building*, August 1938, p. 50.
3 *Stonnington History News*, Newsletter No. 30, October–November 2000.

Case study: Borambil

1 'Sydney seaside flats', *Australian Home Builder*, February 1924, p. 33.
2 *Building*, January 1921, p. 101.
3 Borambil prospectus, 1929–30, Peddle Thorp Walker archive, Sydney.
4 *Sunday Pictorial*, 23 February 1930, p. 23.
5 ibid.
6 Supplement to *Building*, March 1929.

7 Downtown is a desirable address: Contemporary apartment living

1 Anthony Dennis, 'Concept caught on with celebrities', *Sydney Morning Herald*, 29 May 2003, p. 9.
2 Robert Harley, 'Graf steps down from Stockland helm', *Australian Financial Review*, 12 October 2000.
3 Pollack, *The Accidental Developer*, p. 282.
4 Thompson, 'Sydney's flats: A social and political history', pp. 263–78.
5 Bonnie Malkin, 'Big backyard—otherwise known as a park', *Sydney Morning Herald*, 29 May 2003, p. 8.

6 Costello, 'From prisons to penthouses', p. 55.
7 Belle property real estate advertisement for an apartment in the Horizon, 301/184 Forbes Street, Darlinghurst.
8 Deirdre Macken, 'The inner circle', *Good Weekend*, 19 June 1999, p. 14.
9 Guy Allenby, 'High society', Spectrum, *Sydney Morning Herald*, 12 June 1999, p. 4s.
10 Elaine Crisp quoted in P. Munro, 'City slickers', *SundayLife!*, p. 9, n.d.
11 Ian Perlman, 'Housing the upwardly mobile', *Sydney Morning Herald*, 7 March 2000.
12 James Weirick quoted in Allenby, 'High society', p. 4s.
13 ibid.
14 From Australian Bureau of Statistics Special Request Matrix, Census of Population and Housing, 1991 and 2001, reproduced in R. Bunker, D. Holloway and B. Randolph, *The Social Outcomes of Urban Consolidation in Sydney*, Research Paper No. 3, City Futures Research Centre, Faculty of the Built Environment, University of New South Wales, December 2005, p. 71, table 20.
15 A. Hughes and N. Bourlioufas, 'Threat to boom in CBD units', *Sydney Morning Herald*, 23 October 1997, p. 10.
16 S. Nicholls and A. Dennis, 'From black hole to the living end town', *Sydney Morning Herald*, 29 May 2003, p. 1.
17 Macken, 'The inner circle', p. 15.
18 J. Dent, 'Sexy selling', Domain, *Sydney Morning Herald*, 24 June 2000, p. 4a.
19 Quoted in Dent, 'Sexy selling', p. 4a.
20 ibid.
21 Kim Dovey, *Fluid City: Transforming Melbourne's Urban Waterfront*, UNSW Press, Kensington, NSW, 2005, p. 82.
22 Anne Susskind, 'Nice tower, shame about the skyline', *Sydney Morning Herald*, 23 May, 1998, p. 6s.
23 ibid., p. 7.
24 'Circular Quay', *Architecture Australia*, January–February 1998.
25 Program transcript, 'In the mind of the architect', program 2, www.abc.net.au/arts/architecture/default.htm.
26 Susskind, 'Nice tower, shame about the skyline', p. 7s.
27 For example, Elizabeth Farrelly, 'Upside all at the down end', *Sydney Morning Herald*, 13 May, 2003.
28 Dovey, *Fluid City*, p. 166.
29 Elizabeth Farrelly, 'The glare of the white revival', *Sydney Morning Herald*, 8 June 2005, p. 19.
30 Development manager of Greencliff, the developer of Surry Hills' Icon.
31 Macken, 'The inner circle', p. 14.
32 Harry Seidler quoted in Jane Burton Taylor, 'Seidler's leap of faith', Domain, *Sydney Morning Herald*, 22 July 2004, p. 16.
33 Bill Randolph, quoted in O'Malley, 'Storm clouds ahead: The cities of our future', p. 8.
34 Chart for Geographic Distribution of People Living in High-rise Units, ABS 1981 and 2001 Censuses of Population and Housing.
35 Urban Frontiers Program, *The Local Impacts of Urban Consolidation: The Experience of Three Councils, Final Report*, University of Western Sydney, Campbelltown, 2001, p. 11.
36 Christopher Proctor, 'Docklands', *Architecture Australia*, March 1997.
37 Dovey, *Fluid City*, p. 201.
38 This consolidation has led to what Graham Jahn calls 'deconsolidation' owing to fragmentation via strata title ownership. Jahn, 'Urban consolidation today', transcript of Urban Development Institute of Australia NSW Making Places Seminar, Sydney, 2004, p. 1.
39 Elizabeth Farrelly, 'Turn of the tide', Domain, *Sydney Morning Herald*, 19–20 June 2004, p. 6a.
40 Kon Vourtzoumis of Tonkin Zulaikha Greer, quoted in Dugald Jellie, 'Industrial bent', Domain, *Sydney Morning Herald*, 25–27 March 2005, p. 4a.
41 Laurence Nield, 'Observatory Towers re-birth as residential', *Architecture Bulletin*, June 1997, p. 11.

42 Australian Bureau of Statistics, *Australian Social Trends, 2003*, cat. no. 4102.0, www.abs.gov.au/ausstats/abs@.nsf.
43 Judith Yates, *Housing Implications of Social, Spatial and Structural Change*, Australian Housing and Urban Research Institute, Sydney, 2002.
44 Jahn, 'Urban consolidation today'.
45 R. Bunker, D. Holloway and B. Randolph, 'The expansion of urban consolidation in Sydney: Social impacts and implications', *Australian Planner,* vol. 42, no. 3, September 2005, p. 16.
46 Chris Paris, *Housing Australia*, Macmillan Education Australia, Melbourne, 1993, p. 126.
47 Dovey, *Fluid City*, p. 198.
48 Bunker, Holloway and Randolph, 'The expansion of urban consolidation in Sydney', p. 24.
49 Bill Randolph, 'The haves and have-nots do not meet in the new suburbia', *Sydney Morning Herald*, 19 May 2004, p. 17.
50 Public housing tenants accounted for only 10 per cent of apartment dwellers in 2001, down from 28 per cent in 1981.
51 Randolph, 'The haves and have-nots do not meet in the new suburbia', p. 17.
52 ABS, *Australian Social Trends*, 2003. The lowest proportions of higher-density housing were in Hobart (16 per cent) and Brisbane (18 per cent).
53 *The Draft Canberra Spatial Plan*, ACT Planning and Land Authority, 2003, Map 9, p. 18.
54 *Kingston Foreshore the Place to Be*, Canberra, Land Development Agency, 2005.
55 Quoted in Jane Burton Taylor, 'High ideas', Domain, *Sydney Morning Herald*, 3 March 2001, p. 4a.
56 Graham Jahn quoted in Susan Owens, 'Brave new buildings', *Australian Financial Review*, 30 July 2005.
57 Pollack, *The Accidental Developer*, p. 320.
58 Graham Jahn quoted in Allenby, 'High society', p. 4s.
59 Quoted in Burton Taylor, 'High ideas'.
60 Paola Totaro, 'The buildings that ate Sydney: How the city's heritage is buried in the rush', *Sydney Morning Herald*, 17 November 1997, pp. 1, 9.
61 Geraldine O'Brien, 'Storm over the Horizon', *Sydney Morning Herald*, 24 June 1999, p. 11.
62 Jonathan Chancellor, 'Event Horizon: Rich rush for the high life', *Sydney Morning Herald*, 26 October 1998.
63 Megan Mason, 'Fairy storeys', Spectrum, *Sydney Morning Herald*, 6–7 August 2005, p. 10.
64 ibid.
65 Quoted in Mason, 'Fairy storeys', p. 10.

Case study: Mondrian

1 Susan Wellings, 'Common ground', Domain, *Sydney Morning Herald*, 7 June 2006.
2 Geraldine O'Brien, 'Architects' great storeys are a tale of world success', *Sydney Morning Herald*, 30 July 2002.
3 'RAIA Jury Report 2003', *Architecture Bulletin*, July–August 2003.
4 Perlman, 'Housing the upwardly mobile'.
5 Geraldine O'Brien, 'Bold and glassy: Sydney living's brave new face', *Sydney Morning Herald*, 21 July 2003.

Picture credits

Chapter 1
Slums of the future?: A century of controversy

page 3
Mr F. A. Franklin
'Sketch plan of building areas as rearranged', 1901
from *Remodelling of "The Rocks" Resumed Areas*
Published by the Legislative Assembly of New South Wales
Royal Australian Historical Society

page 4
'New-law Tenements, Brooklyn'
New South Wales. Report of the Commission of Inquiry into the Question of the Housing of Workmen in Europe and America, NSW PP, 1913, vol. 2, part 1, William Applegate Gullick, Government Printer, Sydney, 1913
State Reference Library, State Library of New South Wales

'Plan of New York Tenement House, new type'
New South Wales. Report of the Commission of Inquiry into the Question of the Housing of Workmen in Europe and America, NSW PP, 1913, vol. 2, part 1, William Applegate Gullick, Government Printer, Sydney, 1913
State Reference Library, State Library of New South Wales

page 5
Eric Sierins
Strickland Flats, Chippendale
digital photograph, 2006
Max Dupain & Associates

The enemy within our gates
Cover image from Housing Commission Victoria booklet, 1966
La Trobe Collection, State Library of Victoria
© Office of Housing

pages 6–7
Eric Sierins
Erskineville Rehousing Scheme
digital photographs, 2006
Max Dupain & Associates

page 8
Cavendish Hall, Elizabeth Bay
glass negative
Tyrrell Collection, Powerhouse Museum

page 9
'Film still at Bellevue Gardens'
from *The Hayseeds*, 1933
National Film and Sound Archive

Russell Roberts
'Mrs Roy Chisholm, who lives at Darnley Hall, Elizabeth Bay'
The Home, July 1935, p. 35
Caroline Simpson Library & Research Collection, Historic Houses Trust

'Cast photograph'
Number 96, 1972
National Film and Sound Archive

page 10
Gladys Owen
The heights of Darlinghurst, 1931
pen and wash on paper
Mitchell Library, State Library of New South Wales
© Estate of David Moore

page 11
H. C. Durant (pilot)
'Aerial view of Elizabeth Bay'
The Home, October 1936, p. 37
Powerhouse Museum

Florence M. Taylor and Francis G. Hood
'View of beautification scheme for Woolloomooloo'
Building, August 1935, p. 36
Caroline Simpson Library & Research Collection, Historic Houses Trust

page 12
Eric Sierins
Blues Point Tower from Balls Head
type C photograph, 1996
© Penelope Seidler

Harry Seidler
MC. M. Pt. 2 [sketch diagram of Blues Point Tower orientation]
Mitchell Library, State Library of New South Wales
© Penelope Seidler

page 13
Max Dupain
Blues Point Tower interior
gelatin silver photograph, 1962
© Penelope Seidler

Harry Seidler
MC. M. Pt. 1 [sketch diagrams of Blues Point Tower orientation]
Mitchell Library, State Library of New South Wales
© Penelope Seidler

page 15
Max Dupain
'Background for bachelors' for KG Murray/*House and Garden*
gelatin silver photograph, 1956
Max Dupain & Associates

page 16
Max Dupain
Doors and windows with models for Hawkesley P/L
gelatin silver photograph, 1962
Max Dupain & Associates

page 17
David Mist
David Mist on roof of Kirribilli flat, c. 1960s
gelatin silver photograph
Powerhouse Museum
© David Mist

page 18
'Dwelling types diagram'
Originally published in *Architectural Forum* reproduced in Walter Bunning, *Homes in the Sun*, 1945, p 46.
Powerhouse Museum Library

George Molnar
'Sorry. I thought it was a dole queue.'
Sydney Morning Herald, 19 February 1981
pen and ink on paper, 20.0 x 25.9 cm
George Molnar Collection, National Library of Australia
© NLA

page 19
Stephenson and Turner
'Victoria Street development proposal'
from *Architecture Australia*, June/July 1976, p. 38
Powerhouse Museum Library
© Architecture Australia

Jan Mackay
In memory of Victoria Street, Kings Cross, c. 1975–76
screenprint, 64.0 x 50.9 cm
Gift of the artist 1981
Art Gallery of New South Wales
© Jan Mackay

The Killing of Angel Street, 1981
Donald Crombie, Director; Anthony Buckley, Producer
Powerhouse Museum
© Donald & Judith Crombie

pages 20–1
Eric Sierins
Melbourne Terrace
Courtesy Pam and Garry Emery
type C photographs, 2006
Max Dupain & Associates

page 22
Eric Sierins
Portrait of Harry Seidler with model of Emu Brewery apartments complex, Perth
type C photograph, 2005

Max Dupain & Associates

Patrick Cook
'Harry Seidler Retirement Park'
Sydney Morning Herald, 27 June 1984, p. 1
State Library of New South Wales
© Patrick Cook

page 23
'Aerial view of slum reclamation'
from *Housing Commission Victoria Annual Report 1969–70*
© Office of Housing

Marinco Kojdanovski
Self-portrait
digital photograph, 2006

page 52
James Russell
Architectural rendering: Lawson flats, 1936
watercolour, pencil, 56.8 x 38.1 cm
Gift of Geoffrey Summerhayes, Perth 1988
National Gallery of Australia, Canberra
© Estate of the artist

page 53
'Lawson Flats Floor Plan'
from *Lawson: managing agents: Robertson Bros. Limited* prospectus
Courtesy Battye Library, State Library of Western Australia

Chapter 3
The pulsing heart of city life: Inner-city apartments 1920–50

page 57
Craigend Estate, Darlinghurst
Auction prospectus, 1922
Mitchell Library, State Library of New South Wales

page 58
Sydney Ure Smith
'Garden Island from Onslow Gardens'
sketch
reproduced in *The Sydney Book*, 1947
Caroline Simpson Library & Research Collection, Historic Houses Trust

page 59
Rah Fizelle
Elizabeth Bay, c. 1931
oil on canvas mounted on composition board, 45.0 x 38.0 cm
National Gallery of Australia, Canberra
© Estate of Rah Fizelle

page 60
Norman Carter
Sydney Ure Smith's flat in 'Manar', 1939
oil on canvas 56.0 x 46.3 cm
Private collection
© Estate of the artist

Sydney Ure Smith
View from 'Manar', 1948
Pen and wash 53.8 x 58.7 cm
Private collection

Harold Cazneaux
'Molly Grey in her flat at Greenknowe Avenue'
The Home, September 1935, p. 29
gelatin silver photograph
Mitchell Library, State Library of New South Wales

page 61
Russell Roberts and John Scott Simmons
'The modern note in two interiors'
The Home, May 1934, p. 21
Caroline Simpson Library & Research Collection, Historic Houses Trust

Hera Roberts
The Home, July 1930, cover
Caroline Simpson Library & Research Collection, Historic Houses Trust
Cover art © Estate of the artist

page 62
Harold Cazneaux
Portrait of Ruby Rich at "The Astor", 1926
gelatin silver photograph, 28.5 x 19.0 cm
Australian Judaica Collection, University of Sydney

page 63
Eric Sierins
Castle Villa and Clyde, Kensington Road, Toorak
digital photograph, 2005
Max Dupain & Associates

page 64
Eric Sierins
Amesbury House, Domain Road, South Yarra
digital photograph, 2006
Max Dupain & Associates

page 65
Eric Sierins
Langi, Toorak Road, South Yarra
digital photograph, 2005
Max Dupain & Associates

page 66
Eric Sierins
Elvada, Glenferrie Road, Malvern
digital photograph, 2005
Max Dupain & Associates

page 67
Eric Sierins
Beverley Hills, Darling Street, South Yarra
digital photograph, 2005
Max Dupain & Associates

page 68
Eric Sierins
Castle Towers, Marne Street, South Yarra
digital photograph, 2005
Max Dupain & Associates

page 69
Eric Sierins
Park Towers, Adam Street, South Yarra
digital photograph, 2005
Max Dupain & Associates

page 70
Siemensstadt, Berlin, Grosssiedlung, 1930 [Walter Gropius architect]
Photograph reproduced in F.R.S. Yorke and Frederick Gibberd, *The Modern flat*, published by The Architectural Press, 1937, p. 54
Powerhouse Museum Library
© Royal Institute of British Architects

page 71
Lawn Road flats Hampstead 1934
Photograph and floor plan reproduced in F. R. S. Yorke and Frederick Gibberd, *The Modern Flat*, published by The Architectural Press, 1937, p. 153
Powerhouse Museum Library
© Royal Institute of British Architects

page 72
'Residential flats being erected facing the Exhibition Gardens …'
Journal of the Royal Victorian Institute of Architects, July 1936, p. 95
State Library Victoria

page 73
Eric Sierins
Woy Woy, Marine Parade, Elwood
digital photograph, 2005
Max Dupain & Associates

pages 74–5
Unknown photographer
Cairo flats
from *Australian Home Beautiful*, April 1937, p. 43
Caroline Simpson Library & Research Collection, Historic Houses Trust

Eric Sierins
Cairo, Nicholson Street, Fitzroy
digital photographs, 2006
Max Dupain & Associates

Margarete Schütte-Lihotzky, designer
'Modern kitchen'
Archiv Ernst May, Germanisches Nationalmuseum Nurnberg
Powerhouse Museum

page 76
Eric Sierins
Quamby, Glover Court, Toorak
digital photograph, 2005
Max Dupain & Associates

Lyle Fowler
Interior of "Clendon" flats, corner Clendon and Malvern Road Armadale, designed by Roy Grounds, c. 1940
gelatin silver photograph, 20.3 x 25.4 cm approx
Harold Paynting Collection, State Library of Victoria

page 77
Eric Sierins
Glenunga, Horsburgh Grove, Armadale
digital photograph, 2005
Max Dupain & Associates

Eric Sierins
Newburn, Queens Road, South Melbourne
digital photograph, 2006
Max Dupain & Associates

page 78
Eric Sierins
Stanhill Flats, Queens Road, South Melbourne
type C photograph, 1999
Max Dupain & Associates

page 79
Wolfgang Sievers
Mr and Mrs Korman at their "Stanhill" flat, 1959
gelatin silver photograph
National Library of Australia
© Wolfgang Sievers. Licensed by Viscopy, Australia, 2006

Eric Sierins
Caringal, Tahara Road, Toorak
digital photograph, 2006
Max Dupain & Associates

page 80
R. A. Prevost & Cyril Ruwald Architects
'Residential Flats No.16 Macleay Street, Darlinghurst'
diazo prints, elevations and floor plans, c. 1930
Powerhouse Museum

page 81
Eric Sierins
Rutland Gate, Fairfax Road, Double Bay
digital photograph, 2006
Max Dupain & Associates

Eric Sierins
Macleay Regis, Macleay Street, Potts Point
digital photograph, 2006
Max Dupain & Associates

page 82
Dudley Ward
'Flats designed by Dudley Ward …' (Gowrie Gate)
Cover from *Decoration and Glass*, August 1936
Caroline Simpson Library & Research Collection, Historic Houses Trust

Aaron Bolot
'Hillside'
Cover from *Decoration and Glass*, February 1936
Caroline Simpson Library & Research Collection, Historic Houses Trust

page 83
Eric Sierins
Birtley Towers, Birtley Place, Elizabeth Bay
gelatin silver photographs, 1999
Max Dupain & Associates

page 84
Max Dupain
Wyldefel Gardens, Wylde Steet, Potts Point
gelatin silver photograph, 1937
Max Dupain & Associates

page 85
John R. Brogan
Block plan, Wyldefel Gardens
John Brogan collection, Mitchell Library, State Library of New South Wales
© John R. Brogan & Associates

page 86
Max Dupain
George Edwards' flat at Darjoa for Lipson & Kaad
gelatin silver photographs, 1938
Max Dupain & Associates

page 87
Eric Sierins
The Broadway, O'Sullivan Road, Bellevue Hill
digital photograph, 2006
Max Dupain & Associates

Eric Sierins
Segenhoe Apartments, Wolfe Street, Newcastle, 1998
type C photograph
Max Dupain & Associates

page 88
Eric Sierins
Cliffside, Lower River Terrace, Kangaroo Point
digital photograph, 2006
Max Dupain & Associates

'Bachelor flats … to be erected at Brisbane'
Advertisement from *Decoration and Glass*, May 1936
Caroline Simpson Library & Research Collection, Historic Houses Trust

page 89
Eric Sierins
Greystaines, Kingsford Smith Drive, Hamilton
digital photograph, 2006
Max Dupain & Associates

Marinco Kojdanovski
Geoff Cousins
digital photograph, 2006

page 90
Emil Sodersten
Elevation, Marlborough Hall, *Decoration & Glass*, June 1937, p. 17
Caroline Simpson Library & Research Collection, Historic Houses Trust

page 91
Eric Sierins
Marlborough Hall, Ward Avenue, Kings Cross
digital photographs, 2006
Max Dupain & Associates

'Luxury flats for moderate incomes'
Prospectus for Seven Elizabeth Street, Sydney, 1937
Caroline Simpson Library & Research Collection, Historic Houses Trust

page 92
Eric Sierins
Green Gables, Julius Street, New Farm
digital photograph, 2006
Max Dupain & Associates

Eric Sierins
Evelyn Court, Julius Street, New Farm
digital photograph, 2006
Max Dupain & Associates

page 93
Eric Sierins
Coronet Court, Brunswick Street, New Farm, 1998
type C photograph
Max Dupain & Associates

page 94
Max Dupain
Deep Acres, Melbourne Street, North Adelaide
gelatin silver photograph, c. 1950
Max Dupain & Associates

page 95
John Oldham
Illustration for 'Proposed block of Bachelor Flats', 1936
Originally published in *Riviera Investments Prospectus*
Private collection
© Tish Oldham

John Oldham
Illustration for interior view, 'Proposed block of Bachelor Flats', 1936
Originally published in *Riviera Investments Prospectus*
Private collection
© Tish Oldham

Chapter 4
A new style of living: Inner-city apartments 1950–80

pages 98–9
Eric Sierins
Domain Park, Domain Road, South Yarra
type C photographs, 2006
Max Dupain & Associates

Domain Park
Cover from buyers' prospectus, c. 1960
Private collection
© Reproduced courtesy Civil & Civic Pty Ltd and Lend Lease Development Pty Ltd

Domain Park
'Floor plan' from prospectus, c. 1960
Private collection
© Reproduced courtesy Civil & Civic Pty Ltd and Lend Lease Development Pty Ltd

page 100
Max Dupain
McMahons Point and Lavender Bay redevelopment model
gelatin silver photograph, 1957
© Penelope Seidler

Cover, *Urban redevelopment concerns you!*, 1957
Mitchell Library, State Library of New South Wales
© Penelope Seidler

page 101
Harry Seidler
Sketch of Blues Point Tower, September 1958
Mitchell Library, State Library of New South Wales
© Penelope Seidler

Max Dupain
Blues Point Tower exterior
gelatin silver photograph, 1962
© Penelope Seidler

page 102
Harry Seidler
Unite d'Habitation
type C photograph
© Penelope Seidler

Highpoint, Highgate, 1935
Photograph reproduced in F. R. S. Yorke and
Frederick Gibberd, *The Modern Flat*, published by
The Architectural Press, 1937, p. 135
Powerhouse Museum Library
© Royal Institute of British Architects

page 103
Harry Seidler
Alton Estate, Roehampton
type C photograph
© Penelope Seidler

page 104
Max Dupain
Ithaca Gardens units, Elizabeth Bay
gelatin silver photograph, 1960
© Penelope Seidler

page 105
Eric Sierins
Seven Seas, Upper Pitt Street, Kirribilli
digital photograph, 2006
Max Dupain & Associates

Marinco Kojdanovski
Marita Leuver and Sylvia Weimer
digital photograph, 2006

page 106
Max Dupain
Etham Avenue, Darling Point home units
gelatin silver photograph, 1959
Max Dupain & Associates

Max Dupain
Quarterdeck units, Carrabella Street, Kirribilli
gelatin silver photograph, 1965
Max Dupain & Associates

page 107
Eric Sierins
Oceana Apartments, Elizabeth Bay Road
digital photograph, 2006
Max Dupain & Associates

pages 108–9
Max Dupain
Wylde Street home units
gelatin silver photographs, 1953
Max Dupain & Associates

Aaron Bolot
Floor plans, Wylde Street Co-operative home units
Building, May 1948, p. 20
Powerhouse Museum Library

page 110
Max Dupain
Home Units, Bayswater Road
gelatin silver photograph, 1961
Max Dupain & Associates

Max Dupain
Bibaringa apartment building
gelatin silver photograph, 1963
Max Dupain & Associates

page 111
Max Dupain
Broadwaters, Sutherland Crescent, Darling Point
gelatin silver photograph, 1960
Max Dupain & Associates

page 112
David Mist
Apartments at Kirribilli, 1960s
gelatin silver photograph
Powerhouse Museum
© David Mist

Unknown photographer
*Using a Hydromat washing machine on the roof of
a block of flats, Potts Point*, 1954
gelatin silver photograph
Australian Photographic Agency collection, State
Library of New South Wales

page 113
Eric Sierins
Fairlie, Anderson Street, South Yarra
digital photograph, 2005
Max Dupain & Associates

Wolfgang Sievers
View across Melbourne from Fairlie Flats, 1961
gelatin silver photograph
National Library of Australia
© Wolfgang Sievers. Licensed by Viscopy, Australia,
2006

page 114
Wolfgang Sievers
Pool area and landscaping, Kilpara flats, 1971
gelatin silver photograph
State Library of Victoria
© Wolfgang Sievers. Licensed by Viscopy, Australia,
2006

page 115
Eric Sierins
15 Collins Street, Melbourne
digital photograph, 2006
Max Dupain & Associates

Eric Sierins
Edgewater, Marine Parade, St Kilda
digital photograph, 2006
Max Dupain & Associates

pages 116–17
'Aerial perspective'
from *Torbreck, a new concept in modern living*
pamphlet
State Library of Queensland

Eric Sierins
Torbreck, Dornoch Terrace
type C and digital photographs, 1998, 2006
Max Dupain & Associates

page 118
Peter Wille
Orrong Tower under construction
type C photograph, 1960
State Library of Victoria

page 119
Max Dupain
Rocks redevelopment model
gelatin silver photograph, 1963
Max Dupain & Associates

page 120
Max Dupain
The Penthouses, Darling Point
gelatin silver photograph, 1967
Max Dupain & Associates

Eric Sierins
City Edge, Kingsway, South Melbourne
digital photograph, 2006
Max Dupain & Associates

page 121
Eric Sierins,
Glenfalloch, Oxlade Drive, New Farm
digital photograph, 2006
Max Dupain & Associates

Chapter 5
**Homes for working couples: Public
apartments**

page 124
Changing face of a City…
Cover of Housing Commission promotional
booklet, 1960
NSW Department of Housing Library
© NSW Department of Housing

page 125
Eric Sierins
Public housing, High Street, The Rocks
digital photograph, 2006
Max Dupain & Associates

page 126
Eric Sierins
Public housing, Lower Fort Street, The Rocks
digital photograph, 2006
Max Dupain & Associates

Government Architect
'Plans of Lower Fort Street, No. 1 (First and
ground)'
from *Workmen's dwellings in Lower Fort Street*
diazo print, 1910
State Records NSW

page 127
Max Dupain
Ways Terrace, Point Street, Pyrmont
gelatin silver photograph, 1982
Max Dupain & Associates

page 128
Lipson, Kaad, Fotheringham and Partners Pty Ltd
Perspective view of proposed workmen's flats, Paddington, c. 1934
Mitchell Library, State Library of New South Wales

page 129
Eric Sierins
Philomene Watson
digital photograph, 2006

page 130
Sam Hood Studio
Erskineville Housing Scheme
gelatin silver photographs, 1938
Hood Collection, State Library of New South Wales

page 131
NSW Government Printing Office
Flats with car-park at Redfern, c. 1955
gelatin silver photograph
NSW Department of Housing Library

pages 132–3
Max Dupain
Northbourne Housing complex for National Capital Development Commission
gelatin silver photographs, 1966
Max Dupain & Associates

page 134
Eric Sierins
Greenway, Kirribilli
digital photograph, 2006
Max Dupain & Associates

page 135
Unknown photographer
View from window, Wandana Flats in Subiaco, 1956
gelatin silver photograph
Herb Graham collection of photographs, State Library of Western Australia

Unknown photographer
Front facade, Wandana Flats in Subiaco, 1956
gelatin silver photograph
Herb Graham collection of photographs, State Library of Western Australia

page 136
Unknown photographer
'Moe – Lone Person and Darby & John (sic) flats'
from *Housing Commission Victoria Annual Report 1962*
© Office of Housing

'Cover image'
Housing Commission Victoria Annual Report 1962
© Office of Housing

page 137
Unknown photographer
'Debney's Estate, Flemington'
Housing Commission Victoria Annual Report 1968–69
© Office of Housing

page 138
Unknown photographer
'Hotham Estate, North Melbourne'
from *Housing Commission Victoria Annual Report 1968–69*
© Office of Housing

page 139
Unknown photographer
Terraces and City Council tower, Mitchell Street, Glebe, 1960s
© NSW Department of Housing

pages 140–1
Max Dupain
John Northcott Place Units
gelatin silver photographs, 1962
Max Dupain & Associates

pages 142–3
Eric Sierins
Atherton Gardens Estate, Fitzroy
digital photographs, 2006
Max Dupain & Associates

page 144
David Woodhead
Construction of apartment buildings at Dundas, 1970s
gelatin silver photograph
NSW Department of Housing Library
© NSW Department of Housing

page 145
Unknown photographer
Construction picture of Waterloo housing
gelatin silver photograph
NSW Department of Housing Library
© NSW Department of Housing

page 146
Max Dupain
William McKell Place
gelatin silver photograph, 1964
Max Dupain & Associates

Douglas Baglin
Opening ceremony, Purcell flats, Redfern
gelatin silver photograph
NSW Department of Housing Library
© NSW Department of Housing

page 147
Max Dupain
Housing Commission unit blocks, Redfern, under construction
gelatin silver photograph, 1965
Max Dupain & Associates

page 148
Unknown photographer
'Waterloo: location shot of a building in Raglan Street, with people leaning out of upper-storey windows holding protest banners'
National Film and Sound Archive
© Tom Zubrycki

Unknown photographer
Matavai and Turanga
from Waterloo Endeavour Towers promotional booklet, 1976
NSW Department of Housing Library
© NSW Department of Housing

page 149
Phil Campbell
Sirius Tower, Cumberland Street, The Rocks
digital photograph, 2005

Sirius
from Sirius Tower promotional booklet, 1979
© NSW Department of Housing

page 150
Max Dupain
Housing Commission Units, Brougham Street, Woolloomooloo
gelatin silver photograph, 1982
Max Dupain & Associates

page 151
Eric Sierins
Kay Street housing, Carlton
digital photograph, 2005
Max Dupain & Associates

page 152
Dave Tacon
Flemington Eagles striker Osman, representing the Flemington high rise Housing Commission flats, lets fly with a corner cross, Atherton Reserve, Fitzroy, Victoria, September 10, 2005
type C photograph
National Library of Australia
© Dave Tacon

Unknown photographer
'Presentation of architecture aware for Park Towers'
from *Housing Commission Victoria Annual Report 1969–70*
© Office of Housing

page 153
Eric Sierins
Newcastle East public housing
gelatin silver photograph, 1998
Max Dupain & Associates

Chapter 6
A series of three-storey buildings: Suburban and seaside apartments

page 157
Charles Pickett
Walk-up flats, Petersham
type C photograph, 2006

Unknown photographer
Stevens Buildings, Windmill Street, c. 1900
Mitchell Library, State Library of New South Wales

page 158
Eric Sierins
Summerland Mansions, Acland and Fitzroy Streets,
St Kilda
digital photograph, 2006
Max Dupain & Associates

page 159
Eric Sierins
Marli Place, The Esplanade, St Kilda
digital photograph, 2006
Max Dupain & Associates

page 160
Eric Sierins
The Canterbury, Canterbury Road, St Kilda
digital photograph, 2006
Max Dupain & Associates

page 161
Mick Kanis with his Pontiac outside his block of flats
in Punt Road, Richmond, 1940s
gelatin silver photograph
Kominos & Zervos, Building a Country Archive
State Library of Victoria

page 162
Eric Sierins
Denby Dale
digital photograph, 2006
Max Dupain & Associates

page 163
'Denby Dale, Glenferrie Road', 1938
photograph
City of Stonnington Archives

Robert Hamilton, architect; Marcus Norris,
associate architect
'Proposed residential flats at Glenferrie Road,
Kooyong, for Mrs JLB Perry', 1937
Hand-coloured plans
City of Stonnington Archives

page 164
Eric Sierins
Walk-up flats at Brighton-Le-Sands
digital photograph, 2006
Max Dupain & Associates

page 165
Max Dupain
The Chilterns, New South Head Road, Rose Bay
gelatin silver photograph, 1954
Max Dupain & Associates

page 166
Max Dupain
Delcana, Spit Road, Mosman
gelatin silver photograph, 1959
Max Dupain & Associates

Marinco Kojdanovski
Carmen and Leon Donovan
digital photograph, 2006

page 167
Dean Sewell
Photographs from the series *Hillsdale*
digital photographs, 2005
© Oculi, 2006

page 168
Eric Sierins
Flats and people at Eastlakes
digital photograph, 2006
Max Dupain & Associates

page 169
Max Dupain
The Oaks, Roscoe Street, Bondi
gelatin silver photograph, 1968
Max Dupain & Associates

page 170
Mt Eliza Apartments in Mount Street
digital photograph, 2006
© Terrace Photographers, Perth

Windsor Towers in South Perth
digital photograph, 2006
© Terrace Photographers, Perth

page 171
Eric Sierins
Meriton Street, Gladesville
digital photograph, 2006
Max Dupain & Associates

page 172
Bookalil Brothers
'Manly Jan 1956 No 3 (Borambil)'
standard kodachrome H photograph
© Robert McGrath Photographic Exhibitors

page 173
'Perspective front elevation, Borambil', 1930
PTW Archives
Reproduced with permission

'Typical floor plan, Borambil', 1930
PTW Archives
Reproduced with permission

page 174
Eric Sierins
Meriton development at Rockdale
digital photograph, 2006
Max Dupain & Associates

page 175
Eric Sierins
Colebrook, Double Bay
digital photograph, 2006
Max Dupain & Associates

Max Dupain
Copy of perspective drawing of Colebrook
apartments
gelatin silver photograph, 1961
Max Dupain & Associates

Marinco Kojdanovski
Abdul Alizada, Homa Shojaie, Omid and Navid
Alizada
digital photograph, 2006

page 176
Eric Sierins
The Montreaux, West Esplanade, Manly Cove
digital photograph, 2006
Max Dupain & Associates

Advertisement for 'Montreaux Flats, Manly'
from *Where to Live in Sydney*, 1917, p. 12
Mitchell Library, State Library of NSW

page 177
Eric Sierins
Bellaire, Cowderoy Street, St Kilda
digital photograph, 2006
Max Dupain & Associates

page 178
Eric Sierins
The Belvedere, Upper Esplanade, St Kilda
digital photograph, 2006
Max Dupain & Associates

page 179
Unknown photographer
*View of Kinkabool Units and Tahitian Sun Private
Hotel, Hanlon Street, Surfers Paradise*
type C photograph, 1960s
Gold Coast City Council Local Studies Library

Unknown photographer
*Alston and Halmar Flats, Marine Parade, Labrador,
1965*
type C photograph, 1965
Gold Coast City Council Local Studies Library

Unknown photographer
*View of holiday makers at one of the many
apartment buildings in Surfers Paradise*
gelatin silver photograph, 1970
Gold Coast City Council Local Studies Library

page 180
Graham Weeks
*Focus Holiday Apartments, 114 The Esplanade,
Surfers Paradise*
type C photograph, c. 1999
Collection of the photographer
© Graham Weeks

page 181
Eric Sierins
Grand Mariner, Commodore Drive, Paradise Waters
type C photograph, c. 1991
Max Dupain & Associates

page 182
Eric Sierins
The Moroccan, View Avenue, Surfers Paradise
digital photograph, 2006
Max Dupain & Associates

page 183
Eric Sierins
Q1, Surfers Paradise Boulevard, Surfers Paradise
digital photograph, 2006
Max Dupain & Associates

Chapter 7
**Downtown is a desirable address:
Contemporary apartment living**

page 186
Max Dupain
The Connaught units
gelatin silver photograph, 1984
Max Dupain & Associates

page 187
Max Dupain
Park Regis units, Park Street
gelatin silver photograph, 1968
Max Dupain & Associates

page 188
Eric Sierins
Century Tower, Pitt Street
type C photograph, 1998
Max Dupain & Associates

Eric Sierins,
World Tower, World Square
digital photograph, 2006
Max Dupain & Associates

page 189
Eric Sierins
East Circular Quay
type C photograph, 2000
Max Dupain & Associates

page 190
Eric Sierins
Macquarie Apartments, Macquarie Street
type C photographs, 2000
Max Dupain & Associates

page 191
Eric Sierins
Cove apartments, Harrington Street, Sydney
type C photographs, 2003
Max Dupain & Associates

James Houston, photographer
Prospectus for Republic 2, 1998
Dakota Creative

page 192
Eric Sierins
Docklands, Melbourne
digital photograph, 2006
Max Dupain & Associates

page 193
Eric Sierins
Yarra's Edge and Eureka, Southbank Promenade
digital photograph, 2006
Max Dupain & Associates

page 194
Eric Sierins
Pyrmont apartments
type C photograph, 2004
Max Dupain & Associates

page 195
Eric Sierins
Wolli Creek development, Tempe
digital photograph, 2006
Max Dupain & Associates

Eric Sierins
Balmain Shores
digital photograph, 2006
Max Dupain & Associates

Eric Sierins
Tribeca East Melbourne, Victoria Parade, East
Melbourne
digital photograph, 2006
Max Dupain & Associates

pages 196–7
Brett Boardman
Mondrian
digital photographs
© Brett Boardman Photography

Stanisic Associates
section, Mondrian
© Stanisic Associates

page 198
Eric Sierins
Silos residential apartments, Richmond
type C photograph, 1998
Max Dupain & Associates

Eric Sierins
The Melburnian, St Kilda Road
digital photograph, 2006
Max Dupain & Associates

page 199
Eric Sierins
Riparian Tower, Eagle Street, Brisbane
digital photograph, 2006
Max Dupain & Associates

page 200
Eric Sierins
Observatory Tower
type C photograph, 1996
Max Dupain & Associates

Prospectus for the Dorchester, 2003
Caroline Simpson Library & Research Collection,
Historic Houses Trust

page 201
Marinco Kojdanovski
John A. Pickles
digital photograph, 2006

page 202
Eric Sierins
Horizon apartments, East Sydney
type C photographs, 1998, 2001
Max Dupain & Associates

page 203
Roslyn Sharp
'Wally Murray stands outside the Elan, the
apartment block built over the underground
dwelling in Kings Cross'
gelatin silver photograph, 2000
National Library of Australia

page 204
Prospectus for Kingston Foreshore, 2004
Land Development Agency, ACT

page 205
Marinco Kojdanovski
John Sharpe, Claire Armstrong and Rosie Sharpe
digital photograph, 2006

Acknowledgements

Any book of this size with a large pictorial content draws on a wide net of people and institutions.

We must first acknowledge the Historic Houses Trust of NSW for embracing the project. Our particular thanks go to Peter Watts, Director, and Helen Temple, Deputy Director.

Many thanks also to Historic Houses Trust's two senior curators, Caroline Mackaness and Susan Hunt, who made it possible for time and resources to be allocated to Homes in the Sky. Thanks also to Charmaine Moldrich, formerly at HHT, and Peter Barnes, who were enthusiastic supporters of the book throughout. We are indebted to two other HHT staff, Megan Martin and Alice Livingstone. Research Librarian at the Caroline Simpson Library & Research Collection and a powerhouse of knowledge, Megan provided a thorough and constructive reading of the first draft of the manuscript. Alice's spirited nature, professional integrity and sheer intelligence assisted us in many ways beyond the immense task of copyright clearance and image collection.

We are also grateful to Susan Sedgwick, Head of Exhibitions and Publications, and Vani Sripathy, Publications Officer, who handled HHT's final editorial and production liaison with MUP. We are also grateful to the staff of the Caroline Simpson Library & Research Collection, Matthew Stephens and Penny Gill, who were always generous in their support throughout the long duration of this book and exhibition project. Others at HHT provided specific support on their areas of specialty, including Joanna Nicholas, Richard Silink and Scott Carlin. And particular thanks to Sally Webster and family, who kindly scouted Perth flats for us.

To all the institutions, companies and individuals who have loaned material for the associated exhibition, Homes in the Sky: Apartment living in Sydney (Museum of Sydney, 19 May to 26 August 2007), we are immensely grateful. We also thank the HHT exhibition team for all their fantastic expertise and help, in particular: Tim Girling-Butcher, Wendy Osmond, Bruce Smythe, Caroline Lorentz, Charlotte Grant and Ruth Williams. Special thanks also to Sydney University intern Ida Strøm-Larsen, who was a huge support in the research of pictorial material for the book and exhibition.

At the Powerhouse Museum we wish to thank Dr Kevin Fewster and Jennifer Sanders for permitting Charles to work on this project. Special thanks go to Michael Desmond and Dr Kimberley Webber for supporting us; to Karen Johnson and the PHM research library staff for all their help; to Marinco Kojdanovski, Ryan Hernandez, Beatrice D'Souza—and to Dr Ann Stephen who, as always, had something to say on the subject.

The research for this book has a long history dating back to the 1990s when we received a grant from the University of Western Sydney to develop a database of significant apartment buildings in New South Wales. We are grateful to Tim Marshall, formerly of UWS, now Dean of Parsons The New School for Design, New York, who started us on the road towards this book; and to the research assistants who began the hard slog of research for the UWS grant, Dr Chiara O'Reilly and Dr Nicola Teffer.

Academics at several institutions have been pivotal to the research process. At the University of New South Wales, where Caroline is completing her PhD on apartment living in Sydney, Associate Professors Robert Freestone and Bruce Judd, who have provided critical feedback on research; and Professors Bill Randolph, James Weirick and Ian Burnley, whose insights on apartment living have been particularly useful. Also to Philip Thalis and Peter John Cantrill, who taught an excellent course on urban housing to fourth-year BA Architecture students at University of Technology, Sydney. Thanks for inviting us in to talk and share the case studies by students. Thanks also to Professor Philip Goad at the University of Melbourne, who has always shown interest and support for the project.

Dr Fran Tonkiss of Adelaide, Sydney, Barcelona, Paris and the London School of Economics (among other addresses) deserves a special thank you for her special brand of intellectual power, friendship and encouragement.

Many people provided their own records and/or collections and new insights into individual apartment buildings and architects, including Professor Richard Clough, Penelope Seidler, Doug Farram, Sam Ure Smith and Tish Oldham, among others. We are also grateful to all those other researchers and writers who have worked on aspects of the history of apartments: Richard Cardew, Donald Dunbar, Terry Sawyer, Ruth Thompson, Deborah Dearing, Graham Jahn, Jennifer Hill, Scott Robertson, Winston Barnett, Howard Tanner, Seamus O'Hanlon, Davina Jackson, Chris Johnson, Peter Spearritt, Max Kelly, Gina Ghioni and Kim Crestani.

We are immensely grateful to all those featured in the 'apartment living' vignettes, who welcomed us into their homes and participated enthusiastically. We also thank those who assisted us with locating these interesting people: Nigel Lincoln, Michelle Cannane, Terry and Louise Mooney, Wayne Tunnicliffe, Elizabeth Schaeffer, Felix Ryan, Dr Annabel Kain and Glenn Smith.

We are indebted to the apartment owners who discussed and/or let us visit and photograph their 'homes in the sky': David Webb, Kate Mountstephens, Terence Maloon, Pam and Garry Emery, Sir Ninian and Lady Stephen, Jim O'Donnell, Steve Taylor, Caroline Fry, Les and Greeba Pritchard, Amanda Findlay, Don Stewart and Mrs Stewart. The Board and management of The Astor, in particular Helen Neale, Laraine Gray and Robert Kroening, have been particularly helpful in assisting us with research and public programs for the exhibition. Particular thanks also to Dr Jan Roberts for all her research and advice about this famous Sydney building.

Thanks must go to staff at the NSW Department of Housing: to Director Mike Allen for supporting the project; to the terrific Library Manager Penelope Campbell; to John Gregory, historian of public housing, and to Adam Murray, who gave us access to a number of public housing records and buildings. Likewise, Sherri Bruinhout from the Victorian Office of Housing was helpful in providing access to the Atherton Gardens Estate. Colleagues and friends at a range of cultural institutions and companies provided crucial advice and assistance, including Anna McFarlane and Garth Nix for advice about publishing and publishers; Wayne Tunnicliffe, Judy Annear, Anne Ryan and Barry Pearce at the Art Gallery of New South Wales; John McPhee; Stephen Rogers; Gail Davis at State Records NSW; Geoffrey Smith at the National Gallery of Victoria; Sylvia Carr at the National Library of Australia; Margot Riley and Helen Harrison at Mitchell Library; Simon Drake at the National Film and Sound Archive; Dr Sherry McKay at the University of British Columbia, Vancouver; Mark Stevens at City of Sydney Archives; Michial Farrow at City of Adelaide Archives; Di Foster at Stonnington Council Archives; Kate Gray and Michael Galimany at Lovell Chen; Claire Armstrong at *Art & Australia*; Dr Ian Hoskins and Leonie Masson at Stanton Library, North Sydney Council; Dr Marianne Dacy at the Archive of Australian Judaica; Frank Stanisic at Stanisic Associates; Dirk Meinecke at Harry Seidler & Associates; Phillip Rossington at Alexander Tzannes Architects; Neale Towart at Unions NSW; Ian Stapleton at Clive Lucas, Stapleton & Partners; Doug Djorcevic and Anna Brogan from JR Brogan & Associates; Arijana Hodzic at Peddle Thorp Walker; and Karl Fender at Fender Katsalidis.

At Melbourne University Publishing we are grateful to a range of people, notably Louise Adler, CEO, and Tracy O'Shaughnessy, Associate Publisher, The Miegunyah Press, for having faith in our proposal and providing encouragement along the way; to Felicity Edge for production management; to Cathryn Game for editing the manuscript; and to Phil Campbell for his terrific book design. Especially, we are grateful to Eugenie Baulch, who finalised the book with such commitment and expertise.

Above all we are indebted to Eric Sierins of Max Dupain & Associates, our supremely gifted photographer, who was both good-humoured and indefatigable in producing new work and delving into the Dupain archive. Eric has helped us on numerous projects over the years; we are pleased to be able to give him due recognition this time.

Marinco Kojdanovski, photographer (and star) of the apartment-living sections, was also persistent and imaginative.

This book is dedicated to Dr Phillip Kent (1958–2003), who inspired and encouraged it. Another inspiration was Caroline's father, Anthony Butler-Bowdon (1913–2001), whose discussion of architecture and cities, and whose stunning elevation of the Mimosa apartment building he designed at Sea Point, Cape Town, as a young architect in the late 1950s, helped sow the seeds of this book.

Lastly and most of all to our families: Marion Butler-Bowdon clipped many pieces from newspapers on the subject and as always, provided love, intelligence and endured too many conversations about our workload; Joan Pickett's love and devotion to us and our children was unstinting. To Richard, Piers, Edward, Charles, Teresa and Tom Butler-Bowdon and partners, to Fran and Stuart Jones, our thanks for all the encouragement along the way. Thanks also to Alex, who probably can't remember life before this project. Our beautiful children, Toby and Claudia, were simply essential to this book, and to everything else.

Index

Page numbers in bold refer to illustrations.

The Miegunyah Press

This book was designed and typeset by Phil Campbell
The text was set in 9 point Avenir with 14 points of leading
The text is printed on 130 gsm matt art

This book was edited by Cathryn Game

THE
MIEGUNYAH
PRESS